Jonathan Edwards
and the Catholic Vision
of Salvation

Jonathan Edwards
and the Catholic Vision
of Salvation

Anri Morimoto

The Pennsylvania State University Press
University Park, Pennsylvania

Library of Congress Cataloging-in-Publication Data

Morimoto, Anri, 1956–
  Jonathan Edwards and the Catholic vision of salvation / Anri Morimoto.
     p.   cm.
  Includes bibliographical references and index.
  ISBN 978-0-271-02816-3
  1. Edwards, Jonathan, 1703–1758—Contributions in concept of salvation. 2. Salvation—History of doctrines—18th century. I. Title.
BT751.2.M58 1995
234'.092—dc20   94-40824
                                                                    CIP

Copyright © 1995 The Pennsylvania State University
All rights reserved
Printed in the United States of America
Published by The Pennsylvania State University Press,
University Park, PA 16802-1003

It is the policy of The Pennsylvania State University Press to use acid-free paper for the first printing of all clothbound books. Publications on uncoated stock satisfy the minimum requirements of American National Standard for Information Sciences—Permanence of Paper for Printed Library Materials, ANSI Z39.48–1984.

Contents

Acknowledgments	vii
1 Introduction	1
2 Conversion: The Infusion of Grace	13
3 Conversion: The New Internal Principle	37
4 Justification: God's Crowning of His Own Gift	71
5 Justification: Systemic Comparison	103
6 Sanctification and Glorification	131
7 Conclusion	157
Bibliography	165
Index	175

Acknowledgments

Japanese Christianity owes much to Puritan America, and Jonathan Edwards is the prime subject of inquiry if we want to set out on a long-overdue reflection on our Puritan heritage. My first expression of gratitude must therefore go to all those who motivated me to study closely the theology of Edwards in its original context.

To faculty and friends at the International Christian University, I owe everything that I am as a Japanese Christian scholar. The university, founded in the aftermath of World War II as an act of reconciliation between Japanese and North American Christians, provided war-stricken people with the gleaming ideal of an academic and intellectual endeavor in which they could learn about democracy and Christianity firsthand. "What great historical significance a Christian Japan would have for the world of today," commented Emil Brunner, who in 1953 accepted a call from this little-known institution in the Far East to teach there for two years, postponing the completion of his magnum opus (see the preface to volume 3 of his *Dogmatics*). As I now preach regularly from the same pulpit from which Dr. Brunner preached, I am keenly aware that his vision is yet to be realized.

This book is based on my doctoral dissertation presented to the faculty of Princeton Theological Seminary in 1991. My sincere appreciation is extended to all faculty members who taught me the rigor and enjoyment of scholarship. In particular, I can think of no better guide than Sang H. Lee, Kyung-Chik Han Professor of Systematic Theology. I hope the reader will find evidence of a unique succession from a Korean to a Japanese in the study of an American Puritan—a lineage that illustrates the wide relevance of Edwards's theology. It was in the course of a private tutorial with Dr. Lee that I was first introduced to the heart of Edwards's dispositional ontology. Without his warm encouragement I could not have survived the kind of life one has to lead apart from his or her homeland. E. David Willis-Watkins, Charles Hodge Professor of Systematic Theology, gave me invaluable suggestions in Reformation and post-Reformation theology, which constitutes an essential part of this book. John F. Wilson, Agate Brown and George L. Collord Professor of Religion at Princeton University and member of the editorial committee for the Yale Works of Jonathan Edwards, was an important resource person on whose broad scholarship I could rely with regard to anything related to Edwards. I am also deeply indebted to Thomas A. Schafer, member of the Yale editorial committee, who not only granted me permission to read his transcription of Edwards's "Miscellanies" but also answered in letters and conversation many complicated questions concerning Edwards's theology, especially in the early stages of this project.

I am grateful to the Japan–United States Educational Commission for granting me a Fulbright scholarship in order to study Edwards at Princeton, where his last thoughts are buried with other presidents of the University. I would also like to express my gratitude to the Japan–North American Commission on Cooperative Mission for the financial support I received during the last year of my research.

A very special word of appreciation is due to Philip Winsor, senior editor at Penn State Press, who gave me sustained and unfailing support and patiently waited for several revisions of the manuscript. I am thankful for the friendship of Professors Clair Hughes and Virginia LoCastro, and Ms. Marie Bedell for reading my manuscript in whole or in part and giving me numerous suggestions for stylistic improvements. To Ms. Patricia A. Mitchell of Penn State Press, who kindly undertook the editorial work on my final manuscript, I owe my heartfelt thanks.

Writing a book proved to be more of a family project than my own. There are no words that can express my indebtedness and gratitude to my wife, Eriko, who has juggled multiple roles at home and outside, in Japan and in the States. I wish that someday my daughters, Shoko and Akiko, will come to share my vision and grow as their names signify—manifesting and glorifying God's grace in their lives. May all be, as Edwards said, "interested" in Christ and his salvation.

1
Introduction

"Puritanism is the essence of Protestantism, and Jonathan Edwards is the quintessence of Puritanism,"[1] wrote Perry Miller. To Miller, Edwards was the theologian who defined both Protestantism and Puritanism. Another critic, Robert Jenson, recommended Edwards as "America's Theologian"—not just *an* American theologian who happened to be born and to live in America, but *the* most American of theologians, a man whose theology "meets precisely the problems and opportunities of specifically American Christianity and of the nation molded thereby."[2] If we give credit to these characterizations, we find in Edwards Puritanism, Protestantism, and American Christianity all realized in their purest forms.

1. Perry Miller, *Jonathan Edwards* (1949; reprint, Amherst: University of Massachusetts Press, 1981), 301. Note also "Puritanism is what Edwards is," and "he extracted the essense of Puritanism" (194).
2. Robert Jenson, *America's Theologian: A Recommendation of Jonathan Edwards* (New York: Oxford University Press, 1988), 3.

In this book, my question is not whether Edwards encompassed *all* of these forms or *less* of them, but whether he possessed *more*. Learning from Edwards would be of little more than historical interest if Edwards were a mere representative—even the best representative—of a particular school of thought within a particular time and context. Naturally, his thought is somewhat defined by the context and the agenda of his own day. Yet, like Augustine, Thomas Aquinas, and John Calvin, Edwards offers us insights that are applicable beyond his own temporal, spatial, and confessional limitations. What is truly representative of a particular type always has a quality that transcends that particularity. With the present study I aim to establish Edwards as a theologian whose vision of salvation is significant not only to eighteenth-century Puritan America but to all people—whether Protestant or Roman Catholic, Puritan or Eastern Orthodox, American or Japanese—who share the basic premise of the Scripture that God's transformative power brings forth a new creation.

As a Calvinist Puritan of eighteenth-century New England, Edwards may not seem very promising for interdenominational dialogue. Yet, contrary to the popular caricature of a narrow-minded, dogmatic "Puritan," Edwards learned much from the theology of the continental Roman Catholic tradition and allowed himself to be profoundly influenced by it. I document examples of unpublicized ecumenical interchanges within Edwards's own theological milieu. His vision of human salvation can therefore offer today's Protestant theology valuable help in reformulating and revitalizing its own understanding of salvation, without forcing it to surrender or compromise its genuine Protestant concerns. Indeed, ecumenical dialogue should not mean watering down the particularities to the lowest common denominator; it should enrich and deepen theological tradition and conviction. It is my hope that the reader will find in Edwards the potential for such mutual enrichment across the presupposed boundaries.

The implication of this dispositional view is not limited to the Christian community. As I argue in Chapter 3, Edwards's soteriology envisions a new and radical paradigm for understanding the salvation of people who are called "non-Christians." Reformed theology has not been very optimistic in this prospect. It teaches that those who die unevangelized or unconverted are destined to eternal damnation. Repugnant to the idea of a God who creates but does nothing to save, theologians of various convictions have recently tried to lay out various paradigms—whether pluralistic, universal, or inclusive—to suggest otherwise. Partly because of my own cultural and religious background, I feel compelled to develop a soteriology that is inclusive yet theologically responsible. Edwards has been regarded as a theologian who peremptorily and almost sadistically condemns unbelievers to eternal damnation. The image of a hell-fire preacher should be carefully relocated in his unexpectedly broad understanding of salvation. By extending the implication of his dispositional view a little further, Edwards's theology could help us reconsider the destiny of those who stand outside the visible circle of Christian faith. Most theologians no longer regard unbelievers as *massa damnata* (damned masses), but would they say that the Christian proclamation is no longer necessary or meaningful? In Edwards's view of faith, the division between Christians and non-Christians is not simply a division between those who have faith and those who do not. Rather the difference lies in whether or not the disposition into faith has been actualized.

Jonathan Edwards lived in an age in which traditional ways of understanding the nature of reality were being radically reconceived in response to the challenges of science and philosophy. In the first two decades of the eighteenth century, books by John Locke (1632–1704) and Isaac Newton (1643–1727) were transported across the Atlantic Ocean to awaken the minds of progressive New England thinkers. Although recent evidence has discounted the legend of a thirteen-year-old Edwards poring over Locke's *Essays* in a dark Yale library room, a young Edwards was no doubt exposed to the thought of both Locke and Newton and became aware of the challenges posed to theology.[3] Edwards was a theologian by profession, but in those days no one could be a theologian without also being a profound metaphysician and, to a varying extent, an amateur scientist; he was no exception. But in Edwards's efforts to restate the traditional doctrines of Calvinist theology in the language of his own time, he accomplished—perhaps without so realizing—what neither Locke nor Newton could accomplish.

While die-hard scholasticism, with its Aristotelian worldview, was on the wane, new theses did not spring automatically from the collapsing

---

3. For Edwards's exposure to the writings of Locke and Newton, see Wallace E. Anderson's Introduction to *The Works of Jonathan Edwards* [hereafter *WY*], vol. 6: *Scientific and Philosophical Writings*, ed. Wallace E. Anderson (New Haven: Yale University Press, 1980), 1–143.

castle of medieval scholasticism. Newton had to struggle hard to work out a nonimpact causation theory. Locke too was still probing, although without reaching a definite conclusion, whether it was really possible to abandon the concepts and paradigms of Aristotelian metaphysics altogether. In such a time of transition, Edwards's reflections on the nature of reality made a qualitative leap from the metaphysics of form and substance to a dispositional ontology that is still relevant today. This dispositional view of reality is carefully described and analyzed in a work by Sang H. Lee, *The Philosophical Theology of Jonathan Edwards*,[4] to which the present study owes its inception. In the following pages, I try to recapitulate Lee's argument, but I refer the reader to this important monograph for deeper understanding. My aim here is to describe more fully the theological implications that this dispositional view of reality has on Edwards's "soteriology," or "theories of salvation"—that is, a theological discipline that deals with ways to understand aspects of human salvation.

At the age of twenty-seven and barely four years into his ministry in a frontier congregation in Northampton, Connecticut, Jonathan Edwards had the honor of being invited to deliver a public lecture in Boston in 1731. This "Thursday Lecture," as it was called, was an occasion for inquiring New England Puritans to listen to their ministers parade the best of their theological talents. Understandably, Edwards prepared his manuscript scrupulously, and within a month after its favorable reception the lecture was published. The title of his first published work is of a typical New England style—long: "God Glorified in the Work of Redemption, by the Greatness of Man's Dependence upon him, in the Whole of it." This lecture represents the gist of Edwards's thought in its formative years, and scholars often recognize important concepts of his later days here in embryonic form. I find Edwards's vision of salvation articulated in it very clearly.

Edwards takes as his scriptural text 1 Corinthians 1:30 (King James),[5] "Christ Jesus is made unto us wisdom and righteousness and sanctification and redemption," and ascribes both justification and sanctification to the grace of God. He defines these two manifestations of grace

4. Sang H. Lee, *The Philosophical Theology of Jonathan Edwards* (Princeton: Princeton University Press, 1988).
5. Biblical quotations are from the New Revised Standard Version unless otherwise stated, as here.

somewhat enigmatically as "objective good" and "inherent good." While not neglecting the objective good, Edwards's soteriology uniquely accents the inherent good that redeemed persons have by salvation. Grace transforms human beings so that they may have "spiritual excellency and joy by a kind of participation [in] God." They are not only *counted* as righteous, but are themselves *made* excellent "by a communication of God's excellency" and *made* holy "by being made partakers of God's holiness."[6] For Edwards, salvation means a palpable reality of regeneration. To be saved is to participate in the fullness of God by the communication of God's own nature to humanity. God "communicates" himself to human beings, and human beings "participate" in the nature of God. This vision of salvation is attested to in Scripture (2 Pet. 1:4) and is shared by the Roman Catholic and Eastern Orthodox churches. According to Thomas Aquinas, the end of grace is to make human beings "partakers of the divine nature," while the Eastern Orthodox term for this vision is "divinization" or "deification" (*theosis*).[7] It is this soteriology of ontological transformation that I analyze in Edwards.

Participation, according to Paul Tillich, is an ontological concept that relates an individual subject to an objective and transcendent reality, without destroying the former's self-identity.[8] It is neither complete "absorption" nor complete "separation," and it is possible only when both elements of transcendence and immanence are present. In Edwards's soteriology, the locus where these two elements meet is the

---

6. Sermon, "God glorified in Man's Dependence," in *The Work of President Edwards in Four Volumes* [hereafter *WW*], (1808–9; reprint, New York: Jonathan Levitt and John F. Trow, 1843), 4:174–75. Perry Miller took advantage of the mysteriousness of these words and interpreted them as "Newton and natural law" and "Locke and perception" so as to suit his own interpretative scheme (Miller, *Jonathan Edwards*, 98). My reading is less constrained, since in another sermon Edwards explicitly uses these words in relation to justification and sanctification. See "The Wisdom of God, displayed in the way of Salvation," *WW*, 4:145.

7. *Summa Theologica*, 1–2.110.3. On *theosis*, see Vladimir Lossky, *The Mystical Theology of the Eastern Church*, trans. The Fellowship of St. Alban and St. Sergius (Cambridge: James Clarke & Co., 1957; reprint, Crestwood, N.Y.: St. Vladimir's Seminary Press, 1976), 196–216 and passim. See also George Maloney, *A Theology of "Uncreated Energies"* (Milwaukee: Marquette University Press, 1978), chap. 3. Jaroslav Pelikan notes its bearing on Edwards's theology in *Christian Doctrine and Modern Culture (since 1700)*, vol. 5 of *The Christian Tradition: A History of the Development of Doctrine* (Chicago: University of Chicago Press, 1989), 161.

8. Paul Tillich, *Systematic Theology* (Chicago: University of Chicago Press, 1951), 1:177.

"new disposition" created by infused grace. In the Boston lecture, Edwards elaborates on the meaning of "participation" and "communication."

> The saints have both their spiritual excellency and blessedness by the gift of the Holy Ghost, or Spirit of God, and his dwelling in them. They are not only caused by the Holy Ghost, but are in the Holy Ghost as their principle. The Holy Spirit becoming an inhabitant, is a vital principle in the soul: he, acting in, upon, and with the soul, becomes a fountain of true holiness and joy, as a spring is of water, by the exertion and diffusion of itself.[9]

God communicates his own nature to human beings, which results in a new "principle" of the heart. This principle is created by the infusion of the Holy Spirit, Edwards says, who then "dwells" in the regenerate persons as "the vital principle in the soul" by which they spontaneously and voluntarily act out in faith and holy practice.

What is important to note here is Edwards's concept of "a vital principle in the soul" that "exerts" itself. Called more often "disposition" or "habit" in other contexts, this "principle" is a key word in his soteriology and ontology. In Edwards's dispositional view, all being—whether corporeal or spiritual—is a disposition, an active tendency to realize itself in certain ways. Being is no longer described as substance and form, as in the Aristotelian tradition. Being is, for Edwards, essentially a network of laws that prescribe certain actions and events to take place on specified occasions. These laws are active and purposive tendencies, or dispositions, that automatically come into "exertion" when the specified circumstances are met. A chair in a room, for example, is not a chair by itself that has certain qualities. It is rather a result of the exercise of laws governing the nature of that particular chair to exist in such and such a manner. This dispositional conception of being can therefore mediate between various categories traditionally thought to be antithetical—such as substance and accident, being and action, or being and becoming.

The theological upshot of this conception of disposition is that it makes all being radically and constantly dependent on the causal power and activity of God, while at the same time affirming the relative

---

9. "God glorified in Man's Dependence," 175.

permanence of the created world. On one hand, the existence of the world is totally dependent on God. It is God who has established and who works in and through these laws, bringing entities into being according to the conditions that specify the enactment of these laws. On the other hand, the specific integrity of the created world is secured and upheld by the permanence of the laws that have an objective and ontological reality. The laws that God has established are essentially permanent, and they necessarily and unfailingly come into exercise as specified. This permanence and certainty gives being an integrity of its own.[10]

Translated into soteriological language, this conception of being as the exercise of laws has two aspects. First, it affirms the immediate and continual activity of God in and through the reality of the new creation. By the infusion of grace, God creates in human nature a new disposition. In order for this new disposition to exist and operate, God must be continually at work in and through it. In this sense, the reality of human salvation is totally dependent on the sovereign activity of God. Divine grace never becomes encapsulated in a static human quality. Salvation is not something achieved once and for all and then relegated to human possession. It must be given anew every moment by God's immediate and continual activity from above. I call this the "Protestant concern" in soteriology.

Second, this new disposition is an active and purposive tendency that is exercised necessarily and without fail when conditions are met. Contrary to common understanding, a disposition or habit, according to Edwards, is not a description of likelihood; a disposition as a prescriptive law exerts itself unfailingly and necessarily upon preordained occasions. God works according to the laws he has established, and these laws, once established, are essentially permanent (*potentia ordinata*). This certainty gives the reality of salvation an enduring character. The transformative power of grace effectuates in human nature a real and qualitative change—something tangible and palpable—that is far more than a hypothesis. The regenerate persons enjoy an abiding reality of salvation created within them. I call this the "Catholic concern" in soteriology.

The strength of Edwards's soteriology is that it fuses Protestant and

---

10. See Lee, *Philosophical Theology*, 34–75. See also Anderson's Introduction to WY, 6:68–136. See Chapter 3 of this volume for further discussion.

Catholic concerns into one form. To use Tillich's terms, Edwards's soteriology is a well-balanced combination of "Protestant Principle" and "Catholic Substance."[11] The same combination can be expressed by the scholastic terms *gratia increata* (uncreated grace) and *gratia creata* (created grace). Uncreated grace (the Holy Spirit) operates in and through created grace (the new disposition). One can also associate these two aspects of grace with Peter Lombard and Thomas Aquinas: Lombard represents the "Protestant concern," or the tradition of uncreated grace, and Thomas represents the "Catholic concern," or the tradition of created grace. With his dispositional view of reality, Edwards succeeds in mediating the truths of both traditions, arguing for an abiding reality of salvation in humanity, while not undermining God's sovereign grace.

The kind of emphasis Edwards put on the human reality of salvation has often caused suspicion and misgiving in Protestant circles; his genuine theological concerns have been sadly misrepresented. In the middle of the nineteenth century, Tryon Edwards surreptitiously tampered with the text of Edwards's *Charity and Its Fruits* before publication in order to conceal his great forefather's emphatic use of the word "infusion," which to Tryon sounded too "Roman Catholic."[12] George Boardman recognized the precedence of regeneration to justification in Edwards's theology and thought that an explanation was due.[13] In this century, Perry Miller notes that Edwards felt "a necessity of saying something more" than the standard Protestant doctrine of forensic justification.[14] Thomas Schafer also writes that Edwards "went beyond the doctrine of justification."[15]

Comparable efforts to "defend" Edwards's "Protestantness" have been made as well. Conrad Cherry argues that Edwards remained Protestant by underscoring the direct indwelling of the Holy Spirit in the regenerate.[16] Paul Ramsey emphatically reassures his readers that,

---

11. Tillich, *Systematic Theology*, 3:223,245.
12. See Paul Ramsey's Introduction to *Charity and Its Fruits*, in *WY*, vol. 8: *Ethical Writings*, ed. Paul Ramsey (New Haven: Yale University Press, 1989), 59–60 n. 5.
13. George Nye Boardman, *A History of New England Theology* (New York: A. D. F. Randolph, 1899; reprint, New York: Garland, 1987), 155–56.
14. Miller, *Jonathan Edwards*, 76.
15. Thomas A. Schafer, "Jonathan Edwards and Justification by Faith," *Church History* 20 (1951): 64.
16. Conrad Cherry, *The Theology of Jonathan Edwards: A Reappraisal* (Gloucester, Mass.: Peter Smith, 1974), 29–31, 37, 41–43.

despite the seeming coincidence of Edwards's thought with the Roman Catholic position, Edwards has a "deep family resemblance" to Calvin and other Reformed theologians.[17]

There is truth in each of these assertions. Two preliminary remarks, however, should be made for the sake of clarity. First, Edwards himself seems not to have noticed the obvious similarity his theology has with Roman Catholic theology. His writings hardly show any effort to differentiate or contrast his thought to Roman Catholic understandings of salvation. This may sound surprising in view of Edwards's thorough acquaintance with the anti-Roman polemics of the preceding generation. Even his most explicitly Protestant discourse, "Justification by Faith alone," was directed against those Edwards called "Arminians," not against Roman Catholics.[18] On Edwards's theological horizon, Roman Catholicism did not present itself as something to be confronted or to be reconciled with.[19] The reader should therefore keep in mind that any comparative statement I make in the following pages is instead part of my own effort to better understand Edwards's soteriology on a broad scale.

Second, a distinction should be made between interpretation and value-judgment. It is one thing to say that Edwards's soteriology has a substantial affinity with Roman Catholic soteriology, and quite another to say that it is therefore to be praised or condemned. Though at some points my interpretation concurs with the results of previous studies, my attitude toward the perceived facts is different from those who have seen this affinity as a problem—or even a "scandal" in the biblical sense of the word—that should be concealed or circumvented. As I point out in several contexts, this defensive motivation has often placed undue pressure on the text to make it *look* "Protestant," resulting in misrepre-

17. See Appendix 4 to WY, 8:739–50.
18. See, for example, Preface to "Justification by Faith alone," in *The Works of President Edwards in Ten Volumes* [hereafter WD] (New York: S. Converse, 1829–30), 5:349.
19. "Papists," as Edwards calls them, are classified in the same category with "heathens or atheists" (Sermons, "Natural men in a dreadful condition," WD, 8:12; "Man's Natural Blindness in the things of Religion," WW, 4:22). This was not uncommon for a New England Puritan. See, for example, Harry S. Stout, *The New England Soul: Preaching and Religious Culture in Colonial New England* (New York: Oxford University Press, 1986), 48–49. Edwards's firsthand knowledge of Roman Catholic theology did not go beyond conventional literature. See John F. Wilson's Appendix B, "Jonathan Edwards' Notebooks for *A History of the Work of Redemption*," WY, vol. 9: *A History of the Work of Redemption*, ed. John F. Wilson, 547.

sentations of Edwards's true concerns. Furthermore, in light of recent successes of ecumenical dialogues between Protestants and Roman Catholics, it would be indeed unfortunate if the opportunity that Edwards's soteriology offers for a reevaluation of the strengths of both soteriologies is ignored. I want to reconfirm and give positive recognition to the contiguity of Edwards's soteriology with the Roman Catholic tradition, especially as represented by Thomas Aquinas, without depreciating the essential continuity of his theology with that of Calvin and other Reformed theologians. To achieve this task, I look to recent ecumenical interchanges for support. Edwards's concern for the reality of ontological transformation is consonant, I believe, not only with contemporary Roman Catholic theology but also fundamentally with biblical testimony regarding the transformative power of divine grace.

The methodological framework of this study is provided by what traditional Reformed theology calls "the application of redemption," or the teaching of the ways in which Christ's redemption is applied to individual believers. According to Edwards's own definition of redemption, it consists of four phases: conversion, justification, sanctification, and glorification.[20] Of these, I treat conversion and justification more extensively, not because they are more important than the other two but because they illuminate the basic pattern and structure of Edwards's soteriology.

This does not mean that I force Edwards's thinking and utterances into four static categories, which is impossible in view of the complexity and interrelatedness of the subject matter. Edwards did not leave a systematic treatise on soteriology, nor did he feel it necessary to write one in the manner and language of traditional Reformed theology. The classical method of *ordo salutis* (order of salvation) functions here as a guideline along which to bring his fragmentary thoughts together into a meaningful whole, one that allows close research and systemic comparison. Thus integrated, Edwards's soteriology appears as an organic body of thought that is consistent within itself and rich in implication, while less attended to by recent scholarship.

Chapters 2 and 3 deal with Edwards's thoughts on conversion. Conversion is brought about by the infusion of the Holy Spirit, whose indwelling creates in human nature a new internal principle. Chapter 4

20. *History of the Work of Redemption*, 120–21.

analyzes Edwards's thoughts on justification in relation to his overall paradigm of soteriology and to the polemical context of his day. Chapter 5 attempts to compare his soteriology with that of Roman Catholicism. In Chapter 6, Edwards's thoughts on sanctification and glorification are reviewed as the continuation and perfection of conversion and justification. Through their participation in the being and goodness of God, human beings fulfill the ultimate end of creation, God's self-glorification.

2

Conversion
The Infusion of Grace

The Concept of Infusion

When Edwards speaks of the saving operation of grace in human nature, he almost invariably uses the word "infusion."[1] However, the standard Reformed teaching often pairs "infusion" with another word, "illumination," to describe the same work of grace in conversion.[2] An explanation is called for here; why did "infusion" come to assume such predomi-

---

1. Infusion was a focal issue in the Reformation controversy over the cause of justification, that is, the Roman Catholic insistence on the "infusion" of righteousness versus the "imputation" of righteousness asserted by Protestant Reformers. However, infusion has its own place in Protestant theology as well, in the context of conversion. This is how Edwards uses the word.
2. See, for example, the Synod of Dort (1619), article 11, in *Creeds of Christendom*, 3 vols., ed. Philip Schaff (New York: Harper & Row, 1931; reprint, Grand Rapids, Mich.: Baker Book House, 1985), 3:590. However, the Westminster Confession (1647), chap. 10, cautiously avoids the word "infusion" in order to prevent confusion with its next article on justification (624–26).

nance in Edwards's soteriology? Tracing the short history of the concept will offer a good starting point to the study of Edwards's theology, as it locates him in the context of seventeenth-century Reformed and Roman Catholic traditions.

First of all, Edwards's use of the concept of "infusion" makes an interesting contrast with Calvin's use of "illumination." While Edwards emphasizes that our will must be transformed by the infusion of grace, Calvin stresses that our understanding should be illumined by grace before conversion.[3] The contrast between the two positions is so dramatic that some prominent twentieth-century theologians have labeled Calvin as "intellectualist" and Edwards as "voluntarist."[4] However, difference in language does not always mean difference in the reality to which it refers. Terrence Erdt traces Edwards's extensive use of the "heart-language" ("the sense of the heart") back to Calvin's concept of *suavitas*, a sweetness that men and women of faith taste and relish.[5] This "heart-language" helps Edwards transcend the conventional division of the intellect from the will that was assumed by the faculty-psychology of the day. While at times he refers to this division to explain the basic configuration of the human mind, he is by no means bound by it. He does not materialize intellect and will into two "faculties," and he does not think them to be in sharp dichotomy.[6] With the sense of the heart,

---

3. John Calvin, *Institutes of the Christian Religion*, ed. John T. McNeill, trans. Ford Lewis Battles (Philadelphia: Westminster Press, 1960), 1.5.14, 1.7.5, 1.9.1, 2.2.20, 25, 3.1.14, 3.2.7, 19, 33–35, 3.14.5, 3.18.1, 3.24.2, 8. In contrast, "infusion" is rarely used, if ever (*Institutes*, 3.6.2 [Latin, *perfundo*]). Calvin's commentary on Romans 5:5 adopts "shed abroad" (Latin, *diffusa*). See his *The Epistles of Paul The Apostle to the Romans and to the Thessalonians*, ed. David W. Torrance and Thomas F. Torrance, trans. Ross Mackenzie (Edinburgh: Oliver and Boyd, 1960; reprint, Grand Rapids, Mich.: Wm. B. Eerdmans, 1990), 107–8.

4. Vernon J. Bourke, *Will in Western Thought: An Historico-Critical Survey* (New York: Sheed & Ward, 1964), 41, 141. Miller, *Jonathan Edwards*, 252, seems to have the same preconception. For a survey of the issue of the will and the intellect in Edwards's background, see Norman Fiering, "Will and Intellect in the New England Mind," *William and Mary Quarterly*, 3d ser., 29 (1972): 515–58.

5. Terrence Erdt, *Jonathan Edwards: Art and the Sense of the Heart* (Amherst: University of Massachusetts Press, 1980), 1–20. Erdt seems to presume that Calvin is in dispute with medieval Scholastics. By "philosophers," however, Calvin is referring to Greek ethicists, and he is rather in basic accord with the "Schoolmen" on this point (see *Institutes*, 1.15.7, 2.2.26).

6. There can be no "clear distinction between the two faculties of understanding and will, as acting distinctly and separately in this matter" (*WY*, vol. 2: *Religious Affections*, 272). Hence Edwards's tart remark, "How the Scriptures are ignorant of the philosophic distinction of the understanding and the will" ("The Mind," no. 14, *WY*, 6:389). See also

"the mind don't [sic] only speculate and behold, but relishes and feels."[7] Faith for Edwards is not mere speculative knowledge. Rather, it is the "sensible knowledge"—sensible of "beauty, amiableness, or sweetness," of "pleasure and delight."[8]

Calvin also knows that faith is not just an intellectual assent to doctrine. Saving faith is "a firm and certain knowledge of God's benevolence toward us."[9] God is not known where there is no piety. The knowledge of God is always accompanied by, or is itself *pietas*, which Calvin defines as "that reverence joined with love of God which the knowledge of his benefits induces."[10] In fact, Erdt's insight could be extended beyond Calvin to Anselm and Augustine. Calvin's vocabulary reflects the Augustino-Anselmian dicta, *credo, ut intelligam* (I believe, so as to understand) and *fides quaerens intellectum* (faith seeking understanding), in which *intelligere* or *intellectus* does not privilege the faculty of understanding over the will. While at times Calvin refers, just as Edwards, to the division of understanding and will, for him the division is merely an expedient for a discussion that has a limited scope. According to T.H.L. Parker, Calvin "will not allow the rigid division of man into intellect, affection, senses, etc."[11] Conversion, for Calvin, is more a matter "of the heart than of the brain."[12] The knowledge of faith is always an "existential" knowledge, as Edward Dowey called it,[13] in the sense that it determines the whole existence of the knower.

This explains why for Calvin the word "illumination" means much more than simply the enhancement of the power of reasoning and

---

Roland Andre Delattre, *Beauty and Sensibility in the Thought of Jonathan Edwards: An Essay in Aesthetics and Theological Ethics* (New Haven: Yale University Press, 1968), 5–8, 41–44.

7. *Religious Affections*, 272.

8. Ibid. See also Sermons, "A Divine and Supernatural Light," *WW*, 4:442; "Concerning Faith," *WW*, 4:623, 625, 639; "Miscellanies," no. 540, Beinecke Library, Yale University; *The Philosophy of Jonathan Edwards from His Private Notebooks*, ed. Harvey G. Townsend (Westport, Conn.: Greenwood Press, 1955), 250.

9. *Institutes*, 3.2.7.

10. Ibid., 1.2.1. See also E. David Willis, *Calvin's Catholic Christology: The Function of the So-called Extra Calvinisticum in Calvin's Theology*, Studies in Medieval and Reformation Thought, vol. 2, ed. Heiko A. Oberman et al. (Leiden: E. J. Brill, 1966), 107–8, 127.

11. T.H.L. Parker, *The Doctrine of the Knowledge of God: A Study in the Theology of John Calvin* (Edinburgh: Oliver and Boyd, 1952), 100–102, 106–7.

12. *Institutes*, 1.5.9, 3.2.8, 3.6.4.

13. Edward A. Dowey Jr., *The Knowledge of God in Calvin's Theology* (New York: Columbia University Press, 1952), 26.

knowing. The saving operation of the Spirit cannot remain external, but thrusts itself into the innermost being of the person. Hence Calvin calls the Holy Spirit the "inner teacher," who "opens the eyes of the mind."[14] "Infusion" may not be Calvin's preferred term, but the same powerful and effectual operation is affirmed when he speaks of the Holy Spirit's "penetrating" and "instilling" the heart.[15] As far as an understanding of the nature of saving faith is concerned, the similarities between Edwards and Calvin are obvious.[16]

Given the congruity between Calvin and Edwards, one wonders why they use different words. It is unlikely that the words were arbitrarily chosen. Edwards carefully chooses "infusion" rather than "illumination" to denote the same operation of the converting grace on the whole person. The change of language from Calvin to Edwards indicates that something happened during the two centuries that separate them. It is important to know the rationale for the shift in terminology, since it defines in an essential manner the way Edwards uses the word "infusion" in his own context.

Part of the reason for the shift may be explained by the gradual decrease in the breadth of meaning that *intellectus* originally had for Augustine, Anselm, and Calvin. An obvious example is found in the work of William Ames (1576–1633), who was convinced that the Ramist logic of division and dissection could provide the essential "method" by which to know the nature of things.[17] Ames made a clear-cut distinction

---

14. *Institutes*, 1.7.5, 2.2.21, 3.1.4, 3.2.7, 33, 34.
15. Ibid., 1.7.4, 3.1.4, 3.2.34; see also Calvin, *Epistles of Paul The Apostle to the Romans*, 107.
16. It should be noted, however, that Calvin and Edwards coincide from opposite directions. Calvin thinks that the intellect is the "directing part" of a person, the approval or disapproval of which the will must follow. He calls this intellect, following Aristotle, "the appetitive understanding," which involves certain volitional inclinations induced by the positive or negative judgment toward the object. For Calvin, therefore, the assistance of "illumination" first illumines the intellect, and then, through this illumined intellect, directs the will (see *Institutes*, 1.15.6, 7). Edwards has a vision of the will that subsumes part of the understanding faculty. The infusion of grace cures the will, and, through this cured will, transforms the person's understanding faculty, so that the convert may see the beauty and holiness of God (see "Miscellanies," no. 123 [*Philosophy of Jonathan Edwards*, 246]). For both theologians, conversion is an event that involves the whole person, but the presuppositions each treads to this conclusion are different.
17. Karl Reuter, *William Ames*, trans. Douglas Horton (Cambridge: Harvard Divinity School Library, 1965), 182–96, describes the process of "the whole of orthodoxy decay[ing] into an intellectualization of faith," and how Ames came to oppose it. See

between the faculties of understanding and will, and, within that division, accorded the will the primary *Sitz* of faith.[18] When he says that "to believe signifies *ordinarily* an act of the understanding as it gives assent to evidence" and then raises objections to this "ordinary" view, he takes Calvin's "knowledge" to mean something in opposition to the "will" or "heart."[19] As I have shown above, this interpretation does not fully represent Calvin's concept of *intellectus*. The distinction Ames makes originates not in the "ordinary" view as he understood it, but in his own mind. Ames still describes conversion as an act "of the whole man," including both the understanding and will, but within this totality the understanding is depreciated to something merely external and preliminary, something that is "common to us along with unbelievers, heretics, apostates, and the devils themselves." This depreciation of the understanding corresponds to the elevation of the will to "the proper and prime subject of this grace."[20]

As the breadth of the word *intellectus* narrowed, so did the concept of "illumination," which was supposed to operate on it. Illumination came to be seen as something that is merely external and preparatory to the work of conversion. The status of the concept of "infusion," on the other hand, was elevated to mean "conversion" in its full sense. When one takes into account the extent of influence that Ames's *Marrow*

Keith L. Sprunger, *The Learned Doctor William Ames: Dutch Background of English and American Puritanism* (Chicago: University of Illinois Press, 1972), who calls Ames a "voluntarist" and says that "his emphasis on the will rather than intellectual assent pulled Ames from the mainstream of Reformed theology" (146). R. T. Kendall, *Calvin and English Calvinism to 1649* (New York: Oxford University Press, 1979), 13–28, 151–64, et passim, traces the changing concept of faith from Calvin to Ames. The "Ramist" logic originates in a French Calvinist logician, Petrus Ramus (1515–72), who vigorously opposed the Aristotelian logic in favor of deduction as scientific method. His writings include *Aristotelicae Animadversiones* (Paris, 1543), and *Dialecticae Institutiones* (Paris, 1543). See Perry Miller, *The New England Mind: The Seventeenth Century* (Cambridge: Belknap Press of Harvard University Press, 1939), 111–80, 493–501.

18. Faith is primarily "an act of choice." William Ames, *The Marrow of Theology*, ed. and trans. John Dykstra Eusden (Boston: Pilgrim Press, 1968; reprint, Durham, N.C.: Labyrinth Press, 1983), 1.3.3. When his contemporary theologians made faith reside in the understanding or in the intellect *and* in the will, Ames was known to attribute faith "to the will *alone*." See Kendall, *Calvin and English Calvinism*, 152.

19. Ames, *Marrow of Theology*, 1.3.2. John Eusden in his Introduction to Ames, 48–49, is also plagued by the same misunderstanding. Ames may have had William Perkins in mind. See also Kendall, *Calvin and English Calvinism*, 152.

20. Ames, *Marrow of Theology*, 1.3.3, 2.5.13, 1.26.23.

of Theology (Medulla Theologica) was to exercise over New England theological education in general, it is not surprising that his vocabulary set the standard for later generations of theologians, including Edwards.[21]

Another factor that lies behind Edwards's preference for the word "infusion" over "illumination" is the Roman Catholic *de auxiliis* controversy, which took place at the turn of the seventeenth century and centered on the mode of divine operation in conversion.[22] It may sound odd for Puritan theology to be so profoundly influenced by an internal controversy between Roman Catholic orders, but, as I contend throughout this book, this was precisely what happened before Edwards's century. Prominent Reformed theologians such as Francis Turretin (1623–87) and Peter van Mastricht (1630–1706) took great interest in this controversy, and their arguments on conversion faithfully reproduce it. Turretin, whom Edwards prized for his thorough explication of controversial issues of theology, relied heavily on *de auxiliis* in discussing effectual calling and conversion in his dogmatics.[23] Mastricht, another of Edwards's favorite theologians, reflected the terminology of *de auxiliis* by arguing that the work of regenerating grace is "not a moral act, exercised in offering and inviting, as is the case with the external call," but "a physical act powerfully infusing spiritual life into the soul."[24] In

---

21. Ames's *Marrow of Theology* was first published in 1623 and quickly became the standard textbook of divinity throughout New England. The English translation appeared as early as 1643. Edwards owned a copy by the age of eighteen. See Eusden's Introduction to Ames, *Marrow of Theology*, 2 n. 3.

22. On the *de auxiliis* controversy, see the entry "congregatio de auxiliis," by T. Ryan, *New Catholic Encyclopedia*, ed. Editorial Staff at the Catholic University of America (New York: McGraw-Hill, 1967); also Alister E. McGrath, *Iustitia Dei: A History of the Christian Doctrine of Justification*, 2 vols. (Cambridge: Cambridge University Press, 1986), 2:86–97; James Brodrick, S.J., *The Life and Work of Blessed Robert Francis Cardinal Bellarmine*, 2 vols. (London: Burns Oates and Washbourne, 1928), 2:1–69; idem, *Robert Bellarmine: Saint and Scholar* (Westminster, Md.: Newman Press, 1961), 189–216.

23. Francis Turretin, *Institutio Theologiae Elencticae* (reprint, New York, 1847), 15.4. Turretin's argument is reviewed in detail in Chapter 3. The translation used here is taken from George Musgrave Giger's unpublished manuscript deposited at the Speer Library, Princeton Theological Seminary. For Edwards's relation to Turretin, see "Six Letters of Jonathan Edwards to Joseph Bellamy," ed. Stanley T. Williams, *New England Quarterly* 1 (1928): 230. Edwards calls him "the great Turretine" (*Religious Affections*, 289).

24. Peter van Mastricht, *Theoretico-Practica Theologia* (reprint, Amsterdam, 1715), 4.3.9. The English translation of Mastricht's work used in this book, unless otherwise noted, is taken from the anonymously translated *A Treatise on Regeneration: extracted*

the terminology of the controversy, "moral suasion" means an operation of grace on the intellect, and "physical infusion" on the will. Sinners are first externally illumined with "rational teaching, offering, and persuading" and called with "moral suasion." Yet, since prior to regeneration they are spiritually as dead as Lazarus in the tomb, this external illumination is bound to fail, unless the Holy Spirit further carries it out to "implant in the heart or will . . . a new inclination or propensity."[25] Mastricht calls this the "physical operation," or simply "infusion."[26] While these theologians knew well that the operation of grace cannot be divided, the terminology they took from the *de auxiliis* controversy prompted the word "infusion" to gain precedence over "illumination" for this undivided and integral operation.[27] I will have more to say about this Roman Catholic controversy in Chapter 3.

The *de auxiliis* controversy took on a new significance in the New England setting. A section on regeneration from Mastricht's *Theoretico-Practica Theologia* was translated into English for general readers as *A Treatise on Regeneration*, and the anonymous translator explained the motive of his work in the following words: "The reason for translating and publishing the following Treatise at this time, is principally a hope, that it may have a tendency to put a stop to the controversy, which seems to be growing among us, relative to regeneration; whether it be wrought by the immediate influences of the divine Spirit, or by light as the means?"[28] By the controversy "which seems to be growing among us," the translator is not referring to the original Jesuit-Dominican controversy that had been settled more than a century and a half before. He had rather in mind the growing number of Arminians who contested the idea of God's Spirit influencing immediately on the human mind. Their theological contentions will be examined in Chapter 4. As it was

from his system of divinity called theologia theoretico-practica and faithfully translated into English (New Haven, n.d. [1769]).

25. Mastricht, *Theoretico-Practica*, 6.3.15.

26. Ibid., 6.3.6. See also *Reformed Dogmatics: Set Out and Illustrated from the Sources*, ed. Heinrich Heppe and Ernst Bizer, trans. G. T. Thomson (reprint, Grand Rapids, Mich.: Baker Book House, 1978), 522, for another example furnished by Leonard Riissen.

27. The translator of Mastricht listed a number of contemporary Reformed theologians such as Ridgeley, Charnock, Willard, Flavel, Witsius, Le Blanc, Ames, Burman, Braunius, and Brine, who all underscored in one way or another the determining power of the will, and, accordingly, physical infusion. See Mastricht, *Treatise*, appendix.

28. Mastricht, *Treatise*, Preface, v.

used in eighteenth-century New England, "Arminianism" is neither the name for any specific brand or school of thought, nor does it have any substantial connection with the theology of Jacob Arminius (1560–1609), although the term originated from him. It is rather an atmosphere or climate, a general intellectual attitude that is antipathetic to the hegemony of Calvinist doctrines. "Arminianism," paraphrases Paul Ramsey, is "but a loose term for all forms of the complaint of the aggrieved moral nature against the harsh tenets of Calvinism."[29] Thomas Schafer aptly called it "a native American variety of human self-sufficiency."[30]

The concept of supernatural infusion particularly ill-fits this Arminian idea of "human self-sufficiency." The Arminians maintained in one way or another that human nature needs divine betterment, but if any change is to take place at all, they insisted, it has to be brought about by personal decision, not by an alien force that is beyond human control. God's regenerating grace should therefore work within the domain of "natural assistance," that is, assisting and illuminating human reason to make right decisions. All God does in regeneration, according to Daniel Whitby (1638–1726), is to "bring moral motives and inducements to mind, and set them before the understanding."[31] Here again, the debate is between physical infusion and moral illumination. Mastricht's treatise thus found a ready audience in New England.

It was in this context that Jonathan Edwards preferred "infusion" to "illumination." Mastricht's translator, who seems to be a devoted Edwards reader, quotes Edwards in a footnote, hoping to strengthen the author's argument for physical infusion.[32] While it may not be totally contrary to his understanding and intention, Edwards's own reflection on the issue is more properly represented in the following argument:

> Those that deny infusion of grace by the Holy Spirit, must, of necessity, deny the Spirit to do any thing at all. Those who say

---

29. Introduction to *WY*, vol. 1: *Freedom of the Will*, 3. Clyde Holbrook uses the term as "a complex of notions involving an elevated confidence in freedom of choice, a sharply upward revised estimate of human nature, and a form of commonsense moralism, all of which were related to an acute dissatisfaction with Calvinism" (Introduction to *WY*, vol. 3: *Original Sin*, 4–5 n. 9). See also John F. Jamieson, "Jonathan Edwards's Change of Position on Stoddardeanism," *Harvard Theological Review* 74 (1981): 82–83.

30. Schafer, "Jonathan Edwards and Justification by Faith," 55.

31. "Concerning Efficacious Grace," *WW*, 2:547. See also *Freedom of the Will*, 218–22, for Daniel Whitby's argument on moral illumination.

32. See Mastricht, *Treatise*, 37.

there is no infusion, contradict themselves. For they say the Spirit doth something in the soul; that is, he causeth some motion, or affection, or apprehension to arise in the soul. . . . For suppose the Spirit of God only to assist the natural powers, then there is something done betwixt them. . . . Now, that part that the Spirit doth, how little soever it be, is infused. . . . For they say, the Holy Spirit assists the man in acquiring the habit; so that it is acquired rather sooner than it would be otherwise. Or, to act more lively and vigorously than otherwise. . . . Then that liveliness and vigorousness must be infused; . . . It is grace, and therefore infused grace. . . . So that, if any operation of the Holy Spirit at all is allowed, the dispute is only, How much is infused? The one says, a great deal, the other says, but little.[33]

Here Edwards upholds "infusion" as a comprehensive term that includes not only "the infusion of a new habit" but also "the moral suasion upon the understanding." It is nonsensical for him to make a distinction between physically creating a new heart and morally persuading the heart, since for him both are the result of one and the same work of divine infusion; they are different not in kind but in degree, and both are named "physical infusion."[34] On another occasion he repeats that if God's regenerating act consisted merely "in exciting ideas of motives, or in any respect assisting or promoting any effect," it is still named "physical" infusion, not "moral" illumination, because the help is of supernatural origin.[35]

In this way Edwards's use of the word "infusion" carries unmistakable signs of the terminology he learned from the *de auxiliis* controversy, most probably through Turretin and Mastricht. Edwards was, however, more concerned with refuting the Arminian position than with contrasting "infusion" and "illumination." The difference in context required Edwards to use a term different from Calvin's, but his understanding of the operation of grace remained identical with that of the Genevan Reformer, namely, that the converting grace operates integrally upon the entire personality. The effect of infusion is by no means confined to

---

33. "Efficacious Grace," 566–67.
34. Hence Edwards could speak of "the degree of grace which is infused," that is, "weaker" and "stronger" infusion. See Sermon, "Hope and comfort usually follow genuine humiliation and repentance," *WD*, 8:81.
35. "Efficacious Grace," 569.

the understanding or the will alone. It brings forth the knowledge of divine beauty and glory, which is the subject matter of our next discussion.

Conversion as Change of Disposition

How, then, does the work of infusion affect the convert? Fundamental to Edwards's thoughts on conversion is that the infusion of grace causes a radical and abiding change in the *disposition* of the person: "The prime alteration that is made in conversion, that which is first and the foundation of all, is the alteration of the temper and disposition and spirit of the mind."[36]

It is first of all self-evident to Edwards that human beings cannot convert on their own. If ever they are turned from sin, God must be the cause of their conversion.[37] Human beings have no natural capacity for religion. They are "naturally blind" to the things of religion. Not merely are they incapable of turning to God; they are "naturally God's enemies" who "cannot overcome their enmity" by themselves.[38] This is all because there prevails in their hearts "a spirit of atheism" or "a principle of atheism."[39] Edwards calls it "a strange disposition," for "no good reason can be given why men should have such an inward disposition to deny."[40] Furthermore, as with all other dispositions, this strange disposition to atheism increases its strength by exerting itself day by day. "The longer it continues, the worse it grows," says Edwards. It grows like a cancer or gangrene, increasingly polluting and hardening the heart.[41]

Infused grace operates on this utterly helpless disposition of the unconverted. The grace infused, as I will argue in more detail in the next

---

36. "Miscellanies," no. 397 (*Philosophy of Jonathan Edwards*, 249).
37. "Efficacious Grace," 547; *Treatise on Grace*, ed. Paul Helm (Greenwood, S.C.: The Attic Press, 1971), 37–38.
38. Sermons, "Man's Natural Blindness," 17; "Men Naturally God's Enemies," *WW*, 4:40.
39. "Natural men in a dreadful condition," 7; "Men Naturally God's Enemies," 46.
40. *Treatise on Grace*, 53. Even at the last stage of his life, Edwards could not explain how the first parents fell into sin when there was no prior evil disposition that should have induced it. See Holbrook's Introduction to *Original Sin*, 49–53.
41. "Natural men in a dreadful condition," 25.

chapter, is nothing but the Holy Spirit himself opening the eyes of the mind and enabling the person to see divine beauty and excellency. No human effort, not even "the best and most-able men in the world with their greatest diligence and laboriousness," can cause this perception of divine beauty and excellency, since there is no *disposition* in their heart. Unconverted persons may hear the words of the Gospel, but since they do not have the right disposition, they do not see "the beauty of the things of the Gospel" and "the excellency of holiness and of God."[42]

Behind this assertion lies Edwards's innovative conceptualization of imagination as a habit of mind, a unique epistemology that he forged out of Locke's empiricism, which I do not propose to deal with here.[43] What is important to see at this juncture is that conversion consists of the change in disposition, which enables one to see the beauty and excellency of divinity. One's "internal feeling and sense of the mind," or "internal disposition," must first be changed.[44] In the words of Harold Simonson, "what we know" depends in the final analysis on "what we are."[45] To Edwards, the perception of beauty and excellency comes only through the renewed disposition. "The sanctifying influence of the Spirit of God rectifies the taste of the soul, whereby it savors those things that are of God, and naturally relishes and delights in those things that are holy and agreeable to God's mind."[46] Edwards often deplores the shortcomings of language when he attempts to explain "spiritual knowledge." It is "incommunicable" and "ineffable," not merely because the subject is difficult to put into words, but primarily because it does not "make sense" for those who do not share this "internal disposition."[47] This disposition is the ability to form a meaningful perception by ordering and relating the information one receives in "simple ideas." Unregenerate persons may possess sense data but lack the "imagination" to assemble that data into a meaningful whole that

42. "Miscellanies," no. 123 (*Philosophy of Jonathan Edwards*, 246).
43. Locke's empirical theory of perception cannot give an account of how the mind assembles the sense data of "simple ideas" into meaningful "complex ideas." For a detailed argument, see Sang H. Lee, "Mental Activity and the Perception of Beauty in Jonathan Edwards," *Harvard Theological Review* 69 (1976): 369–96; idem, *Philosophical Theology*, chaps. 5 and 6.
44. "Miscellanies," no. 123 (*Philosophy of Jonathan Edwards*, 246).
45. Harold P. Simonson, *Jonathan Edwards: Theologian of the Heart* (Grand Rapids, Mich.: Wm. B. Eerdmans, 1974), 70.
46. "Some Thoughts Concerning the Revival," *WY*, 4:437. See also *Religious Affections*, 283.
47. "Miscellanies," no. 201 (*Philosophy of Jonathan Edwards*, 246–47).

they are meant to convey. To explain divine things to those who do not have this "internal disposition" is like trying to explain the sweet taste of honey to those who have never tasted it.[48] The biblical notion of the "testimony of the Spirit" may also be understood in this sense: When the Holy Spirit is infused, the person is transformed so that he or she is able to see the force of the evidence presented.[49] Conversion means this alteration of one's disposition. "The change of the disposition of the soul, in any case, is the very same as the causing that for the future the mind shall have more lively ideas of such a sort of good. Therefore conversion is nothing but God's causing such an alteration with respect to the mind's ideas of spiritual good."[50]

This also explains at a deeper level why Edwards regarded infusion as the integral operation of grace that unites the division of understanding and will. For Edwards, as for Calvin, the "illumination *by* the Spirit" takes place precisely as the "infusion *of* the Spirit." The light must shine from within. It is "the spiritual light that is *let into the soul* by the Spirit of God," enabling one to discover "the excellency and glory of divine things."[51] The concept can be restated as the interdependence of the immediate inworking of the Holy Spirit and the proclaimed Word as its vehicle. In his well-known sermon "A Divine and Supernatural Light," Edwards explains, "It is not intended that outward means have no concern in this affair. . . . The mind cannot see the excellency of any doctrine, unless that doctrine be first in the mind; but the seeing of the excellency of the doctrine may be immediately from the Spirit of God; though the conveying of the doctrine or proposition itself may be by the word."[52] The "outward means," of which the proclamation of the Word is the principal one, provides the mind with the "subject matter" on which the Holy Spirit works. The Holy Spirit cannot work fittingly if there is no such subject matter in the mind.[53] But the excellency of the

48. *Religious Affections*, 206.
49. "Miscellanies," nos. *aa* and 201 (*Philosophy of Jonathan Edwards*, 244–45, 247).
50. "Miscellanies," no. 284, Yale MSS.
51. "Miscellanies," no. 628 (*Philosophy of Jonathan Edwards*, 251).
52. "A Divine and Supernatural Light," 444.
53. "Miscellanies," no. 539, Yale MSS. See also nos. 325, 542, 629, 1157, Yale MSS. In several "Miscellanies" entries, Edwards speculates about the possibility of the Spirit working without the Word. No doubt God is free to infuse grace where there is no matter to act upon at all. But in such a case grace would have to act "very lamely or monstrously, and so unsuitably," that God ordinarily does not see it "meet" to do so. Just as Elijah prepared the wood orderly on the altar before the fire came down from heaven to set it aflame (1 Kings 18:30–39), there must be a matter on which grace operates properly and

subject matter can only be appreciated by the power of the Holy Spirit working immediately with the Word. The Spirit gives "a due apprehension of the same truths that are revealed in the word of God."[54] The Spirit itself reveals *no new truths,* as Edwards pointed out repeatedly against enthusiasts during the height of the Revival; it rather gives "the true sense of the divine excellency of the things revealed in the word of God, and a conviction of the truth and reality of them thence arising."[55] It makes sense out of what is conveyed by the Word. This is what Edwards calls "infusion of the new principle," or "renewing and sanctifying work of the Holy Ghost."[56]

The operation of the Spirit in the altered disposition of the regenerate is therefore nothing but the orthodox Reformed teaching of the inseparable relationship between the Word and the Spirit, reframed in Edwards's unique language of "beauty" and "excellency." And indeed he was well aware of the Reformed heritage on this issue. In support of his argument, Edwards quotes from the *Institutes*—one of his few references to Calvin—in which Calvin states that the office of the Spirit is not "to make new and before unheard of revelations," but "to seal and confirm to us that very doctrine which is by the gospel."[57] The observation of David E. Willis about the Word joined to the Spirit applies here to Edwards as well: "The Word is self-authenticating only insofar as the Holy Spirit is self-authenticating."[58] Chapter 3 will further examine the nature of this altered disposition. Before we move on to discuss the result of infusion in humanity, however, some questions have to be addressed in order to better understand Edwards's conception of infusion per se. Three questions present themselves here: Is this change of disposition really the work of the Holy Spirit? Does the Spirit work in any way other than infusing and indwelling in human nature? Can the new disposition remain dormant and unexercised?

---

fittingly. In this sense, the Word of God is a means of grace, as it gives opportunity for its proper exercise.

54. "A Divine and Supernatural Light," 444.

55. Ibid. See also *Religious Affections:* "Spiritual understanding does not consist in any new doctrinal knowledge, or in having suggested to the mind any new proposition, not before read or heard of" (278). See also *Faithful Narrative:* "The arguments are the same that they have heard hundreds of times; but the force of the arguments, and their conviction by 'em, is altogether new" (180).

56. "A Divine and Supernatural Light," 439–41; *Religious Affections,* 307.

57. *Religious Affections,* 278 n. 2. Edwards here supplies his own English translation. Cf. *Institutes,* 1.9.1.

58. Willis, *Calvin's Catholic Christology,* 119.

Aspects of Infusion

Infusion and Preparation

The first question to be addressed concerning Edwards's conception of infusion is the origin of the new disposition: How do we know that such a transformation is supernaturally "infused" and not brought about by a natural process as Arminians assert? To this question Edwards replies that an irreparable contradiction will arise if one supposes that the saving disposition is acquired by repeated exercise of holiness. "If the first virtuous act of will or choice be from a preceding act of will or choice, that preceding act of choice must be a virtuous act of choice, which is contrary to the supposition. For then there would be a preceding act of choice before the first virtuous act of choice. And if it be said the first virtuous act of choice is from a preceding act of will which is not virtuous, this is absurd."[59] Therefore, one concludes that the first virtue comes into being by a supernatural operation. If so, this act of infusion must be performed instantaneously and immediately under the absolute initiative of the sovereign God.[60] With this conclusion the question about whether divine calling is "resistible" or not is also answered. Perhaps with Mastricht's work laid open before him, Edwards argued the case with an illustration from Lazarus's resuscitation. Since the unregenerate person is spiritually as dead as Lazarus was in the grave, he or she can resist being called no more than a dead person can.[61] One also concludes that the work of infusion is instantaneous because there is no intermediary moment between life and death.

Such an assertion of the immediate and instantaneous work of conversion may also be found with other theologians. Yet, in the final analysis, Edwards's theological conviction draws its strength from his own personal experience. As he recalled vividly in his personal narrative twenty

---

59. "Efficacious Grace," 569, also 581. See also *Original Sin,* 226. Arguments more or less similar to this are found in early "Miscellanies" entries, for example, nos. *1,* 73, 147 (137), Yale MSS.

60. *Treatise on Grace,* 35; "Efficacious Grace," 592. "Miscellanies," no. 967, Yale MSS, quotes from Plato on the issue; no. 1028, Yale MSS, is his study note from Doddridge's sermon that deals with Xenophon, Seneca, Simplicius, and Maximus Tyrius, all in support of his theory of infused virtue. One may also want to add Thomas Aquinas to the list (*Summa Theologica,* 1–2.113.7).

61. "Efficacious Grace," 592–93. Cf. Mastricht, *Theoretico-Practica Theologia,* 6.3.20.

years after the event, his own conversion was indeed an abrupt change, occasioned by the reading of a scriptural passage (1 Tim. 1:17). It enabled him all of a sudden to see the "horrible" doctrine of God's sovereignty as "exceedingly pleasant, bright, and sweet." Since that time, "a *delightful* conviction" became for him the hallmark of genuine conversion. He was unable for a long time to give an account of how or by what means he had become so convinced, yet finally he concluded that there was an "extraordinary influence of God's Spirit in it."[62]

Probably this personal experience underlies his subtle distantiation from a long and impressive Puritan tradition that Edmund Morgan called "the morphology of conversion."[63] Puritan divines in Old and New England had described—and even *prescribed*—in detail the steps of preparation a person should pass through in order to receive the grace of conversion.[64] Being instantaneous and immediate, however, Edwards's own conversion did not quite match up with the pattern and steps that were considered standard by these divines. Recalling his own conversion in his personal narrative, Edwards could only say to himself that "the chief thing, that now makes me in any measure to question my good estate, is my not having experienced conversion in those particular steps, wherein the people of New England, and anciently the Dissenters of Old England, used to experience it."[65] Since he could not doubt the truthfulness of his own "delightful" conversion experience, he had no alternative but to continue searching for the reason why others spelled out the process in the way they did. One may find the result of his persistent inquiry in his later works during the Revival, including *Faithful Narrative* and *Religious Affections*.[66]

Throughout his inquiry, however, Edwards remained unpersuaded by the idea of presenting any normative "morphology" by which one can judge the saving status of oneself, let alone others. As he clearly states,

---

62. *Life of President Edwards*, 60.
63. Edmund S. Morgan, *Visible Saints: The History of a Puritan Idea* (New York: New York University Press, 1963), 66, 151–52.
64. For an overview of so-called preparationist theories prior to Edwards, see Norman Pettit, *The Heart Prepared: Grace and Conversion in Puritan Spiritual Life* (New Haven: Yale University Press, 1966); Perry Miller, " 'Preparation for Salvation' in Seventeenth-Century New England," *Journal of the History of Ideas* 4 (1943): 253–86.
65. *Life of President Edwards*, 93.
66. *Faithful Narrative*, *WY*, vol. 4; *Religious Affections*, *WY*, vol. 2; see also Sermons, "Pressing into the Kingdom of God," *WW*, 4:382–86; "The manner of seeking salvation," *WW*, 4:370; "Miscellanies," nos. r, 116b, 255, 286, 295, 328, 483, Yale MSS.

"no order or method of operations and experiences, is any certain sign of their divinity."[67] Such human endeavors for conversion may be deemed necessary *as a whole* insofar as this whole is not broken down to particular steps and method. It may be God's *usual* and *ordinary* way "to humble the soul first before he bestows salvation." Yet, as Edwards repeatedly reminded, it is after all *God's* manner, and human beings are in no position to line it up in casuistry for easy reference.[68] It is even "unscriptural," he says, to insist on "a particular account of the distinct method and steps" that the Spirit takes to bring the soul into the state of salvation. The way of grace is "unsearcheable" and "untraceable," and the operation of infusion supernatural and instantaneous, effectuating a radical change in the convert.[69] It may not be totally unexpected, but nonetheless it cannot be demanded or deserved.

Infusion as Indwelling

If such is the case, another question arises: Does the Holy Spirit work at all in the unregenerate? The "preparationists" claimed that it is the Spirit that prepares men and women for conversion. Does Edwards, by keeping this preparationist theory at arm's distance and emphasizing instead the radical change effected by the infused grace, deny that there is any operation of the Holy Spirit prior to conversion? By searching for an answer to this question, one finds a narrower definition to Edwards's concept of infusion.

Edwards's answer is that the Spirit does work on the unregenerate and that it does prepare them for the grace of conversion. The apostle Paul writes that there remains in the hearts of unregenerates a natural conscience even after the Fall, which, being greatly impaired and blinded, needs the "assistance" of the Holy Spirit to become aware of God's deserving wrath and impending punishment (see Rom. 2:14–15). However, this "assistance" of the Spirit *on* the unregenerate is radically

---

67. *Religious Affections*, 151–63. See Edwards's letter to Gillespie, in appendix to *Religious Affections*, 502–3, for his disbelief of "introspection" and "practical syllogism."

68. *Religious Affections*, 416; Sermons, "God makes men sensible of their misery before he reveals his mercy and love," WD, 8:45; "Hope and comfort," 72. Note Edwards's careful expression, "great probability," in "Pressing into the Kingdom of God," 392; "The manner of seeking salvation," 370.

69. *Religious Affections*, 418, 162, respectively. See also "Miscellanies," nos. 675 and 899, Yale MSS, wherein Edwards compares the undiscernible manner of "the formation of X [Christ] in the soul" with "the formation of a child in the womb."

different, Edwards argues, from the work of the Spirit *in* the regenerate, since "no new principle is infused" in the former.[70] The "convincing influence of his Spirit" leads them to "a discovery of God's awful and terrible greatness . . . to excite their terror," which is what Luther called "the second *usus* [use] of the Law." In the regenerate, by contrast, the Spirit brings about the delightful "discovery of God's glory and excellency and grace."[71] Edwards calls this work of the Spirit in the regenerate "evangelical repentance" or "evangelical humiliation," distinguishing it from the work of the Spirit that causes "legal repentance" or "legal humiliation" in the unregenerate.[72] The legal conviction is "but short-lived": it can be easily lost, and once it is lost, backsliding is even more virulent and pernicious. It is short-lived and easily lost because the natural operation of the Spirit acts on them only as "an extrinsic, occasional agent."[73] In contrast, the saving operation of the Holy Spirit is characterized by its constant and steady indwelling within the soul. "The Spirit of God is given to the true saints to dwell in them, as his proper lasting abode; and to influence their hearts, as a principle of new nature, or as a divine supernatural spring of life and action."[74] In the regenerate, the Spirit operates not only by "occasionally influencing the saints," lasting and abiding, the Spirit functions in them "as a vital principle, or as a new supernatural principle of life and action."[75]

One might further ask what the difference is between the "external" and the "indwelling" works of the Spirit. Here is Edwards's crucial answer: When the Holy Spirit "dwells" in the human soul, there is a communication of God's own holiness to the person. At issue here is the theme of "participation" that I mentioned in Chapter 1. Human beings are allowed to participate in the divine nature through the Spirit's self-communication. The preparatory work is indeed the work of the Spirit, Edwards argues, "tho[ugh] there be no holiness in it & so nothing of the nature of the holy Spirit communicated to the soul or exerted in the soul in it."[76] In the unregenerate, the Holy Spirit acts according to

---

70. "God makes men sensible of their misery," 55. See also "Miscellanies," no. 626, Yale MSS.
71. "God makes men sensible of their misery," 56–57, 65.
72. Ibid., 57, 65–69. See also "Hope and comfort," 78, 88, 96; *Faithful Narrative*, 170; *Religious Affections*, 311–40 (sixth sign).
73. "A Divine and Supernatural Light," 440.
74. *Religious Affections*, 200.
75. "Miscellanies," no. 471, Yale MSS.
76. "Miscellanies," no. 734, Yale MSS.

human nature, "assisting the natural principles of reason and conscience," thus awakening them to the terror of dreadful wrath and judgment. But "he [the Holy Spirit] don't [sic] exert his proper nature in them and in union with their souls, so that there shall be a communication of his own natural, essential and eternal act."[77]

In other words, there are two ways in which the Spirit operates: it acts, either in an uninvolved way from outside as "an extrinsic agent," or it communicates and imparts its own nature. The second way of operation is "infusion" in the proper sense of the word. In the unregenerate, "the Spirit may act, and not, in acting, communicate itself," just as the Spirit of God moved upon the face of the waters at the time of creation. In regenerates, the Spirit not only *assists* them in doing better what they ordinarily do, it also *restores* them to the original purposes for which they were created; they are enabled once again to do what they are meant to do.[78] In another context Edwards illustrates this difference with two similar but contrasting words: "lightsome" and "luminous." A thing may be lit up by a light that shines upon it, becoming "lightsome." But, in the case of true saints, God so communicates his nature to them that they become the source of light themselves, becoming "luminous."[79] Precisely speaking, "infusion" means for Edwards this self-communication and self-impartation of the nature of the Holy Spirit to humanity. In this affirmation of an abiding reality of salvation lies the heart of Edwards's soteriology.

Infusion and Sensibility

If conversion is such a drastic and tangible change brought about by the self-communication and self-impartation of the Holy Spirit, a third question arises: Is it possible for an infant, who may show no sign of the change, to be the recipient of this grace? And if it is possible, then does that mean the infused grace can remain dormant or inoperative with no outward exercise, notwithstanding Edwards's repeated assertion that grace must be "sensible"? Part of his distinctive understanding of disposition reveals itself in the answer to this question.

Edwards's unambiguous assumption, first of all, is that children are by nature "children of wrath" (Eph. 2:3). They too must be converted

77. "Miscellanies," no. 471, Yale MSS.
78. Ibid. See also "Miscellanies," no. 626, Yale MSS.
79. *Religious Affections*, 343. See also p. 201.

in order to be saved. But conversion, according to his definition, must be "sensible and visible." As he puts it, "We know how very much God seems to insist on it that his mercy & salvation should be sensible & therefore is wont so to order the circumstance of it as to make it most sensible and visible."[80] The only conclusion Edwards could draw from these premises is that "few are converted in infancy."

Later, in another entry, Edwards seems to back down from this conclusion, however, allowing greater efficacy of Christ's work in the salvation of infants. "Salvation is not sensible at that age to the person that is the subject of it. If that be an hindrance then that is a great disadvantage that infants are under arising from their infancy. But we must look upon X [Christ, who] out of his compassion to infants has removed that & all their other disadvantages."[81] Because of the all-sufficient and all-efficacious work of Christ's redemption, he now says, infants' "unsensibleness" should not constitute a "hindrance" to their being in a state of salvation. Is Edwards caught in a blunt self-contradiction? His careful phrasing of the title of this entry, "Conversion, *or rather*, Regeneration of Infants," seems to suggest otherwise. Edwards feels constrained here to make a distinction that he usually does not honor. The orthodox Reformed and Puritan theologians made fastidious distinctions between such terms as calling, regeneration, conversion, and sanctification, but for Edwards they all mean the same reality of grace infused at one instance.[82] In the case of infants, however, he had to admit that "regeneration" is a better word than "conversion." That is to say, infants are, by the infusion of grace, "regenerated" but not yet "converted." The difference between regeneration and conversion lies in the "sensibleness" of the grace. Yes, salvation must surely be palpable and tangible in adults, but with infants it is possible for grace to remain as yet "unsensible."[83] This "sensibility" issue must be further explained in light of Edwards's concept of disposition.

80. "Miscellanies," no. 816, Yale MSS. Unmoved by the touchy issue of the damnation of infants, Edwards wrote peremptorily in a very early "Miscellanies" entry that "it is most just, exceeding just, that God should take the soul of a newborn infant and cast it into eternal torments" ("Miscellanies," no. *n*, Yale MSS). Compare this to a later entry, no. 1129, Yale MSS.

81. "Miscellanies," no. 849, Yale MSS.

82. See *Charity and Its Fruits*, WY, 8:332; *Treatise on Grace*, 39–40. Cf. Turretin, *Institutio Theologiae Elencticae* 15.4.13; Mastricht, *Theoretico-Practica Theologica*, 6.3.5, 6.8.7.

83. *Religious Affections*, 383–461 (twelfth sign); *Charity and Its Fruits*, WY, 8:294; "Miscellanies," no. 289, Yale MSS.

As I argued earlier, Edwards believes that the work of infusion must take place instantaneously and once and for all at a certain moment, for it is not acquired by repeated exercise. Yet the tangible change that follows this instantaneous infusion takes a long and gradual process before it is fully realized. At several occasions Edwards likens this process to the growth of a fetus. Although "there is a certain moment that an immortal spirit begins to exist in it by God's appointment, the vivification of the fetus in the womb is exceeding[ly] gradual."[84] Consequently, he could assert that "a person according to the gospel may be in a state of salvation, before a distinct and express act of faith."[85] In fact, he is even bolder in another "Miscellanies" entry, stating that no act of the disposition whatsoever, neither faith nor humiliation, is necessary at all for one to be in the state of salvation.

> The disposition is all that can be said to be absolutely necessary. The act cannot be proved to be absolutely necessary; that is, it can't be proved that there is not the disposition before there is an act. . . . The Scripture in many places speaks as plainly about the necessity of a holy life as of believing. But by those expressions concerning a holy life, we can understand nothing else but a disposition that would naturally exert itself in holy [living] upon occasion; so we say of the believing disposition.[86]

The act of faith must naturally and necessarily arise out of the disposition on specific occasions, and in that sense the act is an indispensable condition for salvation. Yet, the specific occasion may not always coincide with the time of infusion, and when there is no occasion to exercise itself in faith, the infused disposition remains there unexercised. This lapse of time translates into the difference between regeneration and conversion. Although Edwards usually speaks of these two interchangeably (and they do coincide in adult converts), he thinks that the word "regeneration" is more appropriate to infants for describing their

---

84. "Miscellanies," no. 241, Yale MSS. See also nos. 302, 847, Yale MSS.
85. "Miscellanies," no. 393, Yale MSS. The assertion could critically undermine the cardinal Protestant doctrine of faith as an essential prerequisite for salvation. Chapter 5 will take up this subject.
86. "Miscellanies," no. 27b, Yale MSS. Edwards here is in private dialogue with his grandfather and predecessor, Solomon Stoddard, who insisted that there cannot be gracious disposition prior to the explicit act of faith.

new disposition. It is this disposition, not its "sensible" exertion, that God takes into account when judging one's saving status.

In the same "Miscellanies" entry, Edwards tries out this conception of the unexercised disposition in two other cases. The first case is when a person—an adult person—dies suddenly. "Supposing a man dies suddenly and not in the actual exercise of faith, 'tis his disposition that saves him." The person is saved on account of his disposition, without regard to its exercise at the time of death. The second case is a person who lived and died before Christ. One need not doubt that the ancient Jews in the Old Testament period were saved. They had the saving disposition, but since they did not have the occasion to exhibit it in actual faith in Jesus Christ, they did not exhibit "the sensible exertions" of their disposition. Yet they were saved on account of that unexerted disposition, which alone, according to Edwards, is "absolutely necessary now, and at all times and in all circumstances." The disposition, in other words, has its own mode of reality apart from actual exercise. It is not reduced to nonexistence when it is not exercised. There is "something really abiding" in their minds, he states, even when "there are no acts or exercises" of it.[87] This is a very important feature of Edwards's conception of disposition, which I will explain in more detail in Chapter 3. In other words, the ontological reality of the disposition is not exhausted by its actual exercises.

It is this conception of an unexercised disposition that Edwards applies to infants. Infants are in the state of salvation, he says, even before they come to the actual exercise of the new disposition in conversion and faith. This is indeed a striking remark for a Puritan theologian to make. The Westminster Confession, for example, did hold to the idea that "elect infants dying in infancy" are saved, but, as for its theological warrant, the article could only point to the indistinct work of the Spirit "who worketh when, and where, and how he pleaseth."[88] John Sanders, reviewing all major theories appearing in history on infant salvation and damnation, concludes that "no position . . . is free from serious difficulties."[89] Edwards's dispositional view of salvation, one might say, gave this article a solid theological basis: infants are saved on account of the disposition that is yet unexercised.

87. "The Mind," no. 69 (*WY*, 6:385).
88. Westminster Confession, chap. 10, iii, in *Creeds of Christendom*, 3:625.
89. John Sanders, *No Other Name: An Investigation into the Destiny of the Unevangelized* (Grand Rapids, Mich.: Wm. B. Eerdmans, 1992), 305.

Edwards goes further to speculate on the possibility of regeneration at birth. The infusion of saving grace can happen "not only indefinitely near to the first moment of creation, but . . . in the very moment that the man begins to [be]." This he thinks is to be properly called "conversion and regeneration," because "although he never was in one sense otherwise, so that there is no alteration properly since the time of his birth, yet there is an alteration from his first state in Adam; and if he has grace infused, it is as much new grace as [in] one that is converted when twenty years old."[90] Regeneration can happen, therefore, at birth—regeneration simultaneously with generation, or the second birth simultaneously with the first! Extraordinary as the idea may sound, it renders Edwards's point unambiguous. A newborn infant may indeed be a regenerate, although not exercising its regenerate disposition. The new disposition, effected by God's immediate and instantaneous act of infusion, can remain unexercised for a long time until the actual occasion arises to exert itself—just as a child is endowed with the faculty of reason and other powers at birth but needs time to develop them into actual use.[91]

Seen from the other end, this infused grace never fails to exert itself when the occasion arises. The disposition is an active tendency to realize what it is disposed to realize upon specified occasions. If grace has set up a new disposition in the regenerate person, it must come into practice automatically and without fail at certain times. I contend that this understanding has some bearing on the qualification controversy Edwards got involved in during the last years of his Northampton ministry. Underneath the whole controversy, which developed in such a bitter and costly manner that he was dismissed from the church because of it, lay Edwards's unwavering conviction that infused grace must necessarily exert itself when the occasion arises. His arguments in the published documents are too preoccupied with breaking the spell of Stoddardeanism to hint at this aspect of his conviction. Yet he gave utterance to it in one passage at least (in *Qualifications*), where he refers to the ten sleeping

---

90. "Miscellanies," no. 78, Yale MSS. In the Index of the "Miscellanies," Edwards lists this entry as "Sanctification from the womb." See Index of "Miscellanies," Yale MSS.

91. "Miscellanies," nos. 241, 302, Yale MSS. Edwards may have taken this analogy from Mastricht, *Theoretica-Practica Theologia*, 6.3.17, 22. See also Edwards's letter to Gillespie, Appendix to *Religious Affections*, 507, where he states that grace can remain "asleep and inactive." Also in "Efficacious Grace": "it may be buried up and lie hid . . . it may seem to be dead" (593).

maidens who awaken at the arrival of the bridegroom.[92] In all likelihood, Edwards is inspired here by Thomas Shepard, who in a similar fashion interpreted the "oil" of the wise maidens as "an inward principle of the spirit of Grace."[93] It is possible, Edwards grants, for the disposition to "be asleep," that is, to remain unexercised. Yet, at the time of crucial importance, what distinguishes the wise maidens from the rest is whether or not they have in their heart the oil (the infused grace) that naturally comes to exercise. Some maidens are awakened to the real exercise of the disposition (their lamps shedding light), while the lamps of the others will have to go out, for they do not have this inward reservoir. It would be strange indeed if the saving disposition did not come forth into a reality—"an external show of the oil"—that is visible before the church.[94] The disposition that does not come into exercise upon occasion, Edwards concludes, did not exist from the beginning. In reply to an objection during the qualification controversy, Edwards stated that for children of unconverted parents "there is no manner of reason to expect any other than that such children ordinarily will grow up in irreligion, whether they are baptized or not."[95] Those unable to profess their faith and conversion were not regenerate at all to begin with, regardless of their baptismal status. The baptism in that case is judged as not having had the content it was supposed to seal.

So far my emphasis has been on an analysis of Edwards's thoughts on conversion as the divine work of infusion. I first examined his use of the word "infusion" against the background of the seventeenth-century theology across the Reformed and Roman Catholic traditions. For Edwards "infusion" means the integral work of the Holy Spirit that brings the entire person to conversion. It causes a radical change of disposition in the person by which he or she is enabled to see divine

92. *Concerning the Qualifications Requisite to a Complete Standing and Full Communion in the Visible Christian Church*, in *WW*, 1:101. See also "Hope and comfort," 85.
93. Thomas Shepard, *The Parable of the Ten Virgins Opened & Applied*, reprint, Jonathan Mitchell and Thomas Shepard [son of author], 1695, 169: "Within these Vessels, is an inward Principle of Life and Grace. Or, The burning shining profession of all the faithful. It proceedeth from an inward Principle of the spirit of Grace, by the means of which their Lamp burns; and their profession shines." See also 164. In *Religious Affections*, Edwards quotes from this book more than "any other human production whatever." See Smith's Introduction, 53–56.
94. *Qualifications*, 101. The issue will be dealt with under the subject of Christian practice in Chapter 6.
95. Ibid., 187.

beauty and excellency. Three inquiries are then undertaken. First, the work is characterized as instantaneous and supernatural, not owing to any natural causation or human preparation. Second, the Spirit's operation in the regenerate defines the term "infusion," properly speaking, as "the self-communication and self-impartation of the Holy Spirit." Finally, it is argued, the transformed disposition can remain unexercised until a preordained occasion arises, and it is on account of this unexercised disposition that regenerate persons, including infants, are saved. Chapter 3 will focus on the fruit of infusion in human nature, namely, the internal principle of the new creation.

3

Conversion
The New Internal Principle

The Gift of Infusion

When Edwards says that natural persons have "no interest" in Christ the Mediator, or that the justified are "interested in Christ's merits," by "interest" he does not mean a subjective state of mind curious to know something about Christ.[1] Edwards was certainly a "theologian of the heart" who emphasized the importance of affections and sensations, but he was by no means a "theologian of subjectivity." What he meant by "interest" may be difficult to grasp across the two centuries that saw a constant process of subjectivization in every domain of civil life and thought. The word "interest" for him is not an epistemological concept but an ontological one, and is best rendered as "participation" or "share." *The Oxford English Dictionary* traces the earliest usage of

---

1. Sermons, "Sinners in the hands of an Angry God," *WW*, 4:316; "Natural men in a dreadful condition," 11; "Justification by Faith alone," *WD*, 5:373, 428; "Efficacious Grace," 565; *Qualifications*, 101, 124–25; "Miscellanies," no. 831, Yale MSS.

"interest" to the mid-fifteenth century when it was used to mean "the relation of being *objectively* concerned in something." At the beginning of the seventeenth century, the word began to have a religious connotation, implying "right or title to *spiritual privileges*." It was only in the late eighteenth century that the word acquired the subjective meaning, "a feeling of concern for or curiosity about a person or thing."[2] Edwards's usage follows the classic meaning of the word: a person is "interested" in Christ and his merits, not because he or she is curious, but because that person is objectively related to Christ. The person has an ontological relation to Christ, a "share" and "participation" in his work.[3]

The question is this: Where is the theological locus of such an ontological participation to be found? Where does this divine contact with the human sphere occur? Edwards's answer is that it is in the "new disposition." The new disposition is, in Edwards's soteriology, the fundamental infrastructure on which all the subsequent categories of grace are securely based in a coherent manner. I mentioned in Chapter 2 that this new disposition is created by the infusion of grace. It has an origin beyond human nature, and is kept in operation only by the power of the Holy Spirit. Yet grace does not remain external. The indwelling of the Holy Spirit creates an *internal* principle of action, so that acting and living by it does not mean a heteronomous domination of one's will from outside. This formation of the new internal principle is the sum and substance of the soteriological "interest" as Edwards perceived it.[4] Grace is never "domesticated" by humanity, for it is God's immediate and continual operation. At the same time, however, grace provides an *intrinsic* principle of action by which one acts spontaneously in Christian freedom. The Spirit works, not as "an extrinsic, occasional agent," but as "a vital principle," taking a "proper lasting abode" in the regenerate person.[5] This dialectic of transcendence and immanence, divine initiative

---

2. See "Interest," in *Oxford English Dictionary*, 2d ed. (Oxford: Clarendon Press, 1989). Among the citations of the classic usage were works of Robert South (1634–1716) and John Flavel (1630–1691). Flavel was one of Edwards's favorite sources of inspiration (see Smith's Introduction, *Religious Affections*, 61).

3. The usage was not a theologian's jargon. A four-year-old girl, according to Edwards's report, used the word with this particular meaning during the Northampton Revival. See *Faithful Narrative*, 201.

4. The contrary scheme has the same ontological category: one who has *"the disposition of the devil . . . partakes of his likeness and misery." Charity and Its Fruits*, WY, 8:230.

5. "A Divine and Supernatural Light," 440.

and human spontaneity, is what I now attempt to capture. Chapter 2 dealt with the aspects of God's infusion; this chapter focuses on its human results.

Infused Grace as New Disposition

Edwards does not make the scrupulous distinctions that Reformed theologians before and after him were fond of making concerning the various stages of salvation. Grace "summarily consists in the principle of holy action." Plain and simple, this definition seemed to him quite sufficient.[6] As he does not accept the preparationist idea of chronological steps that a person is supposed to pass through up to the moment of conversion, he does not compartmentalize the postconversion grace into chronological steps. It is common, Edwards notes, "to speak of various graces of the Spirit of God as though they were so many different principles of holiness, and to call them by distinct names as such—repentance, humility, resignation, thankfulness, etc." But he thinks this is misleading. These are in fact different names of one and the same reality. "They all come from the same fountain, and are, indeed, the various exercises and conditions of the same thing; only different denominations according to the various occasions, objects, and manners, attendants and circumstances of its exercise."[7] He does not shuffle cards such as "calling," "regeneration," "conversion," and "sanctification," except when circumstances require it. For him they all mean one and the same grace infused by the instantaneous work of God. "There is not one conversion to bring the heart to faith, and another to infuse love to God, and another humility, and another repentance, and another love to men."[8] All these virtues are infused at the time of conversion, bringing about one change in the regenerate. And the "principle of Divine love" is Edwards's rendition of all these graces.[9]

Underlying such a simplified scheme of salvation is Edwards's view that a holy act—whatever the kind—presupposes a holy disposition. If there is an act of holiness, be it an act of repentance or of love or of thankfulness, it must be a result of a holy disposition. "There can be no

6. *Charity and Its Fruits*, WY, 8:298. See also *Treatise on Grace*, 42–44.
7. *Treatise on Grace*, 39, 40.
8. *Charity and Its Fruits*, WY, 8:332.
9. *Treatise on Grace*, 34, 40. See Chapter 5 for the Catholic concept of *fides caritate formata*.

holy action without a principle of holy inclination."[10] Such an assertion may require some explanation. We know our actions are not always and without exception the result of a certain disposition within us. We sometimes experience sporadic instincts for good and holy action, even though we do acknowledge that we are not angels for most of our lives. When Edwards says "holy action," he seems to have something different from this in mind. Since he does not give illustrations to help our understanding, here is one from Aristotle's *Nicomachean Ethics*, which I think is not totally alien to Edwards's thinking: "Men think that acting unjustly is in their power, and therefore that being just is easy. But it is not; to lie with one's neighbor's wife, to wound another, to deliver a bribe, is easy and in our power, but to do these things as a result of *a certain state of character* is neither easy nor in our power."[11] The "certain state of character" is the Greek word *hexis*, which is also translated as "disposition." Aristotle's point is that justice is not merely acting, but acting in such a way that the act springs out of one's own state of character, or disposition. One particular and isolated action does not constitute "justice," just as a physician's act of healing consists not in "applying or not applying the knife, in using or not using medicines," but "in doing so in a certain way." It is like a healthy man walking healthily.[12] His state of being healthy necessarily results in his walking healthily, whether he wishes it or not. He does not strive to walk healthily, and he is not constrained to do so. He is naturally disposed to walk that way. It is to be in such a state of healthiness or of justice that, Aristotle says, is not easy or within our immediate power. Similarly, Edwards thinks that a holy action, if it is to be truly holy, has to be rooted in a holy disposition. A natural person, that is, a person who is not yet regenerate from Adam's evil disposition, may do what seems to be a holy action, but one that does not arise from his or her nature, since there is in him or her no such disposition. No one can have an "interest in Christ," therefore, "unless he be the subject of that change in the temper and disposition of his heart."[13] One must have the inner principle of holiness, out of which holy actions spring with spontaneity—this is what it means to be "converted."

10. "Efficacious Grace," 570.
11. Aristotle, *Nicomachean Ethics*, book 5, chap. 9, in *The Basic Works of Aristotle*, ed. trans. Richard McKeon (New York: Random House, 1941), 1018–19.
12. Ibid., book 5, chap. 1, 1002.
13. *Original Sin*, 390, 391, 370.

Edwards's concept of disposition differs from that of Aristotle at one important point: namely, it is not acquired by repeated acts. If there is going to be a holy disposition, as I argued in Chapter 2, it has to be supernaturally implanted. The Holy Spirit has to communicate its own holiness to the regenerate, initiating in their disposition a radical change. This change is so radical that the regenerate is now able to "have a relish of the loveliness and sweetness of the supreme excellency of the Divine nature," which was not possible in any ways before.[14] This change of nature is brought about within the depths of the human self. Although "conversion don't [sic] entirely root out the natural temper," Edwards allows, echoing Calvin, "evil dispositions . . . shall no longer have dominion over him."[15] Evil dispositions, in other words, now no longer constitute the person's *hexis*, or "character."

Infused Grace as Uncreated Gift

The second point I have to emphasize about Edwards's concept of infused grace is that what is infused is the Holy Spirit itself. In Chapter 2, the two modes of operation of the Holy Spirit were mentioned. In the unregenerate, the Spirit operates according to *their nature*, assisting their natural reason and conscience.[16] In the regenerate, in contrast, the Holy Spirit operates according to *its own nature*, communicating its own holiness to them and sanctifying them. The "gift" of the Spirit, therefore, is not only "*from* the Spirit, but it also *partakes of* the nature of that Spirit."[17] The gift enables a person to participate in the holiness of God, and if the regenerate person partakes of the essential nature of the Holy Spirit in such a manner, then the infused gift means nothing short of the presence of the Spirit with "its proper, natural and essential acts in itself *ad intra*, or within the Deity from all eternity."[18] The third Person of the Trinity is directly and immediately present in the regenerate, just as it is in the immanent Trinity. Grace in the soul, Edwards writes, "is the Holy Ghost acting in the soul, and there

---

14. *Treatise on Grace*, 49. See also *Charity and Its Fruits*, WY, 8:294, 344; and *Religious Affections*, 340.
15. *Religious Affections*, 341–42. Cf. Calvin, *Institutes*, 3.3.11.
16. See "Miscellanies," nos. 471, 734, 1103, Yale MSS.
17. *Treatise on Grace*, 56 (emphasis mine).
18. "Miscellanies," no. 471, Yale MSS.

communicating his own holy nature," or "the very Holy Ghost dwelling in the souls acting there as a vital principle."[19]

To say that the gift of infusion in human beings (*donum*) is the Holy Spirit itself who is the giver (*donator*) necessarily implies taking a distinctive attitude toward a theological controversy of several centuries in Western Catholic theology. In the twelfth century, Peter Lombard claimed that charity is not something created but is the Holy Spirit itself dwelling in the human mind. This indwelling Holy Spirit is called *gratia increata* (uncreated grace). According to Thomas Aquinas, Lombard did not mean to identify the Holy Spirit with the movement of love, but rather meant that the Spirit works "without any intermediary habit."[20] Thomas, with all due respect to "the Master" Lombard, did not quite concur. If the Holy Spirit moves the human mind in such a way that the mind "be merely moved, without being the principle of this movement, as when a body is moved by some extrinsic motive power," Thomas contends, it would be "contrary to the nature of a voluntary act, whose principle needs to be in itself." In order for the will to be itself, therefore, "there should be in us some habitual form superadded to the natural power, inclining that power to the act of charity."[21] This "habitual form" is called *gratia creata* (created grace). Thomas's objection is based on his apprehension that the unmediated exercise of the Holy Spirit would destroy human spontaneity, which is essential for the movement of charity.

The controversy obviously has some aspects in common with the Reformation debate about the nature of the operation of grace in humanity. Calvin, while strongly emphasizing the palpable reality of regeneration, took sides with the Lombardian concept and chose not to speak of this reality in terms of a new habit.[22] The Council of Trent, on the other hand, endorsed the Thomist view by carefully describing the righteousness of the justified as "the justice by which God *makes us just*."[23]

Edwards may not have been aware of this controversy at all. He does

---

19. *Charity and Its Fruits*, WY, 8:332; *Treatise on Grace*, 74.
20. *Summa Theologica*, 2-2.23.2. Cf. Magistri Petri Lombardi, *Sententiae In IV Libris Distinctae*, Collegii S. Bonaventurae ad Claras Aquas, ed. (Rome: Grottaferrata, 1971), 1.2.142.
21. Ibid.
22. See "Grace, Controversies on," in *New Catholic Encyclopedia*.
23. *The Canons and Decrees of the Council of Trent*, trans. H. J. Schroeder (Rockford, Ill.: Tan Books, 1978), 6th sess., chap. 7.

not use the terms "created grace" and "uncreated grace" characteristic to the controversy. Even though we now know that Thomas Aquinas was part of the standard learning of many New England Puritans, Edwards's direct interaction with the writings of Thomas is still hard to document.[24] Edwards was, however, well aware of the revisionist position he took when he proposed a change to the traditional way of understanding the trinitarian work of redemption. Referring to the classical role of the Holy Spirit as "an applier" of what is achieved by the Son, he says, "merely to apply to us, or immediately to give or hand to us blessing purchased, after it is purchased, is subordinate to the other two Persons." The Holy Spirit, according to Edwards, plays as positive and significant a role as the Father (who paid the price for redemption) and as the Son (who sacrificed himself for the purchase), for the Holy Spirit itself is "the gift purchased." "The price, and the thing bought with that price, answer each other in value; and to be the excellent benefit offered, is as much as to offer such an excellent benefit."[25] His concern in the revision is rather doxological, giving equal glory and honor to the three Persons, yet this reformulation shows Edwards strongly inclined toward the Lombardian motif: grace is the direct presence of the ever-living Spirit, the uncreated grace.

With this enhanced role of the Holy Spirit, Edwards advances a trinitarian formula of redemption. "God the Father is the person of whom the purchase is made; God the Son is the person who makes the purchase, and the Holy Spirit is the gift purchased."[26] The formula was already present in embryonic form in his Boston lecture, in which he stated that the redeemed have all their good "of God" (the Father, who is the author of redemption), "through God" (the Son, who is the medium and price), and "in God" (the Holy Spirit, who is the good purchased).[27] With this trinitarian formulation, Edwards's subscription

24. According to Norman Fiering, Thomas Aquinas was "very well known in early seventeenth-century philosophy and was cited occasionally in student notebooks that have survived from Harvard in this period" (Fiering, "Will and Intellect," 519–20). Stoddard owned a couple of Thomas's works and one of a later Thomist, Francis Suarez. See idem, "Solomon Stoddard's Library at Harvard," *Harvard Library Bulletin* 20 (1972): 262–69.
25. *Treatise on Grace*, 69.
26. *Charity and Its Fruits*, WY, 8:353. See also *History of the Work of Redemption*, 117–18, 375; "Wisdom of God," 141.
27. "God glorified in Man's Dependence," 170–74, 177. "Miscellanies," no. 402, Yale MSS, indicates that Edwards came to this understanding at least a year or two before his Boston lecture.

to the Lombardian understanding seems to be complete. The saving disposition owes its existence and exercise entirely to the working of this indwelling Spirit. "If God should take away His Spirit out of the soul," he says, the saving disposition would "cease as immediately as light ceases in a room when a candle is carried out."[28] The Holy Spirit is not only the giver of the gift, but is the very gift given in salvation.

Infused Grace as Internal Principle

Having said this, I now have to reemphasize the contrary. For all the underscoring of the transcendent and supernatural character of the gift of the Holy Spirit, Edwards did not leave it hovering above human nature. The gift of the Holy Spirit necessarily brings about a new principle by which one naturally and spontaneously acts out holy practice. A passage in *Religious Affections*, quoted above to distinguish the two modes of the Spirit's operation, is worth repeating here to illustrate this abiding and relatively independent reality of the changed disposition. "The soul of a saint receives light from the Sun of Righteousness, in such a manner, that its nature is changed, and it becomes properly a luminous thing: not only does the sun shine in the saints, but they also become little suns, partaking of the nature of the fountain of their light."[29] Saints are not just "a reflecting glass" that is lit up by an external light source, but they become "the lamps in the tabernacle" that burn and shed their own light. Being lit up, they themselves become the source of light. An abiding and enduring reality of the transformed disposition in the regenerate is decisively accentuated here. This abiding reality of regeneration of course does not mean a domestication of the Spirit, who is their ultimate Source and on whose presence their shining is entirely dependent. Yet it is not something extrinsic to the soul. The Spirit is not a sojourner, but an indweller; and the soul is not a temporary abode, but an enduring dwelling.

But how does this view square with Edwards's insistence on the supernatural character of infusion? If the new disposition is set up by God's action, can we really say that it is *our* disposition and *our* principle? An early "Miscellanies" entry shows that Edwards asked this question of himself. In that entry he takes an example of the saints in

---

28. *Treatise on Grace*, 75.
29. *Religious Affections*, 343; see also p. 201.

heaven who have a virtue infused. The virtue "is wrought in the saints immediately by the power of God; *and yet that it is virtue notwithstanding.*" If so, he continues, then "why are not the beginnings of holiness [that is, the holiness of the saints on earth] wrought in the same manner? . . . And why is not the beginning, thus wrought, as much virtue as the perfection thus wrought?"[30] The point of the argument rests in that, while virtue is a product of God's supernatural and immediate work of infusion, it is nonetheless a virtue of one's own. It is so because the infused gift is really *in-fused*, namely, let *into* the depths of human nature and *fused* with it, establishing there an intrinsic principle of action. The grace infused from outside does not eradicate or supplant human freedom. On the contrary, it liberates the person by establishing "a vital principle in the soul."[31] A person is free only when he or she has a principle of action within himself or herself. The infusion of grace is necessary, not because it has to replace nature, but precisely so that nature may be established in its own right. Vernon Bourke describes where the Thomist concern lies on this issue: "It does not diminish the element of voluntary control, or verge upon involuntary, automatic, and so non-human, activity. Rather it represents an increase in the power of intellect and will, a vital growth of originally imperfect potencies."[32] Herein lies the reason why Edwards defines grace as "a principle of holy action." The indwelling grace furnishes the regenerate persons with this genuine Christian freedom in which they will be naturally inclined to holy actions. "Virtue," "principle," and "disposition" are all practically synonymous in Edwards's terminology: grace creates in the regenerate a virtue, a new principle, or a new disposition. It is like a seed implanted in the soul, he explains after the manner of Mastricht, by which is meant an "inward principle of nature . . . from whence all gracious actings flow."[33]

Edwards is here again touching on the Thomist view of "created grace." Grace creates in human beings an abiding reality of salvation in the form of a new disposition. The difference between Lombard and

---

30. "Miscellanies," no. 147 (137), Yale MSS (emphasis mine).
31. "God glorified in Man's Dependence," 175.
32. Vernon J. Bourke, "The Role of Habitus in the Thomist Metaphysics of Potency and Act," in *Essays in Thomism*, ed. Robert E. Brennan (New York: Sheed & Ward, 1942), 106–7.
33. "Efficacious Grace," 593. Cf. Mastricht, *Theoretico-Practica Theologia*, 6.3.13, 22.

Thomas is not whether they think the Holy Spirit *dwells* in the person or not, which both affirm. The real difference lies in whether or not they think this indwelling Spirit creates in the person an "intermediary habit," through which the movement of love occurs. This Lombard denies, and Thomas affirms. Put otherwise, Thomas affirms the presence of uncreated grace (the Holy Spirit), but also affirms the existence of created grace *in addition to* the uncreated grace.[34] If we understand this distinction correctly, Edwards's notion of the internal principle emerges as a close correlative of Thomas's notion of the "intermediary habit," but does not reject the Lombardian motif of the continual operation of the Spirit in and through this habit. The Holy Spirit never *becomes* a created grace, and in that sense it is never domesticated or encapsulated by humanity. But the Spirit *issues in* the formation of a new habit through which it operates. Without this "intermediary habit," Edwards believes with Thomas, only the divine agent would be at work, and no participation could occur from the side of regenerate humanity. Human beings would then be merely moved, as a stone is moved by an extrinsic motive power, which is obviously contrary to what the Holy Spirit achieves by salvation. Here are two aspects combined in one form. First, as Conrad Cherry correctly noted, the supernatural gift does not "collapse into the human faculties."[35] It is not "given over" to human possession. Second, the infused gift does not remain extrinsic to the human self. It creates in human nature an abiding reality of salvation, a new habit or a new disposition, which Edwards does not hesitate to call an inherent quality. "The blessing of the saving grace of God is *a quality inherent in the nature* of him who is the subject of it."[36] The word "inherent" here does not mean inborn or innate; it means intrinsic.[37]

---

34. See Edward Yarnold, *The Second Gift: A Study of Grace* (Slough, England: St. Paul Publications, 1974), 53, for a similar comment.

35. Cherry, *Theology of Jonathan Edwards*, 41; see also 28–29, 30–31, 42–43.

36. *Charity and Its Fruits*, WY, 8:157 (emphasis mine). The word "subject" here denotes the receiver, *not* the giver, of grace. Edwards here speaks of "an inherent quality" in contrast to "extraordinary gifts" such as prophecy, speaking with tongues, and working miracles. These extraordinary gifts, however remarkable, do not make the person holy or excellent, whereas "true grace in the heart is . . . the preciousness of the heart, by which the very soul itself becomes a precious jewel." Grace is an "inherent" quality in this sense.

37. According to *The Oxford English Dictionary* (see "inherent"), "inherent" in Edwards's day primarily and foremost meant "remaining, or abiding in some thing or person," that is, "indwelling," or "intrinsic." It is only in a derivative sense that the word meant "innate" or "inborn."

It is worth recalling again Edwards's understanding of infusion as the self-communication and self-impartation of the Holy Spirit. By communicating and imparting its own holiness and excellency, the Spirit forms in the regenerate an abiding and intrinsic reality, or an intermediary habit in Thomas's words, through which it operates. Because of the holiness and excellency of the gift that is communicated, Edwards says, regenerates also become "little suns," and "the very soul itself becomes a precious jewel."[38] Clearly, he intends in these remarks to emphasize the fact that grace does not dominate the soul extrinsically or heteronomously. "He [the Spirit] don't only live without it [that is, outside it], so as violently to actuate it; but he lives in it; so that that also is alive."[39] The legacy of the medieval Angelic Doctor is retrieved here by the theologian of Puritan New England.

Actually, under the theological climate of New England, Edwards had one other reason to move toward the Thomist understanding. John Taylor, Edwards's archenemy in the original sin controversy, asserted that "*inwrought* virtue, if there were any such thing, would be no virtue; not being the effect of our own will, choice and design, but only of a sovereign act of God's power."[40] Edwards's refutation here reiterates Thomas's conception of voluntariness. For Thomas, as for Edwards, the essence of a voluntary action consists in "having a principle within the agent."[41] In order for an action to be counted as one's own, whether good or evil, one has to have his or her own disposition from which the action arises. It is precisely what Taylor called "inwrought virtue" that functions as such an intrinsic principle. The will is thereby not dominated extrinsically or forced into service; rather, the love of God becomes in the saints the foundation of their true freedom. Only insofar

---

38. *Religious Affections*, 343; *Charity and Its Fruits*, WY, 8:158. In one passage Edwards further hints at the paradoxical fulfillment of Satan's word, "you shall be as gods" (Gen. 3:5). See "Wisdom of God," 158.

39. *Religious Affections*, 342. For this reason Edwards quotes John 14:19, "Because I live, ye shall live *also*," along with Galatians 2:20, "Yet *not* they, *but* Christ lives in them." The Johannine verse has a tone more theonomous than the Pauline one. See *Treatise on Grace*, 73.

40. John Taylor, *The Scripture-Doctrine of Original Sin, Proposed to Free and Candid Examination* (London, 1738 [1740]), 180, 245, 250; quoted in Edwards's *Original Sin*, 359; emphasis in Edwards's text. Edwards himself knew well the force of the opponent's argument. See "Efficacious Grace," 554.

41. *Summa Theologica*, 1–2.6.1, 114.1. See George Tavard, *Justification: An Ecumenical Study* (New York: Paulist Press, 1983), 41.

as it arises freely out of its own principle can love be counted as one's own action and as such a virtue. Thomas's objection to the Lombardian position was also grounded on this consideration: charity must be habitualized, Thomas insisted, for it is the nature of a voluntary act to have a principle with which it works, and love is such a voluntary act par excellence. Robert Scharlemann, a contemporary Thomist, explains this succinctly.

> The Lombardian solution denies what it attempts to affirm. . . . If the impulse of theological love were, as the Lombard maintained, a direct and extrinsic movement on the will by the Holy Spirit without a mediating virtue, then the uniqueness of the movement of the will would be annulled. It is in the nature of the will that it is never simply moved but also self-moving at the same time; there is no such thing as a voluntary movement whose cause is purely external.[42]

This is exactly Edwards's position when he says that grace provides the human agent with an intrinsic principle.

Edwards's often-quoted comment concerning the concurrence of God's activity and human activity can be best understood in the light of this intrinsic principle: "In efficacious grace we are not merely passive, nor yet does God do some, and we do the rest. But God does all, and we do all. God produces all, and we act all. For that is what he produces, viz., our own acts. God is the only proper author and fountain; we only are the proper actors. We are, in different respects, wholly passive, and wholly active."[43] Edwards gives here an example of Titus from the Scripture: God has put into his heart "forwardness" to go to Corinth, but he went there, "being more forward, of his own accord" (KJV, 2 Cor. 8:16–17).[44] "Efficacious grace," therefore, is not inconsistent with human freedom. What God does is no more and no less than to create a new principle of the heart, or a new disposition, by which one acts freely and with spontaneity. Virtues in the saints are first supernaturally

---

42. Robert Scharlemann, *Thomas Aquinas and John Gerhard* (New Haven: Yale University Press, 1964), 131.

43. "Efficacious Grace," 580.

44. Edwards may have taken this example from Witsius. Cf. Herman Witsius, *The Oeconomy of the Covenants Between God and Man: Comprehending a Complete Body of Divinity* (London, 1762), book 3, chap. 5, 472. The original Latin edition was published in Utrecht, 1693.

infused, or "inwrought" as Taylor puts it, yet nevertheless they are real virtues on their own because the infusion establishes within them a new principle by which they spontaneously and freely engage in virtuous acts. Taylor does not understand that human beings are free only when they have this intrinsic principle within themselves.

A comment is to be made here regarding a charge of "spirit-mysticism" directed against Edwards. In making the observation that Edwards does not make the Holy Spirit collapse into something human, Conrad Cherry seems to be embarrassed by Edwards's remarks that accentuate such an "inherent quality" of regeneration. These statements, Cherry worries, are susceptible to being interpreted as "mystical identity" or "absorption" of humanity into deity.[45] Edwards, however, sees the danger creeping in from the opposite direction:

> Some foolishly make it an argument in favor of their discoveries and affections, that when they are gone, they are left wholly without any life or sense, or anything beyond what they had before. They think it an evidence that what they experienced was wholly of God, and not of themselves; because (say they) when God is departed, all is gone; they can see and feel nothing, and are no better than they used to be.

To this Edwards quickly launches a reply, affirming an abiding and inherent reality of the new creation. The mystical enthusiasm must be avoided, not by rejecting the inherent and abiding reality of salvation, but precisely by affirming and underscoring it:

> These persons are mistaken, as to the manner of God's communicating himself and his Holy Spirit, in imparting saving grace to the soul. He gives his Spirit to be united to the faculties of the soul, and to dwell there after the manner of a principle of nature; so that the soul, in being indued with grace, is indued with a new nature: but nature is an *abiding* thing . . . so as through Christ's power, to have *inherent* in itself, a vital nature.[46]

---

45. Cherry, *Theology of Jonathan Edwards*, 31, 37, 85–88. Cherry is here arguing against Douglas J. Elwood, *The Philosophical Theology of Jonathan Edwards* (New York: Columbia University Press, 1960), 145, 157.

46. *Religious Affections*, 342 (emphasis mine). The abiding reality of the transformed nature is the "seventh sign" of genuine religious affections.

With these straightforward words, Edwards affirms a real transformation in the nature of the regenerate. Those who deny the reality of this transformation do not understand "the manner of God's communicating himself and his Holy Spirit." This communication of divine nature is what constitutes the kernel of Edwards's vision of salvation. At the same time, he recognizes that the tangible reality of salvation in the redeemed is sustained and preserved as such only by God's immediate and continual presence. His soteriology does not lose sight of the Lombardian truth, either.

Edwards is thus more attentive to the creaturely reality of salvation in humanity than has been previously suggested. The Holy Spirit may not "collapse" into human existence, but the power of the Spirit is vitally "united" to human faculties in such a way that an abiding and indeed "inherent" or "intrinsic" reality of regeneration is constituted. His use of the word "inherent" may sound obtrusive to some critics, giving an incorrect association with "innate" or "inborn." Yet I believe I have sufficiently shown that this is not what he means by "inherent." Neither does he mean to domesticate the uncreated gift in human nature; the created grace cannot operate without the uncreated grace. The dialectic of Edwards's soteriology is one that is also found in Thomas (and in Turretin, as will be seen below). Once infused, the gift of the Holy Spirit imparts itself and communicates its own nature to human beings, and by so doing transforms them from within and creates an intrinsic principle. Without such a self-communication and self-impartation of the indwelling Spirit, infusion is not a real infusion. And without such participation of humanity in the holiness and excellency of the Spirit, grace would not be savingly present in humanity.

Turretin on Infused Grace

The concept of "disposition" or "habit," needless to say, is not Edwards's invention. Several intellectual streams have been identified as sources of his concept of "habit" as a general term of ontology.[47] But

---

47. Besides Aristotle and Thomas, Lee finds the following sources to be influential in Edwards's formation of the concept: Burgersdicius, John Owen, William Ames, John Flavel, Thomas Shepard, Ralph Cudworth, and John Locke. Locke and Hume even made some abortive attempts to address the questions of comparable nature. Lee, *Philosophical Theology*, 17–34. Lee also lists Ephraim Chambers, but Chambers's *Cyclopaedia* (first published in 1728) was not available in Edwards's formative years.

the use of the concept in soteriology has only few precedents to trace. First used by Thomas Aquinas in this soteriological sense, the concept of disposition did not gain any denotation that can be called new or distinctive. A number of Reformed and Puritan theologians within Edwards's reach also used the concept, largely in accordance with Thomas's usage, but of those the one most prominent and influential on Edwards was without doubt Francis Turretin. Edwards avowedly confessed his indebtedness to this "great Turettine," who, together with Mastricht, furnished the basic categories and theories of theology for subsequent generations of theologians, including Edwards.[48] In spite of such importance, Turretin's influence on Edwards has been more presupposed than actually examined. It is for this reason that I think it appropriate to review Turretin's thoughts on infused grace here. Such an examination will shed light on Edwards's indebtedness to tradition, as well as on his original contribution to it.

What strikes me, first of all, in reading Turretin on calling and conversion is that this grandmaster of Reformed polemics thought it appropriate to discuss the question by depending on the Roman Catholic *de auxiliis* controversy that I mentioned in Chapter 2. He does this by reviewing a book of still another Roman theologian, Cardinal Robert Bellarmine (1542–1621), who was commissioned to write an official report on the controversy.[49] In contrast, Turretin did not find even a single line worth quoting from any of the Protestant theologians or confessions. Not that the Protestant sources do not treat the subject. Calvin and all other succeeding Reformed theologians, and the confessions they formulated, treat the subject thoughtfully and meaningfully. But, in Turretin's judgment, none of them is as important, illuminative, or useful as the arguments made during that Roman Catholic debate. Since his argument has an obvious tilt toward Thomism, it should indicate the extent of influence Thomas's theology exercised upon seventeenth- and eighteenth-century Reformed theology. Edwards himself may not have had direct contact with the writings of Thomas, but, given his thorough reading of Turretin, he may have gone fairly deep

---

48. *Religious Affections*, 289. Williams, "Six Letters of Jonathan Edwards," 230. Mastricht was equally influential on Edwards and his contemporaries, but his writings are less voluminous than Turretin's.

49. See Brodrick, *Life and Works of Bellarmine*, 2:18–22. Turretin's argument is based on Bellarmine's *de gratia et libero arbitrio*, not on his official report, *de Controversia Lovaniensi*. For text, see Robert Bellarmine's *Opera Omnia* (Neapolis, 1856), 4:267–459.

into the heart of Thomist theology without so realizing. Turretin functioned as a hermeneutical funnel through which Edwards received the Thomistic concerns of soteriology.

The questions Turretin had before him to answer were clear alternatives: Does effectual calling consist in "moral suasion" or in "physical operation"? He denies the former alternative, while affirming the latter "against the Romanists and Arminians."[50] What Turretin repudiates under the name of "the Romanists," however, turns out to be a group of Jesuits called Molinists, who asserted in one way or another that effectual calling consists "in the assent and co-operation of man." Turretin charges them for bringing back "the very error of Pelagius," transferring the principal cause of conversion from God to the free will of man.[51] He instead opts for the Thomist view, which affirms "a real and physical action of God." Effectual calling determines the will, not with "mere suasion" but with "an omnipotent and irresistible power."

While Turretin concedes that this opinion "comes nearest to the truth," he qualifies his endorsement of it by registering two complaints. One concerns the word "physical," by which some may "confound the natural acts of Providence with the supernatural acts of grace."[52] What he means here is the *causation* of the first operation of God. Turretin does not want "physical" to imply any "natural" causation. Conversion is wrought in the human subject by the powerful and extraordinary infusion of grace, not by a chain of natural causations that ordinarily prevail in God's providential acts. However, the affirmation of supernatural origin does not entail the denial of ensuing creaturely reality in humanity. The grace that is supernaturally infused by God's "physical" operation brings forth, in Turretin's words, "qualities, or habits, and dispositions," namely, *"something inherent and permanent."*[53] The causation may be indeed supernatural, but the result of this supernatural operation is inherent and permanent, and in that sense "natural." The Spirit's operation is not to "naturalize" the supernatural grace, but to affirm its powerful *effect* in the natural. This process is important in Turretin's view, for, as in Thomas, grace operates "by way of *principle*,"

---

50. Turretin, *Institutio Theologiae Elencticae*, 15.4, title.
51. Ibid., 15.4.2. Turretin actually recognizes Molinaeus ("from the event") and Bellarmine ("from congruity") at variance, depending on the kind of role *scientia media* plays in the picture. But in Turretin's judgment the difference is nominal. Ibid., 15.4.4–8.
52. Ibid., 15.4.9.
53. Ibid., 15.4.13 (emphasis mine).

which enables a person to act voluntarily. Efficacious grace "would flow into the will itself for its renewal and vivification, in order that, itself being renewed and acted upon by God, *it might act as a cause.*"⁵⁴

The other revision Turretin makes concerns the phrase "physical predetermination." He states explicitly that this "physical predetermination" does not lead to the exclusion or denial of the participation of human will in the process of conversion. Interestingly enough, the Thomists with whom Turretin was in accord were so insistent on divine predetermination that their opponents denounced them as Calvinists.⁵⁵ But, in fact, neither Thomas himself nor later Thomists, including Turretin, failed to put great emphasis on the participation of human will in the work of conversion. What they were trying to do was safeguard the movement of free will in conversion in a manner not detrimental to the absolute prevenience of God's converting grace. Turretin does this by making a distinction between "habitual conversion [or regeneration]" and "actual conversion [or conversion in the narrower sense]," the first being totally dependent on divine initiative, while the second is effected by the human will that is vivified by the first.⁵⁶

It is at this juncture that Turretin invokes the Augustinian concept of the "delightful conqueror" (*victrix delectationis*), who moves us "both powerfully and sweetly, pleasingly and invincibly."⁵⁷ What this means is that although the operation of grace is not merely external "teaching" or "persuading," it is nonetheless not coercion of any kind. The soul is sweetly and pleasantly moved—or better, the soul is inclined to move itself voluntarily—"such as becomes the intelligent and rational nature" of human beings.⁵⁸ With the notion of "delightful conqueror," Turretin dismisses the charge of "making man into a log or a trunk"—a charge often directed against Calvinist theology, be it "Protestant" or "Roman Catholic."⁵⁹ The operation of efficacious grace does not injure the will,

---

54. Ibid., 15.4.12 (emphasis mine).
55. See "De auxiliis," in *The Oxford Dictionary of the Christian Church*; McGrath, *Iustitia Dei*, 2:95; Brodrick, *Life and Work of Bellarmine*, 2:14, 32.
56. Turretin, *Institutio Theologiae Elencticae*, 15.4.13. In support of his argument, Turretin quotes a scripture passage that Catholics also favor: "Convert us, O Lord, to thee, and we shall be converted" (Lam. 5:21). Cf. *Summa Theologica*, 1–2.109.6; *Canons and Decrees*, 6th sess., chap. 5.
57. Turretin, *Institutio Theologiae Elencticae*, 15.4.18 (Latin ed., 462).
58. Ibid. The expression is again reminiscent of Thomas's definition of grace. See *Summa Theologica*. 1–2.113.3.
59. Turretin, *Institutio Theologiae Elencticae*, 15.4.16, 21. The charge was commonly directed against Calvinism. See the Synod of Dort, Third and Fourth Heads of Doctrine,

but rather sets up the foundation of the will by making a principle of its own. The more the will is subjected to the actual grace of God, therefore, the more freely it moves.⁶⁰ This is quite in line with Thomas, who defined the nature of voluntariness as "having a principle within the agent."⁶¹ As a consequence, Turretin modifies his initial answer to the question on the operational mode of efficacious grace. He now affirms both moral suasion and physical predetermination: "The movement of efficacious grace is properly to be called *neither Physical nor Ethical*, but supernatural and divine, *which in a measure includes both these relations.*"⁶²

With these qualifications Turretin makes it clear that, although the mode of the operation of efficacious grace is supernatural and physical, infused grace creates an abiding and internal principle of action by which a person freely and voluntarily achieves his or her own conversion. The operation is certainly not "natural," and the grace is not "given over" to human control; nonetheless, it crystallizes into something intrinsic and abiding in human nature. Otherwise, the conversion cannot really be *our* conversion.

Edwards's Dispositional Ontology: A Review

Undoubtedly Edwards learned much from Turretin's Thomistic concern for the human will being actively involved in the work of conversion. Yet Edwards's radically dispositional view of reality did not allow him to remain where Turretin ended. It is necessary to review here Edwards's dispositional ontology, as it has a close correlation with some of the distinctive features of his soteriology, which is to be examined below.

In his list of "Subjects to be handled" attached to "The Mind,"

---

16 (*Creeds of Christendom*, 3:591); Westminster Confession, chap. 10, "Of Effectual Calling" (*Creeds of Christendom*, 3:625). Edwards also had to confront similar charges from Arminians. See "Concerning the Divine Decrees in General and Election in Particular," WW, 2:522.

60. Turretin, *Institutio Theologiae Elencticae*, 15.4.9.
61. *Summa Theologica*, 1–2.6.1.
62. Turretin, *Institutio Theologiae Elencticae*, 15.4.18 (emphasis mine). Efficacious grace moves the will "congruously to consent" (ibid., 15.4.8). In view of these remarks it is regrettable to see the argument represented by Cherry as either-or alternatives. Cherry, *Theology of Jonathan Edwards*, 36.

Edwards wrote: "It is laws that constitute all permanent being in created things, both corporeal and spiritual."[63] A little later he picked up the theme again and said that these "laws" are "stated methods fixed by God," on which "the very being of created things depend."[64] The being of created things depends on these laws, because God exercises his power of resistance and causation in created things through them. Lee calls them "conditional laws," for, according to an early "Miscellanies" entry, "all habits [are] a law that God has fixed, that such actions upon such occasions should be exerted."[65] Habits and dispositions are the laws according to which God causes actions and events. These remarks constitute the axiom of Edwards's dispositional ontology. The dispositional view of reality has within it two contrasting claims that are integrated in a dynamic unity: the world's radical and total dependence on God, and its relative permanence and integrity. These two claims will be reviewed below in some detail.

First, the reality of all created entities, whether corporeal or spiritual, depends entirely and unceasingly on the immediate intervention of God's causal power. If being is essentially laws and habits, as defined in the above quotations, then all created entities tend inherently and unceasingly toward actual existence through the immediate exercise of divine power in them. "Reality is not something that is achieved once and for all but something that is achieved again and again."[66] Although for Edwards laws and habits possess their own mode of reality apart from actual exercise, as will be argued next, their actuation into full existence is moment by moment, contingent upon the power of God who causes them to be and to continue to be according to these established laws.

This theme of the constant and immediate divine intervention appears in Edwards's writings at a number of points. His early interest in metaphysics touches on it when he defines the solidity or "indestructibility" of atoms as "the immediate exercise of God's infinite power of resisting annihilation."[67] For Edwards, the laws of nature are nothing

---

63. "The Mind," no. 36 (*WY*, 6:391).
64. Ibid., no. 50 (*WY*, 6:392). See also "Things to be Considered an[d] Written fully about," short ser. no. 23[a]; unnumbered ser., no. [6] (*WY*, 6:235, 265).
65. "Miscellanies," no. 241, Yale MSS. Also in "The Mind," nos. 36, 40 (*WY*, 6:355, 359). See Lee, *Philosophical Theology*, 72.
66. Lee, *Philosophical Theology*, 50.
67. "Of Atoms," *WY*, 6:208–15; also in 235.

but "the stated methods of God's acting with respect to bodies," according to which the universe is upheld continually every moment.[68] The theme is expressed later in *Original Sin* when he faces the difficult question of personal identity and concludes that created entities cannot cause or expect their existence to continue the next moment except by God's *"immediate production out of nothing*, at each moment."[69] In his favorite metaphor, Edwards describes the seemingly steady and serene appearance of the moon as nothing but the continual effect of the strokes of light rays from the sun, each moment creating and renewing the bright image of the moon.[70] In still another context, *Treatise on Grace*, Edwards calls for the concept of "covenant" to articulate the idea of God's sustaining action. It is owing to his covenant-faithfulness that God keeps the established laws in his dealings with the creature: the habit of grace has an abiding tendency, not "any otherwise than by Divine constitution and covenant."[71] In all of these illustrations the world's radical contingency and dependence on God's causal power is distinctively accentuated, causing Edwards to appear almost as an "occasionalist" or "creationist."[72]

Second, however, Edwards's dispositional ontology as it is expressed in the quotations above contains something beyond the reach of any conventional occasionalism or creationism.[73] Unlike in the common

---

68. Ibid., 216; "Things to be Considered an[d] Written fully about," long ser., no. 47 (*WY*, 6:241); "Miscellanies," no. 346 (*Philosophy of Jonathan Edwards*, 130). This assertion, however, must be carefully distinguished from the occasionalist understanding of continual creation. The existence of the universe is elevated every moment from virtuality to full actuality, but it is not a creation ex nihilo.

69. *Original Sin*, 402 (emphasis original). His theory of personal identity—and its complete failure—is reviewed in Chapter 4.

70. Ibid., 403–4.

71. *Treatise on Grace*, 74–75.

72. Some scholars fail to see the subtle but critical difference between Edwards's position and the "occasionalist" or "creationist" understanding of reality. Norman Fiering puts Edwards in the same category with Malebranche and Hume in *Jonathan Edwards's Moral Thought and Its British Context* (Chapel Hill: University of North Carolina Press, 1981), 51–52, 279–80, 307–8). Conrad Cherry also characterizes Edwards as creationist in *Nature and Religious Imagination: From Edwards to Bushnell* (Philadelphia: Fortress Press, 1980), 46–48.

73. John F. Boler, in *Charles Peirce and Scholastic Realism: A Study of Peirce's Relation to John Duns Scotus* (Seattle: University of Washington Press, 1963), offers a distinction helpful in distinguishing Edwards's dispositional view from the "occasionalist" or "creationist" understanding. Boler maintains that there are two kinds of pragmatism: *"reductionist* pragmatism" contends that "only actual events are real—powers and laws, abstractions of all sorts, are only shorthand expressions for actual events," but *"realist*

usage of the word, "habits" or "dispositions" in Edwards are not just an indication of likelihood that similar events happen in similar circumstances; they are active and prescriptive laws that determine events and actions in specific detail. As conditional laws, habits and dispositions certainly become active when the specified occasions arise. Habits are an "active tendency," that is, always tending to actual existence. Once conditions are met, the exertion of habits is necessary and automatic, to such an extent that they not only describe the past and the present occurrences but also govern and prescribe all future actions and events uniformly and generally in accordance with the conditions.[74]

In other words, habits for Edwards are more than the actual events and actions they govern. They have their own mode of reality apart from the actual exercise. A diamond's character of being hard, to use an often-quoted analogy of Charles Sanders Peirce, is a reality even when that characteristic is not in exercise, for example, as when it is scratched with something. It is a reality in the sense that it *would* necessarily be exercised once the conditions (being scratched in such and such a manner) are fulfilled.[75] Unlike Berkeley and Hume, who took reality to be residing solely within the habits of the perceiver ("customary associations"),[76] Edwards accorded habits an ontological status of their own. Habits are not "meer possibility," but are ontologically present in reality, whether manifest or not, in the mode of "real possibility" or "virtuality," governing the pattern of actions and events of which they are the law. These modes of reality can be explained therefore in a three-tiered structure: (1) A being is *fully actual* when the habit is in actual exercise; (2) When the habit is not in exercise, it is in the mode of *virtual existence*; (3) Yet since the exertion of the habit upon the specified occasion is a real potentiality, this virtual existence is more than a *mere possibility*.[77] The virtual mode of existence stands at the "midpoint between pure potentiality and full actuality."[78] When God created the

---

pragmatism" (Peirce's position) does not reduce the "real" to "actual events" (106). Edwards shares Peirce's "realist" conception.

74. See Lee, *Philosophical Theology*, 40, 44.

75. See Boler, *Charles Pierce*, 17, 94–116. My understanding of Peirce's realism and its coincidence with Edwards's dispositional ontology is owed entirely to Lee, *Philosophical Theology*, 42–46.

76. Cf. David Hume, *A Treatise of Human Nature* (London, 1739–40; reprint, London: Scientia Verlag Aalen, 1964), 1.3.6, 8, 14.

77. Here again I am indebted to Lee, *Philosophical Theology*, 37, 45, 63, 106–8.

78. Ibid., 63. "Actual," "virtual," and "meer possibility" are the words Edwards

world, God constituted the world as a nexus of laws according to which he would exercise his power of causation at certain times and occasions. This nexus of laws, even when the laws are not in actual exercise, gives the creaturely reality a relative yet real permanence in the mode of virtuality.

Edwards came to this understanding only after he graduated from his youthful and eminently idealistic speculation. Earlier on, his position was either to deny flatly any status of existence to the beings that are not perceived, or else to preserve their existence barely in the idea of God, who is the ultimate perceiver of all things at all times (Berkeley's solution).[79] The following passage from "The Mind" indicates, however, that he has departed from such an idealistic bent.

> In memory, in mental principles, habits, and inclinations, there is something really abiding in the mind when there are no acts or exercises of them, much in the same manner as there is a chair in this room when no mortal perceives it. For when we say, there are chairs in this room when none perceives it, we mean that minds *would* perceive chairs here according to the law of nature in such circumstances.[80]

Notice the word "would" here. Although the passage appears to refer to human mental activities, what is at stake here is not merely the order of knowing but primarily the order of being.[81] When certain conditions are fulfilled, the minds *would* necessarily and without fail perceive the existence of the chairs, because there is a nexus of the laws of nature that dictate the occurring of such a perception when those specified circumstances are met. Edwards is here effectively leaving behind his earlier "idealist" or "immaterialist" position. The crucial difference in

---

himself used ("Miscellanies," nos. 729, 1337, Yale MSS). See my argument in Chapter 6 on perseverance.

79. "Nothing has any existence anywhere else but in consciousness . . . either in created or uncreated consciousness" ("Of Being," *WY*, 6:204, 206). "Miscellanies," no. 94 (*Philosophy of Jonathan Edwards*, 254). Cf. George Berkeley, *A Treatise concerning Principles of Human Knowledge*, T. E. Jessop, ed., *The Works of George Berkeley, Bishop of Cloyne* (Dublin, 1710; reprint, London: Thomas Nelson and Sons Ltd., 1949), 2.1.3, 6.

80. "The Mind," no. 69 (*WY*, 6:385). Compare this to his earlier "Miscellanies," no. pp (*Philosophy of Jonathan Edwards*, 74), which has similar setting but affirms no being except in God's consciousness.

81. See Lee, *Philosophical Theology*, 42–45.

his position lies in the ontological status of the laws of nature. Now the world is secured of its reality, not by a perceiving subject, human or divine, but by the nexus of the laws and habits that God has established to determine the occurrence and relation of actions and events in the world.[82] Habits and dispositions are now for Edwards the "general law governing the regular order of antecedent and consequent occurrences."[83] For this reason, Edwards is not an occasionalist. His world is designed to possess relative permanence and integrity of its own.

Soteriological Consequences

These contrasting claims of Edwards's dispositional ontology have direct bearing on the way he conceives of human salvation. His unique contribution in the field of soteriology also consists in these contrasting but mutually complementing claims. I will examine two soteriological consequences in accordance with the two claims of Edwards's ontology.

Protestant Concern

First, as the reality of regeneration consists in the new disposition, this state of regeneration is in need of God's immediate and constant power of causation, not only at the time of inception but continually thereafter in order to exist and function. In the Introduction, I called this the "Protestant concern" of soteriology because of its emphasis on divine initiative. While Turretin and others argued that this new disposition is supernaturally posited by the infusion of the Holy Spirit, they did not clearly see that its existence and operation are still entirely dependent on God's immediate acting in and through it.[84] The internal disposition of the regenerate, as a conditional law of actions, comes to exert itself on

---

82. In a review article, (*Journal of Religion* 70 [1990]: 258), James Hoopes seems to underestimate Edwards's later development. As is obvious from the quotation above on an unperceived room, Edwards's early idealist or immaterialist position was not his final thought. See also Hoopes, "Calvinism and Consciousness from Edwards to Beecher," in *Jonathan Edwards and the American Experience*, ed. Nathan O. Hatch and Harry S. Stout (New York: Oxford University Press, 1988), 206-7.
83. Anderson, Introduction to *WY*, 4:126.
84. Cf. Thomas Ridgeley, *A Body of Divinity: wherein the Doctrines of the Christian Religion are Explained and Defended* (London, 1731; reprint, New York, 1855), 2.64.

the preordained occasion, and God's immediate causal power from above is the prime condition for it. It needs God's direct and constant intervention moment by moment in order to remain what it is and in order to function the way it is designed to.

In other words, grace is first infused and communicated to a person, establishing in him or her the new principle of action. There is no guarantee, however, that it continues to exist and exert itself the next moment by "natural necessity"; its continuation depends solely on God, who remains faithful to his covenant and abides by the constitution of the established laws in order to make it happen. In a "Miscellanies" entry of his maturer years, Edwards observes, "The exercises & operations of this Spirit are after the manner of a natural principle in many respects but yet there is that in it that shews it [to] be something supernatural.... It acts both after the manner of a voluntary agent, yea & a most sovereign agent ... & so every way as a divine agent or as God acting in the soul."[85] Grace operates within the regenerate "after the manner of a natural principle," and this principle has a relative permanence of its own; yet, in and through this natural principle God is acting as a vital agent. Here a pertinent interpretation is provided by Paul Ramsey, editor of the *Ethical Writings* volume: "If no 'steady-state' of the universe was 'matter' on its own once it was created, then no steady-state of the soul or of the moral order could ever be a world on its own without God's sustaining, immediate, continual action.... The preservation of a virtue the next moment is the same as its creation the first moment."[86] This interpretation is pertinent because, first, it points out the essential correlation between Edwards's ontology and his soteriology. Within that correlation, second, it notes the radical contingency and dependence of the created virtues on God, illustrating the Lombardian tradition. Since it is a distinctively Protestant concern to uphold the divine work more than its effect in humanity, Ramsey's reading offers a classic example of defending Edwards's "Protestant" character. The Lombardian tradition thus is much more prominent in Edwards than in Turretin and other Reformed theologians. One might say, as Ramsey did, that the "Protestant Edwards" comes to the foreground here in accentuating God's sovereignty and the creature's radical depen-

---

85. "Miscellanies," no. 818, Yale MSS. See also *Treatise on Grace*, 74–75.

86. Appendix 4 to *WY*, 8:742. Note, however, that this reading does not sufficiently safeguard Edwards from the occasionalist interpretation.

dence on God. The saving disposition (created grace) cannot exist or operate without the Holy Spirit (uncreated grace), who works precisely in and through it. If the Thomist insistence on created grace is susceptible to human supplanting, Edwards's scheme is not.[87]

Catholic Concern

Having said this, I must once again underscore the ontological reality Edwards accorded to the new creation. For all its occasionalist outlook, Edwards's universe is given a relative permanence and abiding reality apart from God's being and acting. This is because of his realist conception of the laws of nature, according to which God acts mostly in this world. Here is an unmistakable correspondence between the affirmation of the relative permanence of the material world (ontology) and the relative permanence of the reality of salvation in human nature (soteriology). God's absolute sovereignty in establishing, upholding, and exerting the laws—whether natural or supernatural—does not demolish the relative independence and integrity of the reality thereby created. I have called this the "Catholic concern" of Edwards's soteriology. I will now examine this aspect in more detail.

The infused habit of grace, as I reviewed earlier, is a law of God that necessarily exerts itself when the specified occasion arises. This active tendency can therefore point to a mode of reality apart from and even *prior to* its actual exercise, as it is the case with Edwards's illustration of the unperceived chairs. The existence of the new habit does not depend on its prior exercise, just as the existence of the chairs is not dependent on a prior perception of them. Here is where Edwards departs from Aristotle. For Aristotle, it is "impossible to be a builder if one has built nothing."[88] The habit of the builder cannot exist prior to its actual exercise, since habit for him is something that is acquired by repeated acts. The ontological status of the infused habit prior to its exercise is a matter of theological question that must go beyond Aristotle.

Reformed or Puritan divines of preceding ages also spoke of the saving disposition as an abiding habit. William Ames called virtue "a state of mind of various degrees of perfection."[89] In another treatise Ames

---

87. The issue will be reviewed in Chapter 7. Suffice it to say here that the recent studies on Thomas do not seem to allow such an easy criticism.
88. Aristotle, *Metaphysics*, book 9, chap. 8 (in *Basic Works*, 829).
89. Ames, *Marrow of Theology*, 2.2.5.

further insisted that good works should take root in such a state of mind because "if the habit of vertue be absent, although we should do some good works, yet we are not rooted and grounded in good, but are rashly carried away with evill, and that goodnesse soone vanisheth."⁹⁰ Thomas Shepard also maintained that "the act of grace ceaseth sometimes, because 'tis opposed by corruption, yet the being of it remains in full power, though not in exercise thereof."⁹¹ In this sense Ames and Shepard did not go an inch beyond Aristotle, who already knew the abiding reality of habits even when they are not in actual exercise. They are present in the person as a "second nature," says Aristotle. A brave person is brave even when he or she is asleep.⁹² A builder, having acquired the habit of building, retains the capacity even when he or she is not actually engaged in the work of building.⁹³

Yet none of these divines (including Ames and Shepard) was so bold as Edwards to assert that the disposition of faith is ontologically present, even "before a distinct and express act of faith."⁹⁴ When certain conditions are met, the disposition as an active and purposive tendency is preordained to come into exertion. If so, the existence of such a saving disposition alone should suffice for salvation, and the act that arises from this disposition—be it faith, love, obedience, or any combination of these—"cannot be proved to be absolutely necessary" in order to be counted in the state of salvation.⁹⁵ It is true that some theologians before Edwards recognized the continual presence of habits when they are in a state of *intermission*, or a lingering residual that characterizes the person "*after* the period of actuation has ceased."⁹⁶ Edwards advanced a step further by affirming that the saving habits are a reality even *before* any exercise takes place.

Such an understanding of the saving disposition results in an unexpected broadness to Edwards's soteriology. All too often we hear about his hellfire and brimstone sermons. The name Jonathan Edwards is

---

90. William Ames, *Conscience with the Power and Cases Thereof* (n.p., 1639; reprint, "The English Experience: Its Record in Early Printed Books Published in Facsimile," no. 708 [Amsterdam: Theatrum Orbis Terrarum, 1975], book 3, chap. 8, "Of Vertue."
91. Shepard, *The Parable of the Ten Virgins*, 173.
92. Aristotle, *Nicomachean Ethics*, book 1, chap. 8 (in *Basic Works*, 944).
93. See W.F.R. Hardie, *Aristotle's Ethical Theory* (London: Clarendon Press, 1968), 108.
94. "Miscellanies," no. 393, Yale MSS.
95. "Miscellanies," no. 27b, Yale MSS.
96. See Bourke, "The Role of Habitus," 104.

remembered today mostly in conjunction with his preaching that peremptorily and almost sadistically condemns unbelievers to eternal damnation. But that alone would hardly be a fair representation of his soteriology. The ontological reality he accorded to the saving disposition attests to the other side of his paradigm, which is radically inclusive.

First, Edwards bases his argument for the salvation of infants on this understanding. The fate of infants who die—baptized or unbaptized—presents theology a tough question that demands careful scrutiny as well as sensitivity. Edward Yarnold states that Anselm of Canterbury and Bernard of Clairvaux taught that a baptized baby is still not in the state of righteousness, since "the psychological capacity to perform acts under the influence of grace has not yet developed."[97] The only recourse Anselm and Bernard could find for the salvation of infants was the faith of others who intercede for them. Lombard and Thomas make an interesting contrast on this issue, also. Lombard, who did not see divine grace in terms of habit, followed Anselm and Bernard in denying the saving status to infants, but Thomas distinguished habit from act and said that children incapable of acts are saved on account of their infused habit.[98] Here again, Edwards sides with Thomas. He has no reservation in affirming that infants who did not "sensibly" exercise the saving habit are saved, because their habit has its own mode of reality even *before* it is exercised in faith or in other virtuous acts.[99] It should be remembered, as reviewed in Chapter 2, that Protestant theology before Edwards did not make much progress on the issue either.[100] Edwards's understanding of the saving disposition is uniquely inclusive for his time, and it has a solid theological ground to be so.

Also treated within this paradigm are the faithful people in the Old Testament period, who pose the same kind of question to Christian theology. They had doubtlessly been given the saving disposition, but did not have actual occasions in which to exert it in faith in Christ Jesus. How can one account for the biblical declaration, "He [Abraham] believed the Lord; and the Lord reckoned it to him as righteousness" (Gen. 15:6)? Edwards replies that "the ancient Jews before Christ were

---

97. Yarnold, *Second Gift*, 53; see also McGrath, *Iustitia Dei*, 1:92–93.
98. *Summa Theologica*. 3.69.6.
99. "Miscellanies," no. 27b, Yale MSS. See also nos. 317, 393, Yale MSS.
100. Mastricht, for example, speaks of "the seed of regeneration," but it is "very imperfect" that this seed alone, when unsprouted, is not sufficient for salvation (*Theoretico-Practica Theologia*, 6.3.13, 22).

saved" because "they had the disposition, which alone is absolutely necessary."[101] Had they seen Jesus in person as Simeon did in the Temple of Jerusalem (Luke 2:22–35), they would have instantly exerted the endowed disposition and begun to have faith in him. Edwards's dispositional view thus offers a definitive answer to the agelong question of the salvation of the Old Testament faithful.

Third, Edward's vision of salvation is relevant even beyond the Judeo-Christian tradition. Edwards lived in a predominantly Christian society that afforded few encounters with other religions. It was a theological milieu entirely different from ours, where the world's major religions and ideologies meet daily with equal claims of ultimacy and finality. One cannot therefore expect him to give direct answers to the kinds of questions that did not exist in his time. One can and should ask, however, what reasonable consequences can be drawn from his theological perspective for today's pluralist society. I believe Edwards's dispositional view has some insights to offer in this respect as well.

On the question of the salvation of non-Christians, a helpful synopsis is offered by John Sanders's *No Other Name*.[102] With a wide array of primary sources from biblical and historical scholarship, Sanders finds three basic categories of theories on the question: restrictivism, universalism, and inclusivism. Restrictivism, most typically represented by Augustine and Calvin, asserts that the unevangelized are destined to perdition. For restrictivists, the revelation and salvific work of Jesus Christ is a unique, once-and-for-all event that has a specific content. There is no possibility of salvation for those who do not possess the knowledge of and faith in this revelation.[103]

101. "Miscellanies," no. 27b, Yale MSS.
102. Sanders, *No Other Name*. Several other theologians have proposed comparable categorizations. Hans Küng has four categories: atheist, exclusivist, relativist, and inclusivist (see his *Theology for the Third Millennium: An Ecumenical View*, trans. Peter Heinegg [New York: Doubleday, 1988], 230–37). See also Leslie Newbigin, *The Gospel in a Pluralist Society* (Geneva: World Council of Churches; Grand Rapids, Mich.: Wm. B. Eerdmans, 1989), 171–83. Daniel L. Migliore lists five categories: exclusivist, developmentalist, transcendentalist, dialogical, and relativist (see his *Faith Seeking Understanding: An Introduction to Christian Theology* [Grand Rapids, Mich.: Wm. B. Eerdmans, 1991], 161–64).
103. Sanders, *No Other Name*, 37–79. On this issue the Roman Catholic Church is more progressive than many Protestant theologians in affirming the possibility of salvation for non-Christians. According to Hans Küng, the Catholic Church had moved from "a narrow-minded, arrogant absolutism" to "an epoch of postcolonialism and postimperialism" by 1952 and especially after the Second Vatican Council. Küng, *Theology for the Third Millennium*, 232–33.

Universalism, on the other extreme, believes that restrictivism is inconsistent with the biblical testimony of God's love for the world. God did not make human beings simply to damn them eternally. The postulate of universalism is, therefore, that all will somehow be saved eventually. Its leading proponents include Origen, a New England Arminian Charles Chauncy, and J.A.T. Robinson.[104]

The third category of theories is called "the wider hope," a generic name for a variety of views that stand between the two extremes of restrictivism and universalism. The common assumption of this group is that God provides all people with an opportunity to be saved at some point—either before, at, or after death. Sanders espouses a more specific version, called "inclusivism," which maintains the finality and particularity of the work of Jesus as ontologically necessary for salvation, but asserts that one need not be aware of it in order to be saved.[105] Clark Pinnock, Sanders's theology mentor, argues that those who are outside the church are saved "by trust" in God who is partially revealed in general revelation and in other religions.[106] Jesus often commended "faithful Gentiles," and Paul says that their conscience "may accuse or perhaps excuse them" on the day of judgment (Rom. 2:15). They can therefore be held accountable for accepting or rejecting the general revelation available to them in one form or another. Those who do accept the general revelation are to be called "pre-Christian" believers: they are already saved through their "faith principle."[107]

In which of these three categories should Edwards be placed? It is indeed easy, as it was for Sanders and Pinnock, to find Edwards's sermons with such titles as "The Justice of God in the Damnation of Sinners" or "Wicked men useful in their Destruction only"[108] in the

---

104. Sanders, *No Other Name*, 81–128.
105. Ibid., 151–280.
106. Clark H. Pinnock, *A Wideness in God's Mercy: The Finality of Jesus Christ in a World of Religions* (Grand Rapids, Mich.: Zondervan, 1992), 104, 157–60.
107. Inclusivists, however, will have to answer Küng's criticism: "The result is that every other religion is de facto reduced to a lower or partial knowledge of the truth, while one's own religion is elevated to a supersystem. . . . What looks like tolerance proves in practice to be a kind of conquest by embracing . . . an integration through relativization and loss of identity" (Küng, *Theology for the Third Millennium*, 235–36). An example of such a relativizing or domesticating integration is observed by Newbigin, *The Gospel in a Pluralist Society*, 3.
108. Pinnock, *A Wideness in God's Mercy*, 157; Sanders, *No Other Name*, 42–43, 95; "The Justice of God," *WW*, 4:226; "Wicked men," *WW*, 4:300. Sanders quotes from the Banner of Truth Edition, vol. 2, 253 ("Man's Natural Blindness," 30–31).

category of restrictivism. Putting him in the restrictivist group on the basis of these sermons, however, does not do justice to the fullness of his entire soteriology. By extending his dispositional view of salvation to its logical consequence, one finds a remarkable opportunity for reconsidering the salvation of those who do not explicitly believe in Jesus Christ. If infants and the Old Testament faithful are saved on account of their unexercised disposition, one must also conclude that non-Christians can be saved on the same grounds. They may not as yet manifest their saving disposition into a faith that is specifically Christian, but they might as well be given the disposition and counted as saved because of that disposition. They may even remain non-Christian for their whole lifetime, and still be saved; if the conditions and circumstances do not arise, their saving disposition will remain unexercised. The point is whether they *have* the saving disposition, not whether they *exercise* it or not.

As one from a society that is overwhelmingly non-Christian, I myself have reason to hope that my fellow people are not totally left out of God's economy of salvation, which is to be carried out throughout this whole creation. But at the same time I am convinced of the meaningfulness of the Christian message to all human beings. Christian theology cannot relinquish its claim that Christ is unique and indispensable for human redemption, since if he was not, he would only be "a parochial god" and not the real God or Savior.[109] How can we maintain the uniqueness and necessity of Christ for salvation and still remain open toward other faiths?

Edwards is by no means a universalist. The fact still remains that salvation depends on the presence of the saving disposition. One may or may not be given that disposition, and it rests with the divine counsel to determine who is to receive the infusion of the disposition. Yet, the line between those who have the disposition and those who don't does not simply divide Christians from non-Christians. The Kingdom of God embraces a group of people much larger than just Christians. Those who appear to be non-Christians now might quite well be its members, being given the saving disposition but not manifesting it in exercise. Edwards's soteriology thus maintains the uniqueness of Christian salvation, while emphasizing God's wide mercy that is not enclosed within the Christian community.

109. Diogenes Allen, *Christian Belief in a Postmodern World: The Full Wealth of Conviction* (Louisville, Ky.: Westminster/John Knox Press, 1989), 186.

Another strength of this dispositional view of salvation is that it does not surrender or diminish the necessity of mission and evangelism. If anything, it emphasizes their importance, since it is only through actual exercise that one realizes and fulfills what is endowed within himself or herself. For universalists, Christian mission is not only unnecessary but also harmful, for it implies disrespect toward other religious traditions. Inclusivists try to affirm the importance and necessity of mission, but they are painfully aware of the difficulty therein.[110] If people are saved apart from Christian faith, why bother to proclaim the Gospel? To this question, Edwards's soteriology replies that the saving disposition still awaits occasion to come into bloom. Proclamation is necessary, since it provides opportunities for the disposition to develop into what it is ordained to be. The purpose of mission is to help people realize themselves.[111] Though mission has often been illustrated as sowing the seeds of faith on a barren field, there is actually no barren field in this creation. The seeds are already there; they only await occasion to sprout. The task of Christian mission, therefore, is not to sow, but to help them grow.

Edwards's soteriology thus prompts today's Western Christianity to reconsider seriously its recent attitude of hesitation and skepticism toward mission and evangelism. Without doubt the guilt-consciousness of past colonialism has contributed to such an attitude. Christian mission can of course be imperialistic and patronizing, as it often has been, but equally uncalled for is the presumption that those living in other contexts should be content with what they have now. Quoting a comment made at a recent General Assembly of the United Reformed Church, Leslie Newbigin points out a curious double-standard "which Asian Christians find exceedingly odd": "When thinking of our unbelieving English neighbors we speak of evangelism; when speaking of our Asian and West

---

110. The fact that Sanders repeats his refutation several times indicates that his argument is not quite convincing (*No Other Name*, 262–64, 266–67, 283–86). Pinnock's only perceivable answer is that the goal of mission is not only baptism and conversion but also "to change life's atmosphere, to infect people with hope, love and responsibility for the world" (*A Wideness in God's Mercy*, 176–80). No doubt these are part of the results, but they cannot be the primary goal of mission's arduous effort.

111. Edwards's dispositional view should not be equated with what Migliore calls the "developmentalist" view (*Faith Seeking Understanding*, 161–62). The latter presupposes a hierarchy of religions in which all other religions are seen as preparatory steps toward the highest religion, that is, Christianity. Edwards's view only maintains that the saving disposition for Christian faith may be divinely infused but remain inactive in people of other faiths.

Indian neighbors we speak of dialogue. The gospel is, like the facilities in the parks in South Africa, for whites only."[112] Christians like myself in Asia are increasingly weary of the repeated assumption that the non-Western world is monolithically non-Christian. "Christianity," says Hans Küng, "is not simply the religion of the West."[113] Asian Christians are not anomalies misled by missionaries to desert their own cultural values in favor of Western values. In Edwards's dispositional understanding of salvation, mission and evangelism does not mean an imperialistic crusade to people viewed as poor pagans otherwise consigned to perdition. The task of Christian mission, whether inland or overseas, is not to impose something alien on others, but to offer a respectful invitation to realize what might already be endowed within them. It provides opportunities for their disposition to develop into what it was originally ordained to be. One does not give faith to others. One helps others develop their God-given faith into actuality. Edwards's is a soteriological paradigm that is surprisingly inclusive and yet theologically responsible.

To recapitulate, this chapter dealt with the result of infusion in humanity. Edwards has a genuine Lombardian concern to avoid positing the supernatural gift of infusion as a creaturely given. The reality of regeneration is totally dependent upon God's power, not only when it is first established, but also as it continues to exist and function as the internal principle of the regenerate. At the same time, Edwards makes sure that grace does not nullify human participation but rather establishes it in this new disposition. In this regard he stands in the Thomist tradition. His Thomistic lineage is further substantiated by an analysis of Turretin's discussion of efficacious grace. In accordance with the two axiomatic claims of his general ontology, Edwards's theories of infused grace exhibit a balanced combination of Protestant and Catholic concerns in one form. Such an ontological understanding of the saving disposition results in a surprising broadness of his soteriology. His paradigm of salvation is even inclusive of people of other faiths while remaining theologically sound. Attention must now turn to his thoughts

---

112. Newbigin, *The Gospel in a Pluralist Society*, 4.
113. Hans Küng, *On Being a Christian*, trans. Edward Quinn (London: Collins, 1977), 113. Küng also avoids what Newbigin calls "a potluck supper" contribution to "the pool of human values" (Newbigin, *The Gospel in a Pluralist Society*, 159). In order to carry out the task of genuine dialogue without falling into "a weak eclecticism accepting a little of everything," one has to define what is central and what is peripheral to one's own belief system (Küng, *On Being a Christian*, 112, 114).

on justification. Chapter 4 will prepare us to attend to some of the questions concerning Edwards's implicit and explicit contiguity with Roman Catholic theology—the questions that have long plagued Edwards scholarship.

4

Justification
God's Crowning of His Own Gift

Justification in Edwards's Soteriology

Compared to the fullness of his arguments on conversion and regeneration, Edwards's pronouncements on justification are surprisingly sparse. When he enumerates the phases of redemption, justification is surely on the list, but he does not spend more than a few lines explaining it, and he never touches it again in the remainder of the discourse.[1] There are a few sermons that contain cursory references to the subject, and a number of "Miscellanies" entries treat it, either as drafts for his own writing or as quotations from the books he read.[2] But as far as a

---

1. *History of the Work of Redemption*, 121. In comparison, conversion is a recurrent subject.
2. Edwards's M.A. thesis at Yale was also on justification. In it he argues against the Neonomian (Arminian) scheme of "justification by sincere obedience." The Latin original is deposited at the Beinecke Library, Yale University, but glimpses of the content can be obtained through his early "Miscellanies" notes, for example, nos. *oo*, 36, Yale MSS.

systematic treatment of justification is concerned, the celebrated series of lectures he delivered in 1734 is the only substantial piece of work devoted to the subject.

What is more surprising than the sparseness of its mention is that Edwards hardly shows any effort to relate the theme of justification to his thoughts on conversion. The pronouncements on justification stand on their own, without being woven into a systematic whole. What is the temporal or logical order between conversion and justification? How does the grace infused at conversion operate in justification? How different are the fruits of justification from those of conversion? These questions, which are essential to understanding any kind of soteriological construction in its entirety, remain tantalizingly unanswered.

One can of course brush aside these questions by saying that there is in fact no discrepancy between the two phases of salvation. A person is not first converted and then justified, or first justified and then converted. The two constitute jointly one and the same instance of a new beginning and new creation: "If any man be in Christ, he is a new creature; old things are passed away; behold, *all things are become new*" (2 Cor. 5:17, KJV). Granted this simultaneity, one can still ask about the logical order, just as many Reformed and Puritan divines did,[3] since Paul also says that we all are "being transformed into the same image *from one degree of glory to another*" (2 Cor. 3:18), and that "those whom he predestined he also called; and those whom he called he also justified; and those whom he justified he also glorified" (Rom. 8:30).

In the Redemption discourse, Edwards counts justification as one of the four subdivisions of the "application of redemption," in a loosely temporal order along with conversion, sanctification, and glorification. "And as God carries on the work of converting the souls of fallen men through all these ages, so he goes on to justify them, to blot out all their sins and to accept them as righteous in his sight through the righteous-

---

3. Thomas Shepard, while admitting that "every sinner thus believing in Christ is at that instant translated into a most blessed and happy state," still distinguishes "six privileges or benefits" within that state. See his *The Sound Believer: or a Treatise on Evangelical Conversion, Discovering the Work of God's Spirit, in Reconciling a Sinner to God* (London, 1670; reprint, Aberdeen, 1849), 272. John Flavel teaches "a singular benefit or choice mercy bestowed," in which he counts four successive "privileges of gospel-remission." See his *The Method of Grace in the Holy Spirits Applying to the Souls of Men, the Eternal Redemption Contrived by the Father and Accomplished by the Son* (London, 1699; reprint, 1820), 298. See also Mastricht, *Theoretico-Practica Theologia*, 6.1.9–11.

ness of Christ."⁴ The passage gives no more than a cataloguelike description of soteriological stages, presuming in the standard Reformed fashion that conversion precedes justification. There is also one passage in his Justification discourse that touches upon the relation of justification to conversion. Since faith is "the condition of pardon and justification," it says, conversion must come prior to justification. "Our minds must be changed, that we may believe, and so may be justified."⁵ Conversion initiates faith, and this faith brings forth justification. Beyond these meager references, there is not much help for the reader to relate justification to the rest of his theology. Does the doctrine of justification, then, occupy "an ambiguous and somewhat precarious place" in Edwards's theology, as Schafer once commented?⁶

Edwards did not leave a systematic treatise of soteriology, yet it is possible to conjecture what it might have been like had he ventured to write one. His private note called "Book of Controversies" contains a plan of a major treatise of this kind. According to the sketch, his plan was to treat: "the nature of true virtue," under which is subsumed "God's end in creating the world"; then, the "corruption of nature"; and finally, "infused habits" and "saving grace" as the sole remedy for this corruption.⁷ Although this is no more than a rough sketch of an undeveloped treatise, it adumbrates the major flow of Edwards's thought. It is a move from the corruption of human nature by original sin to the restoration of it by the infusion of grace. As far as one can see from this, the basic structure of Edwards's soteriology is an ontological transition from the state of corruption to the state of salvation—much like in Roman Catholic soteriology. This scheme is in fact materialized, albeit in a concise form, in the structure of his *Original Sin*. "Redemption" there means the "change of state" by regeneration and conversion; grace helps sinners proceed from the state of corruption to the state of renewal.⁸

If such is the structure of Edwards's soteriology, anyone who attempts to understand it will be hard-pressed to ask if there is in his system a

---

4. *History of the Work of Redemption*, 121.
5. "Justification by Faith alone," 431.
6. Schafer, "Jonathan Edwards and Justification by Faith," 57. Lee, too, makes no reference to justification, moving directly from conversion through sanctification to glorification. See Lee, *Philosophical Theology*, 231–36.
7. "Book of Controversies," Yale Collection, folder 28, sec. 4, quoted in Holbrook's Introduction to *Original Sin*, 22–23.
8. *Original Sin*, part 3, esp. 361–62.

place for justification at all. When the actual change of the human state is viewed as the remedy for the corruption, what is the role of the forensic declaration of righteousness in Christ? What significance can legal imputation bear in a system that holds the ontological transformation of the human state in such high regard? To answer these questions, one must first see the structure of his theories of justification as clearly as possible.

Arminian Justification

As noted above, the most significant document reflecting Edwards's systematic thoughts on justification and related issues is his lecture-sermon, "Justification by Faith alone." It instigated a fervent revival of religion in his own parish in 1734, which was "so circumstanced" that he could not doubt it being "the remarkable testimony of God's approbation of the doctrine."[9] In this discourse Edwards appears to be an unwavering orthodox theologian convinced of the truth of the Reformed teaching, namely, forensic and imputatory justification. The "doctrine" of the lecture reads: "We are justified only by faith in Christ, and not by any manner of virtue or goodness of our own."[10]

It is erroneous, however, to suppose that Edwards deliberately attempted here to differentiate himself from the Roman Catholic position on the issue. The title, "Justification *by Faith alone*," may seem to suggest such a calculated confrontation with the Roman theory of "justification by ontological transformation." In fact, the treatise, like all of his later major works, is geared rather exclusively to refuting "the Arminian scheme of justification," with no reference to the Roman Catholic theory at all.[11] The circumstances that surrounded both its actual delivery and publication also testify to this motive.[12] The phrase "by faith alone," in this historical context, stands against the Arminian

---

9. Preface to "Justification by Faith alone," 347. See also Dwight's comment, *Life of President Edwards*, 122.
10. "Justification by Faith alone," 353.
11. Ibid., 349. There is one isolated phrase, "the Popish doctrine of merit" (ibid., 448).
12. The lecture was held when there was a "great noise that was in this part of the country about Arminianism" (*Faithful Narrative*, 148). See also Dwight's similar comment, *Life of President Edwards*, 122.

scheme of justification "by sincere obedience." This will be substantiated by an examination of Edwards's relevant text.

It is not easy to pinpoint the Arminian doctrine of justification that Edwards was refuting here. He does not mention it by name. "Arminianism," as I noted before, was the name for New England's general intellectual climate against Calvinism rather than any particular school of thought. C. C. Goen translated the term as "a subtle form of salvation by works," and "a mood of rising confidence in man's ability to gain some purchase on the divine favor by human endeavor"[13] Edwards himself was personally involved in an Arminian controversy in 1734—the year when this Justification discourse was delivered. That year, a Harvard graduate, Robert Breck, was found unfit for ministry and barred from ordination.[14] The dubious moral character of the candidate aside, the Hampshire Association of Ministers found the following faults with his theology: he denied some of the scriptural texts "to be of Divine Inspiration"; he denied "the necessity of Christ's Satisfaction to Divine Justice for sin," and stated that "God might, consistent with his Justice, forgive Sin without any Satisfaction"; and he preached that "the Heathen that liv'd up to the Light of Nature should be Saved."[15] Of these, only the second point is relevant to the present discussion, and Edwards makes no reference to Breck or his theology in his lecture.

Historians of doctrinal theology provide us with a better view of the Arminian contentions. Charles Hodge, drawing mainly on the works of

13. Introduction to *The Great Awakening, WY,* 4:5–10.
14. Edwards served on the committee that examined Breck. Later on, Breck became a member of the committee that recommended Edwards's dismissal from the Northampton Church. See William Williams et al., *A Narrative of the Proceedings of those Ministers of the County of Hampshire. . . .* (Boston, 1736), 13–14; Breck et al., *A Letter to the Reverend Mr. Hobby in Answer to his Vindication of the Protest, . . .* (Boston, 1751). I would like to express my gratitude to the Speer Library, Princeton Theological Seminary, for allowing me access to these rare books.
15. Williams, *A Narrative of the Proceedings,* 4–5. See also 61. In answer to these charges, Breck recanted, writing: "I do acknowledge that I was too Inconsiderate and Incautious in speaking of them as I did, and although I can't charge my self with believing them then, yet upon my mature Tho't, . . . I reject all Opinions about these things" (ibid., 19–20). For details of the Breck incident, see *Life of President Edwards,* 125–26; O. E. Winslow, *Jonathan Edwards* (New York: Macmillan, 1940), 173–74; Ezra Hoyt Byington, "The Case of Rev. Robert Breck," in *Critical Essays on Jonathan Edwards,* ed. William Scheick (Boston: G. K. Hall & Co., 1980), 8–20; Charles Edwin Jones, "The Impolitic Mr. Edwards: The Personal Dimension of the Robert Breck Affair," in *Critical Essays,* 21–31.

Grotius and Limborch, enumerates three mutually related assertions of Arminianism that can serve as guidelines for identifying their tenets in Edwards's refutation: (1) the Scotist notion of *acceptatio* or *acceptilatio*, according to which Christ's work of satisfaction was not truly an equivalent to the price required, but God as the benevolent ruler accepted it as sufficient; (2) the equation of justification with pardon, which virtually means the denial of the imputation of Christ's righteousness; and (3) "evangelical obedience" as the ground of justification, that is, imperfect human effort rendered sufficient under a new lenient covenant.[16] William Shedd gives another succinct synopsis. "Piscator, Tillotson, Wesley, and Emmons denied the imputation of Christ's active obedience; contending that justification is 'pardon' alone, without 'acceptance,' or a title to life. They maintain that after the pardon of the believer's sin, on the ground of Christ's passive obedience, sanctification by the Holy Spirit ensues, and this earns the title to eternal life."[17] From these descriptions we may summarize the Arminian doctrine of justification in three interlocking pieces of argument: (1) to justify means to pardon; (2) there is no imputation of Christ's righteousness; and (3) sincere obedience is sufficient in order to receive justification understood in this sense, for God of his sovereign grace regards our imperfect human effort as perfect. These three points are internally consistent and meant to complement one another. Taken as a whole, they represent the Enlightenment spirit that believes in the elevated dignity and autonomy of humanity.[18]

Though the presence of the Arminian threat in Edwards's Justification discourse has been well recognized, the difficulty in specifying the particular brand of it has impeded the structural analysis. Here it should

---

16. Charles Hodge, *Systematic Theology*, 3 vols. (Grand Rapids, Mich.: Wm. B. Eerdmans, 1873; reprint, 1989), 3:188–93. For an etiological argument of *acceptilatio* and *acceptatio*, see Robert MacKintosh, *Historic Theories of Atonement* (London: Hoder and Stoughton, 1920), 110–11. See also Heiko A. Oberman, *The Harvest of Medieval Theology: Gabriel Biel and Late Medieval Nominalism* (Cambridge: Harvard University Press, 1963; reprint, Durham, N.C.: Labyrinth Press, 1983), 353–56.

17. William G. T. Shedd, *Dogmatic Theology*, 2 vols. (New York: Charles Scribner's Sons, 1888), 2:547. See also Peter Toon, *Justification and Sanctification* (Westchester, Ill.: Crossway Books, 1983), 105–6.

18. The theme of human autonomy reaches its apex in Immanuel Kant, for whom the idea of substitutional atonement is a "moral outrage." See Kant, *Religion Within the Limits of Reason Alone*, trans. Theodore M. Greene and Hoyt H. Hudson (New York: Harper & Row, 1960), 134. At the same time, Kant knew the abyss of "radical evil" that is "unpardonable."

suffice for our purpose to extract, with the help of the above guidelines, what *Edwards took* to be the Arminian contentions. After all, our interest lies not in what the Arminian assertions actually were but in how Edwards refuted them.

Three major points of Edwards's refutation suggest themselves, corresponding to the above-mentioned three tenets of Arminianism. First, Edwards does not think that justification is exhausted in the remission of sins. If a person is justified, more than the acquittal of sins is involved. There is a qualitative difference between mere pardon, which acquits sins and brings a person to the state of innocence, and justification, which imputes righteousness and entitles the person to eternal life.[19] Justification brings not only the forgiveness of sins, but also a new righteousness. In justification the person is judged to have "both a negative and positive righteousness," so that he or she is "not only free from any obligation to punishment, but also . . . entitled to a positive reward."[20]

Second, the imputation of Christ's righteousness is reaffirmed fully in both senses as "satisfaction" and "obedience," often called in Reformed theology, "active" and "passive" obedience.[21] Christ's suffering the penalty of the law on the cross is imputed to remove our guilt and establish our innocence, and then his perfect obedience to the law during his lifetime is imputed to us so that we should obtain the reward of eternal life. Christ is "our second federal head" in both these senses.[22] Here is a distinctively legal framework of Christological imputation.

Third, several ways are employed to refute the Arminian insistence on sincere obedience. Their introduction of "a new law, a more mild constitution" that requires only imperfect obedience "contains a great deal of absurdity and self-contradiction."[23] Such a new law, first of all, has never been introduced actually. Edwards argues that the moral law has never been abrogated by the advent of Christ. Likewise, the covenant

---

19. See "Miscellanies," no. 812, Yale MSS: "To suppose a sinner pardoned without a righteousness implies no contradiction; but to justify without a righteousness is selfcontradictory."
20. "Justification by Faith alone," 354.
21. See, for example, *Institutes*, 3.11.2; Thomas Shepard, *The Parable of the Ten Virgins*, 170; Thomas Ridgeley, *A Body of Divinity* (London, 1731; reprint, New York, 1855), 2:91; *Reformed Dogmatics*, 459–60.
22. "Justification by Faith alone," 395, 396, 399–400; "Miscellanies," nos. s, 812, Yale MSS.
23. "Justification by Faith alone," 375.

of works has never been abrogated by the installation of the covenant of grace. Granted that there be such a new law, it still cannot escape a contradiction, since every law, whether stringent or mild, insofar as it is a law, requires perfect obedience, and, should there be a breach, that breach is still a sin against the law.

The bottom line of the refutation is Edwards's repugnance of the Arminian assumption that sinners can do something worthy of God's respect and favor. These "modern divines," in so assuming, lay "another foundation of man's salvation than God hath laid."[24] To be sure, any Arminian of those days would still affirm human corruption to some degree. Yet, as Edwards sums up their thesis, "after all, it is our *virtue*, imperfect as it is, that recommends men to God, by which good men come to have a saving interest in Christ."[25] The Arminian theory is thus manifestly against "the design of the gospel-grace," derogating both "the freedom and riches of his grace . . . appointed in the gospel-covenant" and also "the honour of the Mediator," to whose righteousness we owe our justification exclusively.[26]

Forensic Justification

Viewed in such an anti-Arminian setting, the import of Edwards's emphasis on the forensic character of justification takes on a meaning entirely different from ordinary Protestant assertions against the Roman emphasis on inherent righteousness. Edwards is certainly not averse to the orthodox Protestant language of legal justification. Justification is first and foremost a judicial and declaratory act of God that does not take into account the goodness or value of the person to be justified. Indeed, he says, justification is "manifestly a *forensic* term, as the word is used in scripture, and a judicial thing, or the act of a judge."[27] God is a just Judge who rules over the case in a judicial manner, "according to the law . . . established beforehand."[28] That is to say, justification has

---

24. Ibid., 375, 391, 424, 447. Edwards's position on the notion of *meritum de congruo*, though, is not totally consistent through these pages.
25. Ibid., 448.
26. Ibid., 375, 392, 394.
27. Ibid., 397. See also "Miscellanies," no. 1101, Yale MSS.
28. "Justification by Faith alone," 398.

more to do with declaring a sentence than with actually altering the reality of the person to be justified.

These expressions, however, can be easily misread if one loses sight of the opponent Edwards was arguing against. A careful reader may notice that there is a slight shift in Edwards's imagery of God the Judge. Earlier on, he described justification as the act of "sovereign grace" that sentences those who are *not* just as just, and justifies "the breakers of the law" as righteous, transcending the human parameters of legality and justice.[29] But later in the treatise, he seems to move away from this imagery of a transcendent Judge toward that of a just and lawful Judge, who abides by established laws, even to such an extent as to say that "God *neither will nor can* justify a person without a righteousness." A just judge *must* legitimately determine the case "according to rule, or according to the law," and it is "impossible," says Edwards, even for God to judge without such a legal basis.[30] He did not retract the first image, yet some consideration prevented him from developing it any further. What was this consideration?

The answer lies in the third point of the Arminian understanding of justification, especially as it was advocated by Grotius and those under his influence.[31] An expert in Roman law, Grotius thought that the law God applies in judging sinners is not an unalterable decree but a posited law. Put otherwise, God is not absolutely bound by it; God can, if he pleases, modify it in part or abrogate it altogether—and that is what happened on the cross. God as the supreme Ruler and Judge deemed it best, for the sake of the moral government of the universe, to take a nominal equivalent of Christ's satisfaction as sufficient, and to relax the strict requirements of justice, dispensing with the penalty normally imposed on the sinners and accepting their imperfect obedience.

It is this theory of leniency and relaxation that made Edwards express his thoughts on justification in strict legality. God must be a strict and law-abiding Judge, not because Edwards does not believe in God's

---

29. Ibid., 352.
30. Ibid., 397, 398 (emphasis mine).
31. For succinct epitomes of the Grotian theory of atonement, see Louis Berkhof, *The History of Christian Doctrines* (Grand Rapids, Mich.: Baker Book House, 1937), 186–88; H. D. McDonald, *The Atonement of the Death of Christ: In Faith, Revelation, and History* (Grand Rapids, Mich.: Baker Book House, 1985), 203–7. It is only surprising to see how quickly Jonathan Edwards Jr., and the New England theology reversed the case and moved to this governmental theory. See Dwight's comment in *Life of President Edwards*, 618.

supremacy and prevenience over the law, or because he wants to portray God as an unforgiving and revengeful Monarch. God is a law-abiding Judge because God justifies sinners on the basis of the strictest requirement of justice, which is fulfilled by the perfect righteousness of Christ. This righteousness is then transferred to the sinners, making them perfectly righteous and qualified for eternal life. The point is, God does it all *legitimately* according to the law, not by relaxing or abrogating the demand of the moral law as the Arminians assert.

Edwards further sustains his opposition with a lengthy discussion on the biblical meaning of "the new order of law."[32] The whole purpose of this exegesis is to show that only the ceremonial law was abrogated in the New Testament. The moral law, typically represented by the Mosaic Decalogue, is not abrogated or relaxed, and still demands our full compliance.[33] Regardless of God's varying dispensations in history, "there is but one great law of God, the eternal and unalterable rule of righteousness between God and man," which says, "if thou sinnest, thou shalt die."[34] The only question now is Who renders such a perfect obedience to fulfill the demand of the law? Herein comes the concept of the imputation of Christ's righteousness.[35] The legal framework of Edwards's justification theory, therefore, is just another testimony of his ongoing confrontation with the Arminian theory of justification. It is directed against the scheme of sovereign leniency that pardons sinners on the basis of their imperfect obedience. Within this legal framework, the concept of imputation plays an indispensable role. This concept will be further examined.

Imputation and Its Ontological Basis

"Imputation" is a forensic concept Reformed theology favored in order to explain not only justification but also original sin, the soteriological

---

32. "Justification by Faith alone," 375–91.
33. This is also the orthodox understanding of Reformed theology. See, for example, *Institutes*, 2.7.12–17; Westminster Larger Catechism, QQ. 39–81 (see Samuel Willard, *The Compleat Body of Divinity* [Boston, 1726] 147–212); Heidelberg Catechism, QQ. 86–115 (see *Creeds of Christendom*, 3:338–49). The controversy was reproduced in Edwards's lifetime. See Samuel Wigglesworth and Joseph Chipman, *Remarks on Some Points of Doctrine, Apprehended by many as Unsound.* . . . (Boston, 1746), 14–15.
34. "Justification by Faith alone," 406.
35. Edwards's covenant thought places greater emphasis on Christ's fulfillment of

counterpart of justification. In both cases the guilt *(peccatum alienum)* or righteousness *(iustitia aliena)* that originates in one is legally predicated to others. The doctrine was of crucial importance in the Reformation period, when the Roman emphasis on the transformative power of God's absolution in Christ became indistinguishably close to the denial of the grace-character of justification. As the Enlightenment dawned, however, the concept grew increasingly disturbing to the humanist spirit of the age. From the Arminian standpoint of human autonomy, such an alien predication can only be ridiculed as illogical or resented as unjust. It was under this theological climate that Edwards engaged in polemics and defended the reasonableness of the doctrine of imputation—in both cases, Adam and Christ. Yet he did not defend it without also securing it on an ontological basis.

Adamic Imputation

The intimate correlation of the two phases of imputation, Adamic and Christological, is plainly shown in the Pauline account of original sin (Rom. 5:12–21). Edwards was also keenly aware of the correlation and defended the doctrine of Adamic imputation, perhaps with the apprehension that its denial would eventually lead to the denial of the Christological counterpart.[36] At the same time, however, his polemics are not the product of a dogmatist who is altogether insensitive to the atmosphere of modern thinking. His private notes reveal that Edwards himself knew the force of his opponents' argument.[37]

Edwards's published argument reverberates with this sensitivity. Although he does not forget to use the standard terminology of federal representation, what is implied by it is somewhat untraditional: there is no imputation of Adam's sin to his descendants. Imputation does occur, but it is the imputation of one's own guilt to oneself. The guilt of Adam's first apostasy is imputed to Adam himself, causing the loss of the righteousness he was originally endowed with. In the same manner,

---

justice. One is "saved on the account of works," he says, for salvation has "a fixed price"; and it is Christ who pays the price, fulfilling the condition of the covenant of works to the fullest measure. See "Miscellanies," nos. 2, 30, 35, 1030, 1091, Yale MSS; "Justification by Faith alone," 427; "The Manner of seeking Salvation," 371.

36. *Original Sin*, 103. See also the title of part 3 (*Original Sin*, 351); "Miscellanies," no. 33, Yale MSS.

37. "Miscellanies" no. 654, Yale MSS. Original sin, he says, is "most difficult to reconcile to Gods justice & goodness." See also Holbrook's Introduction to *Original Sin*, 19.

the descendants are also imputed the guilt of their own sin, for they participated in Adam's transgression with their own act of consent.[38] In other words, there are two parallel tracks of imputation, one from Adam to Adam himself, and the other from the descendants to the descendants themselves. The two tracks of imputation are kept apart throughout and never intersect with each other. What is imputed to the posterity is the sin that is committed by themselves, in the same manner as Adam's sin is imputed to Adam himself. One gets just what he or she deserves. Edwards therefore emphasizes that it is "a *just* imputation," not *peccatum alienum*.[39] Imputation in this paradigm is dramatically deprived of its original "stumbling-block" character.

Coupled with this paradigm of parallel imputation is Edwards's thesis of the primordial identity of all humankind with Adam. His opponents claimed that the doctrine of original sin "implies *falsehood*, viewing and treating those as one which indeed are not one."[40] But for Edwards, Adam and the posterity are united in one organic body, sharing responsibility for the joint act of sinning. They are, according to his varying similes, like a head to the body or a root to the tree, existing "as if he and they had all coexisted."[41] The identification is therefore legitimate. "The first depravity of heart, and the imputation of that sin, are both the consequences of that established union."[42] Edwards then introduces a unique theory of personal identity to explain this divinely constituted union. The details of this personal identity theory and its fate in a complete fiasco are not our primary concern here.[43] What must be

---

38. *Original Sin*, 391.
39. Ibid., 412 (emphasis mine). This does not, as often claimed, prove Edwards's endorsement of the Saumur theory of mediate imputation. Cf. John Murray, "The Imputation of Adam's Sin," *Westminster Theological Journal* 19 (1956): 141–63; Louis Berkhof, *Systematic Theology*, 4th ed. (Grand Rapids, Mich.: Wm. B. Eerdmans, 1949), 243. Mediate imputation is for Edwards no more than a sideline illustration of his own thesis, parallel imputation supported by the physico-theological theory of personal identity. See *Original Sin*, 392–93.
40. *Original Sin*, 395 (emphasis original).
41. Ibid., 389, 391.
42. Ibid., 391. Frank Hugh Foster, though outdated in other aspects, correctly pointed out the importance of the "constitution" in Edwards's argument. Foster, *A Genetic History of the New England Theology* (Chicago: University of Chicago Press, 1907; reprint, New York: Garland Publishing, 1987), 87–88.
43. Dwight seems not thoroughly satisfied with Edward's personal identity theory and counted Jonathan Edwards Jr.'s modification as an "improvement" (*Life of President Edwards*, 557, 618–19). See Hodge, *Systematic Theology*, 2:220, for another perceptive criticism. According to Shelton Smith, the theory "fell flat so far as his theological

recognized is that he tried, though unsuccessfully, to create an alternative to Augustine's theory of biological propagation. He knew well the inadequacy of the Augustinian explanation, and in his whole treatise he did not make any mention of it. Nevertheless, he could not give up the element of truthfulness contained in the theory, namely, posterity's real participation in Adam's sin. It offers the Adamic imputation a solid ontological foundation.[44] Humankind in all ages and places truly "partake of the sin of the first apostasy," Edwards explains, "so as that this, in reality and propriety, shall become *their* sin; by virtue of a real union between the root and branches of the world of mankind."[45] Imputation is not a transaction that attributes an alien guilt to uninvolved others. Rather it is grounded in the ontological participation of the posterity in Adam's sin. "The sin of the apostasy is not theirs, merely because God *imputes* it to them; but it is *truly* and *properly* theirs, and on that ground, God imputes it to them."[46] Their participation in Adam's sin

---

successors were concerned" (Smith, *Changing Conceptions of Original Sin: A Study in American Theology Since 1750* [New York: Charles Scribner's Sons, 1955], 35–36). If Edwards's theological followers were unconvinced, his opponents were more than glad to seize the opportunity to pounce on him. See Holbrook's Introduction, *Original Sin*, 97–101.

44. "Imputation" was an unknown concept for the early Church. The developing doctrine of original sin was at first securely embedded in the context of "traducianism," a teaching that all human souls were actually present in the first father's loins. If so, as Tertullian taught, they all participated in Adam's sin, sharing the same guilt with him. But as creationism replaced traducianism, teaching that human souls are created individually at birth, another explanation was called for in order to explain why these individually created souls are all born corrupt. Imputation was the only answer, if one wanted to avoid making God the author of the corrupt souls. For the history of traducianism and creationism, see Berkhof, *History of Christian Doctrines*, 129–30; idem, *Systematic Theology*, 196–201; *Reformed Dogmatics*, 343–44.

45. *Original Sin*, 407. This is not to say that the union is an empirically verifiable fact. Those who criticize Edwards's flawed "empiricism" underestimate his theme of "divine constitution." See Alfred Owen Aldridge, *Jonathan Edwards* (New York: Washington Square Press, 1964), 120; Fiering, *Jonathan Edwards's Moral Thought*, 55, 57; Vincent Tomas, "The Modernity of Jonathan Edwards," *New England Quarterly* 25 (1952): 82; Robert C. Whittemore, *The Transformation of the New England Theology*, American Studies Series, vol. 23, ser. 7 (New York: Peter Lang, 1987), 73. With Edwards, theological truth does not depend on empirical facts. On the contrary, it is the theological truth that grounds empirical facts! "A *divine constitution* is the thing which *makes truth*." (*Original Sin*, 404, emphasis original.) In this respect, Edwards comes very close to Karl Barth who says it is "God's authoritative verdict" that holds all human beings in the bondage of sin. Barth, *Church Dogmatics* 4.1, trans. G. W. Bromiley and T. F. Torrance (Edinburgh: T. & T. Clark, 1956), 499–502.

46. *Original Sin*, 408 (emphasis original).

precedes and grounds the divine act of imputation. Shelton Smith commented appropriately on the importance of this participation theory for Edwards: "He gave little attention to the federal theory, a fact which probably indicates that he doubted that it sufficiently safeguarded the principle of direct participation. He was perceptive enough to realize that when once the principle of direct participation is surrendered, the ground is cut from beneath the doctrine of imputation."[47] His standard use of the "federal" vocabulary notwithstanding, Edwards did not make much use of it. He knew too well that without the underpinning of ontological participation it could not withstand the Arminian charge of unreasonableness. Sensitive to the age's theological climate, his mind "recoiled from the merely legal and arbitrary elements in Calvinistic dogma and in the covenant theology."[48]

Christological Imputation

A similar ontological basis can be found with Christological imputation. Here also, Edwards uses the orthodox terminology of forensic imputation: God "of his sovereign grace is pleased . . . so to regard one that has no righteousness, that the consequence shall be the same as if he had."[49] He affirms the imputation, as noted above, both in passive and active senses: passively, Christ has suffered "the penalty of the law in our stead, in order to our escaping the penalty"; and actively, "Christ's perfect obedience shall be reckoned to our account, so that we shall have the benefit of it, as though we had performed it ourselves." Christ is the "federal head" and "representative" of the human race in these two senses.[50]

Now the Arminian charge against this Christological imputation is essentially the same as the one directed against the Adamic imputation. "It is to suppose God is mistaken," they say, attributing the merit of one to another. But Edwards's refutation here is somewhat milder and moderate. He presents the case by analogy: "Why is there any more absurdity in it, than in a merchant's transferring debt or credit from one man's account to another, when one man pays a price for another, so

---

47. Smith, *Changing Conceptions of Original Sin*, 35.
48. Thomas A. Schafer, "The Role of Jonathan Edwards in American Religious History," *Encounter* 30 (1969): 215.
49. "Justification by Faith alone," 352.
50. Ibid., 395, 394, 396, 400.

that it shall be accepted as if that other had paid it?"⁵¹ Later on, he finds another illustration to explain the same transaction:

> Estates are often & justly settled on the posterity of a person who died in the service of his countrey and they enjoy the benefit of their parent without any merit of their own. . . . This legal imputation of merit or application of the fruits arising from the merit of another is never deem'd unjust among men. . . . The son is often pardon'd even the crime of high treason on account of his fathers services & fidelity and nothing can be more consistent with justice than a pardon so obtain'd. . . . And surely we must own that God is vested with an higher plenitude of power to prescribe terms on which imputed and vicarious merits may be accepted than any earthly legislature or king.⁵²

Edwards does not go further into the logic of such mercantile or legislative transactions as he did in the case of the Adamic imputation. This brevity is probably due to the nature of the charge he was refuting. With the Adamic imputation, the charge was not only of "absurdity" but also of "impropriety." The opponents were more indignant and resentful than merely unconvinced with the unfair attribution of the guilt of the sin they did not commit. John Taylor, a leading Arminian of Edwards's day, exclaimed that "a representation of moral action is what I can by no means digest."⁵³ The charge against the Christological imputation, in contrast, was soft-voiced, for the antagonists still affirmed the imputation of Christ's satisfaction to some extent, making the task easier for Edwards.⁵⁴

However, Edwards is no less assertive when it comes to the ontological basis of this transaction. He defines faith as that which constitutes a union with Christ, providing the faithful with an ontological foundation

---

51. Ibid., 395.
52. "Miscellanies," no. 1237, Yale MSS. The argument is in fact a verbatim quotation from the "fourth Dialogue" of Philip Skelton, *Deism Revealed, or the Attack on Christianity Candidly Reviewed in its real Merits* . . . , 2 vols. 2d ed. (London, 1751), 1:250–51.
53. Taylor, *The Scripture-Doctrine of Original Sin*, 384. Quoted in Holbrook's Introduction to *Original Sin*, 53.
54. According to Edwards's recapitulation, they only denied the imputation of Christ's *positive* obedience. "Justification by Faith alone," 375, 395, 407.

for "their being accounted as one [with Christ] by the judge."[55] "This *relation* or *union* to Christ, whereby Christians are said to be in Christ, is the ground of their right to his benefits."[56] This union is the vital channel through which human beings participate in the life of the ever-living Christ. They become "interested"—in the sense explained at the beginning of Chapter 3—in the merit of Christ by way of this union. Christ's righteousness becomes their property, for there is this real union through which the righteousness of Christ is transferred to them.

Edwards's oft-quoted passage, "what is *real* in the union between Christ and his people, is the foundation of what is *legal*," appears in this context.[57] Miller quoted it in connection with what seemed to him Edwards's sense of "the necessity of saying something more," namely, saying something more than legal and forensic justification. In Miller's interpretation, the phrase implies Edwards's unpretentious revolution from "seventeenth-century legalism" to "eighteenth-century physics" in which "the *experience* of regeneration" came to assume a vital role in religion.[58] Schafer also, more than once, quotes the passage, paraphrasing it as "the natural creates the legal, not vice versa; something really existing in the soul precedes the external imputation."[59] I will reexamine shortly whether these interpretations adequately reflect Edwards's concern in the passage. Nevertheless, they direct our attention properly to his effort to furnish the legal transaction with an ontological basis.

One can even argue that this union with Christ is of such crucial importance that it practically wipes out the concept of legal imputation from Edwards's theory of justification. Dorus Rudisill, based on this concept of union, asserts that Edwards's idea of justification is more of "commendation or influence" than an exchange of merit and sin. Christ's moral quality, says Rudisill, "is not transferred nor adjudged to belong to the sinner."[60] Rather, human beings stand "within Christ's halo," being embraced and enfolded in it. Though Edwards's concept of

55. Ibid., 364.
56. Ibid., 360 (emphasis original).
57. Ibid., 364 (emphasis original).
58. Miller, *Jonathan Edwards*, 76, 77, 78.
59. Schafer, "Jonathan Edwards and Justification by Faith," 58; idem, "Jonathan Edwards' Conception of the Church," *Church History* 24 (1955): 54; idem, "Role of Jonathan Edwards," 215.
60. Dorus Paul Rudisill, *The Doctrine of the Atonement in Jonathan Edwards and His Successors* (New York: Poseidon Books, 1971), 32. His interpretation is based on "Satisfaction for Sin," *WW*, 1:595.

union is too realistic to describe as "halo," and his use of "counted" and "reckoned" too conspicuous to neglect, Rudisill's interpretation is not totally unfounded.

As a matter of fact, Edwards is not advancing a novel doctrine. Contrary to the common presupposition that Reformation theology placed exclusive emphasis on forensic justification, both Luther and Calvin underscored the importance of such a real union with Christ. For Calvin, neither justification nor sanctification is even thinkable without *insitio in Christum* or *unio cum Christo*.[61] The fruits of redemption, in a sense, all hang together on the reality of this union. Ames wrote that *unio* is the basis of *communio*, that is, the sharing of the benefits that Christ has purchased.[62] Mastricht repeated the same proposition on the inseparable connection between *unio* and *communio*.[63] In underscoring the ontological ground of the legal imputation, Edwards was only reiterating what was readily available in tradition. His sentences, like the one following, echo these indubitable precedents rather precisely: "Those that are not in Christ, or are not united to him, can have no degree of communion with him; for union with Christ, or a being in Christ, is the foundation of all communion with him."[64] In repeating the traditional understanding, Edwards had his own agenda in mind. His task was to give a reasonable account of the imputation that seemed so unreasonable and improper in the face of the Arminian charges. He affirmed the concept of legal imputation, but did so only after grounding it in the ontological union with Adam or with Christ. "What is real" is indeed the foundation of "what is legal."

Edwards's Theories of Justification

I have identified Edwards's theological utterances on justification specifically with his polemic agenda in view. Against the Arminian scheme of lenient justification, Edwards took a firm stance on the strictly legal

61. See, for example, W. Kolfhaus, *Christusgemeinschaft bei Johannes Calvin*, Beiträge zur Geschichte und Lehre der Reformierten Kirche, Dritter Band (Buchhandlungs des Erziehungsvereins Neukirchen Kr. Moers, 1939), 19, 85.
62. Ames, *Marrow of Theology*, 1.26.1-2, 1.27.3-5, 1.29.4, 1.30.1.
63. Mastricht, *Theoretico-Practica Theologia*, 6.1.10 (Latin edition, 640, emphasis original).
64. "Efficacious Grace," 596.

justification that requires Christ's complete righteousness to be imputed. At the same time, he showed consistent efforts to ground the legal transaction on a solid ontological foundation in order to fend off the Arminian charge of unreasonableness and impropriety. What, then, does the phrase "by faith alone" mean to Edwards? A person is said to become "interested" in justifying grace "by faith alone." What is the role of faith in justification? How does it form the crucial union with Christ? And if faith is of such importance, how does it square with Edwards's repeated claim that we are not saved by our own virtue or effort? These are the questions that properly belong to the present phase of our inquiry.

Active Role of Faith

First of all, Edwards's concept of faith is very active and volitional in character. In the Calvinist tradition, faith is often defined as "the instrumental cause of justification."[65] Though by that definition Calvin was trying to disprove faith's inherent value, a tendency was inevitable in later generations to see in faith something that merits God's favor, justifying a person in the same sense that works would justify them. It is for this reason that some Reformed theologians thought it wise, despite its wide reception in Protestant confessions, to warn against the instrumental view of faith.[66] Edwards was reissuing this warning afresh when he disapproved of calling faith "the instrument wherewith we receive justification."[67] In his opinion, the "obscurity" and "impropriety" of doing so has to do with the implication that faith has an inherent value or excellency in itself. Justification is owed rather exclusively to the relation that faith has to the fountain of this grace. Hence Edwards defines faith as "the soul's *active* uniting with Christ," or "the very act of unition."[68] Edwards explains the role of faith with a vivid imagery: "If any person that was greatly obliged to me and dependent on me . . . should exceedingly abuse me . . . I should not forgive the person, unless a much dearer friend to me, and one that had always been true to me

---

65. *Institutes*, 3.11.7, 3.14.17; Westminster Confession, Chapter 11 (see *Creeds of Christendom*, 3:626–28).
66. For example, Heidelberg Catechism, Question 61, clearly teaches that "not that I am acceptable to God on account of the worthiness of my faith." See *Creeds of Christendom*, 3:327.
67. "Justification by Faith alone," 357, 359.
68. Ibid., 364 (emphasis original). See also ibid., 409; "Concerning Faith," 611.

... should intercede for him, and, out of the entire love he had to him, should put himself to very hard labors and difficulties, and undergo great pains and miseries to procure him forgiveness."[69] But even so, it is absolutely necessary and imperative, he continues, that the offender "with a changed mind, fly to this mediator . . . seek favor in his name, with a sense in his own mind how much his mediator had done and suffered for him." This act of flying to the Mediator with "a changed mind" and a sense of indebtedness is what Edwards holds to be faith. It is an act of actively uniting oneself with the Mediator, who has all the benefits of salvation. In faith one is united to Christ so that the channel of communion with him should be opened and established. Faith is this act of "the true Christian . . . *on his part*, whereby he is *active* in coming into this relation or union; some *uniting* act, or that which is done towards this union or relation *on the Christian's part*."[70]

With regard to this definition of faith, there is one persistent misconception in Edwards scholarship that has to be corrected here. As I mentioned earlier, his phrase "what is real is the foundation of what is legal" has been repeatedly quoted, with its meaning purported to be that sanctification should precede legal imputation. Something holy that exists in the soul takes precedence over the legal imputation, thus potentially endangering the "Protestant" character of Edwards's theology. A fuller quotation of the context, however, shows that this was not quite his intention.

> God does not give those that believe an union with or an interest in the Saviour as a *reward* for faith, but only because faith is the soul's *active* uniting with Christ, or is itself the very act of unition, *on their part*. God sees it fit, that in order to an union being established between two intelligent active beings or persons, so as that they should be looked upon as one, there should be the mutual act of both, that each should receive the other, as actively joining themselves one to another. God, in requiring this in order to an union with Christ as one of his people, treats men as reasonable creatures, capable of act and choice; and hence sees it fit that they only who are one with Christ by their own act, should be looked upon as one *in law*. What is *real* in the union

---

69. "Satisfaction for Sin," 592. The quoted section also appears in "Miscellanies," no. 245, Yale MSS.
70. "Justification by Faith alone," 363 (emphasis original).

> between Christ and his people, is the foundation of what is *legal;* that is, it is something really in them, and between them, uniting them, that is the ground of the suitableness of their being accounted as one by the judge.[71]

The "what is real" phrase occurs within the context of how this vital union of the believer and Christ can be realized. Faith is necessary for this union, Edwards expounds, because God treats human beings as "intelligent active beings" who are "capable of act and choice," and faith is the expression of this active choice. Edwards is saying that the reality of the union is dependent on how active and voluntary the believer's participation in the union is. By "what is real," he means not the reality of sanctification, but the reality of the union "between Christ and his people" established by this active consenting of the believer. In this scheme, "the minds of men are not only passive, but abundantly active," wherein lies the taxonomic differentiation of human beings from "beasts."[72]

Such an active and voluntary involvement of the believer is important for Edwards, for it expresses an element of human participation in the work of justification. Intelligent beings must actively "consent" to the union in order to be united and justified. Or rather, human consenting is the very principle that constitutes the being of the union, because "consent," in Edwards's aesthetic metaphysics, is "a constitutive principle of intelligent perceiving being."[73] Without active consenting in faith, human beings would be mere receptacles of the grace of justification, or mere spectators of the transaction of guilt and righteousness. Imputation, then, could only be characterized as an arbitrary attribution of alien righteousness, and indeed be "absurd and improper" as Arminians criticize. This is precisely what Edwards wanted to avoid by accentuating the active role of faith in justification. The sentence of "what is real" being the foundation of "what is legal," should therefore be understood as Edwards's continuing effort to give a reasonable account of the doctrine of forensic imputation.

---

71. Ibid., 364 (emphasis original). See also "Miscellanies," no. 568, Yale MSS, for a parallel argument.
72. "The Mind," no. 59 (*WY*, 6:374). See also "Miscellanies," no. 831, Yale MSS.
73. Delattre, *Beauty and Sensibility*, 208. The union, either Adamic or Christological, is made real by human consent. See also "Miscellanies," no. 33, Yale MSS; "Efficacious Grace," 554.

God's Antecedent Acceptance

Edwards's scheme of justification thus avoids making human beings passive onlookers of the drama of salvation. But does not his emphasis on active human participation undermine God's unconditional initiative in justifying the sinners? Faith for Calvin was never a "positive condition" for salvation. It was nothing but "an empty vessel" into which grace is poured, or "a passive work to which no reward can be paid."[74] If Edwards continued to emphasize the active role of faith as he does here, his thesis would eventually be indistinguishable from the Arminian assertion that human beings can on their own make a difference with regard to salvation. Was he so empathetic to the Arminian argument that finally he himself became one of them?

This kind of worry, however, does not seem to have bothered Edwards. For one thing, there is his well-known distinction between natural and moral fitness. The kind of fitness faith has is not *moral*, meaning that it does not carry any meritorious worthiness in itself; it is rather *natural*, in the sense that there is only a "natural concord . . . between such a qualification of a soul, and such an union with Christ, and interest in him."[75] I will review the distinction later in this chapter.

More to the point is his careful phrase, "the very act of unition *on their part.*"[76] What this phrase indicates is that there is the other part to be played out in this picture. If the union is a "*mutual* act of both," then this other part is of course to be played by Christ, the one who offers the deal. That is to say, there is an antecedent offer of Christ in the first place, which is determined from all eternity in the covenant of redemption. "There was a transaction between the Father and the Son, that was antecedent to Christ's becoming man," Edwards expounds, "in which transaction these things were already virtually done in the sight of God, that God acted on the ground of that transaction, justifying and saving sinners, as if the things undertaken had been actually performed long before they were performed indeed."[77] With his absolute initiative, Christ, in establishing the union, has already and fully played out his part in God's triune determination. The human element of consent is

---

74. *Institutes*, 3.11.7, 3.13.5. See Kendall, *Calvin and English Calvinism*, 19–20, 210.
75. "Justification by Faith alone," 369.
76. Ibid., 364 (emphasis original).
77. Ibid., 400–401. See also ibid., 422, for another expression of the theme of antecedent acceptance. Note the word "virtually" in the quotation. For the meaning of the word in Edwards's dispositional view of reality, see Chapter 3.

therefore totally dependent on this antecedent decision of the triune God in eternity.

Here Edwards brings in his favorite metaphor of a marriage contract to further explain the part that is to be played by the believer: "As when a man offers himself to a woman in marriage, he does not give himself to her as a *reward* of her receiving him in marriage. Her receiving him is not considered as a worthy deed in her . . . but it is by her receiving him that the union is made, by which she hath him for her husband. It is *on her part* the union itself."[78] It is true that the woman's active deed concludes this beneficial union, yet this act of receiving is no more than a confirmation of what is already achieved. Human beings play their own part in this mutual act of "unition." But in comparison to Christ's initiating offer, their act of joining is just as slight as "the onward act of a beggar in putting forth his hand," or "as the beggars taking the gift & voluntarily having it."[79] What Edwards is at pains to articulate here might as well be expressed by Paul Tillich's term, "to accept acceptance."[80] The believers are already accepted by Christ when the deal is offered. They still have to accept it, thus fulfilling their own part of unition. This act of accepting is nothing but a delightful recognition of the fact that they are already accepted.

The same structure appears in Edwards's sermons. In a sermon on the excellency of Christ, he delineates the role of faith:

> Let the consideration of this wonderful meeting of diverse excellencies in Christ *induce you to accept him,* and close with him as your Saviour. As all manner of excellencies meet in him, so there are concurring in him all manner of arguments and motives, to *move you to choose him,* for your Saviour, and every thing that tends to *encourage poor sinners to come* and put their trust in him.[81]

In order to establish the saving union with Christ, we do have to accept him, choose him, and come to him, because God treats us as "reasonable creatures, capable of act and choice."[82] The great condition, "if you

78. Ibid., 409 (emphasis original).
79. "Miscellanies," no. 856, Yale MSS.
80. Tillich, *Systematic Theology,* 3:222, 224–26, 228.
81. Sermon, "The Excellency of Christ," *WW,* 4:193.
82. "Justification by Faith alone," 364.

accept," still stands. Yet we are so "enabled," "induced to accept," "moved to choose," and "encouraged to come."[83] Under God's sovereign and prevenient initiative, human beings are installed to be active participants in the work of redemption. Invited, enabled, and encouraged by God the primary Subject, we are made the secondary but nonetheless genuine subjects of salvation. On this Edwards remained unchanged to the very end of his life. He affirmed in one of the last entries of his "Miscellanies" that the human "active and voluntary act of faith" is not in the least inconsistent with "the highest possible freedom of grace."[84]

Human Goodness Prior to Justification

I have examined some of the questions regarding the phrase, "justification by faith alone." But Reformed theology also teaches "justification *of the ungodly.*" I now turn to this aspect of Edwards's justification theory.

Doubtlessly, Edwards thinks that justification is not achieved by the worthiness of the person to be justified. The "doctrine" of the Justification discourse states unequivocally that it is "the ungodly" who are justified.[85] They are "destitute of any righteousness" of their own, and are saved solely on account of Christ's righteousness. Not only are they "wholly without all excellency or beauty," but they are "altogether, yea, infinitely vile and hateful."[86]

One wonders, however, to what extent this explicit denial of human goodness is sustained in Edwards's entire soteriology.[87] Already within the same discourse, a significant equivocation occurs when he states that "there is indeed something in man that is really and spiritually good, prior to justification." He then qualifies the remark by saying, "yet there is nothing that is *accepted* as any godliness or excellency of the person, till after justification."[88] With this statement, the issue of

---

83. Sermon, "The Excellency of Christ," 195, 192. See also "Wisdom of God," 166–67: "There remains nothing wanting but your consent."
84. "Miscellanies," no. 1346, Yale MSS, written probably in or around 1756.
85. "Justification by Faith alone," 353. Also in 351–52.
86. Ibid., 393, 450.
87. Cherry points out an equivocation here: Edwards "risks obscuring" one aspect of justification, namely, that "it is *ungodly* man who is imputed as righteous." Cherry, *Theology of Jonathan Edwards*, 96.
88. "Justification by Faith alone," 374 (emphasis mine). See also "Miscellanies," no. 712, Yale MSS, for a reiteration of the passage.

inherent goodness suddenly slips into a matter of recognition. All it says is that God, in justifying sinners, does not take into consideration their goodness, which is indeed in them prior to justification. The existence of human goodness is not denied or doubted; it is there, but not recognized as such. To be sure, it is not justification *on account of* that goodness, but neither is it justification of *the ungodly* anymore. However small and counterbalanced they are by their "infinite heinousness," there is indeed some real goodness and virtue within the sinner.[89] Edwards's argument rests on one point: inherent goodness becomes "acceptable" and "rewardable" only after justification.[90]

In order to get over this difficulty, scholars have often quoted Edwards's distinction between natural and moral fitness.[91] The distinction, however, is tainted with ambiguity. Edwards himself blurs it at times by affirming the existence of moral fitness prior to justification.[92] His "Miscellanies" notes also reveal hints of ambiguity and indetermination on this matter.[93] The distinction did not survive well after Edwards, either.[94] His disapproval of moral fitness sounds particularly unconvincing in light of these remarks of his own: "Acts of evangelical obedience are indeed concerned in our justification itself, and are not excluded from that condition that justification depends upon. . . . God has respect to this, as that on which the fitness of such an act of justification depends; so that our salvation does as truly depend upon it, as if we were justified for the moral excellency of it."[95] "Holiness and justifica-

---

89. "Justification by Faith alone," 373, 421; and most obviously in "Miscellanies," no. 712, Yale MSS.
90. "Justification by Faith alone," 419–24, 425; "Satisfaction for Sin," 594; "Miscellanies," nos. 627, 688, Yale MSS.
91. This is Cherry's solution (see *Theology of Jonathan Edwards*, 95–98, 105–6).
92. "Justification by Faith alone," 424–25: "I allow that this worthiness does doubtless denote a *moral fitness* to the reward."
93. "Miscellanies," nos. 647 (the first appearance of the distinction), 670, and 829, Yale MSS, deny moral fitness; whereas nos. 687, 688, and 712, Yale MSS, seek to affirm some form of "moral fitness" or "moral valuableness."
94. An anonymous editor (with a signature "W") added a footnote here and argued: "This order, however, is a law to us, and compliance with it necessarily imports moral obedience. Faith may well be an act of moral excellence." ("Justification by Faith alone," 369.) The comment in effect subverts Edwards's import. Hodge, otherwise loyal to Edwards, quietly but completely passes by the distinction (*Systematic Theology*, 3:116–17). Berkhof calls it "an unfortunate distinction" (Berkhof, *Systematic Theology*, 430).
95. "Justification by Faith alone," 417, 446 (emphasis original).

tion shall indeed go together"—his only contention is that these two only coincide, not one causing the other.⁹⁶

Edwards himself seems to be partly aware of the issue. In the last pages of *Religious Affections*, he anticipated some objections with regard to the "twelfth sign" of genuine religious affections (Christian practice). Is his emphasis on holy practice consistent with the doctrine of justification "of the ungodly" and "by faith alone"? Given the importance of the subject, one may say, what is questioned here is the entire construction of his soteriology. Edwards does not draw back, however. It is not scriptural to teach that "no holy and amiable qualifications or actions in us shall be a fruit." The gratuitous nature of grace in the Scripture means rather that "it is not the worthiness or loveliness of any qualification or action of ours which recommends us to that grace."⁹⁷ Holy qualifications are really present in us as evidence of divinely wrought transformation, yet they do not *count* as such in recommending us to justification. What matters in justification is "not the worthiness or loveliness of our works, or anything in us," but solely "the righteousness of Christ" received in union by faith. The existence of "holy and amiable qualifications" is not denied or doubted. Edwards's last appeal in the treatise is quite symbolic: he asks to cast off "a senseless aversion to the letters and sound of the word 'works.' "⁹⁸

Actually, Edwards is not an isolated figure in underscoring the value of human goodness. Most of those involved in the New England Arminian controversy would not disclaim the moral value of human deeds. They would readily line up with Edwards on the issue. Wigglesworth and Chipman, for example, wrote a vindication of orthodox faith against an Arminian, William Balch, and sharply rejected the latter's charge of "the Contempt of Good Works." "We are not those Adversaries that ever yet thought or spake contemptuously of Good Works; So much greater Friends are we to Good Works, than Mr. Balch, that in our Divinity we provide and acknowledge a Principle, whence they may flow; whereas he owns no such Thing."⁹⁹ There is no doubt about the value of good works either in theory or in life. Nonetheless, in the next line, the

---

96. Ibid., 416. See also "Efficacious Grace," 559; "Miscellanies," no. 416, Yale MSS.
97. *Religious Affections*, 455.
98. Ibid., 459.
99. Wigglesworth and Chipman, *Remarks on Some Points of Doctrine*, 31.

authors retort very sharply: "In respect of Justification, we do indeed think of them with Contempt, lest we should put Contempt upon the Grace of God."

These New Englanders are not anomalies in the history of Reformed faith. The Belgic Confession, first composed in 1561 and later revised at the Synod of Dort, affirms in plain and straightforward language that "it is impossible that this holy faith can be unfruitful in man," yet forewarns that "howbeit they are of no account towards our justification."[100] The Belgic Confession does indeed deny the justification by good works, yet it does not deny that we are made good trees that bear good fruits. The concept of "merit" is thereby explicitly excluded, but that does not inhibit one from affirming the presence of goodness in the regenerate humanity. There is a distinction to be made between *regenerate human goodness* and *human meritorious works*. Edwards is avowedly against the latter; he denied the existence of such works that can be termed meritorious at all. This does not lead to the exclusion of the former, however. There is indeed within human beings good works that are of moral value. They are held in high regard. Yet when it comes to justification, they are not counted as meritorious. With Edwards, therefore, piety and morality are not played off against each other. It is piety *in addition to* morality.[101]

God Crowns His Own Gift

The ultimate answer to the above question of inherent goodness must be given with Edwards's entire soteriology in perspective. After all, such a claim is not unexpected, especially in view of his strong emphasis on the reality of the new disposition, as was reviewed in the previous chapters. If he thinks—and obviously he does—that justification follows conversion, then there must be in the convert all the good fruits of God's converting grace. Justification must presuppose the reality of the new creation, that is, the new intrinsic principle of holy action. In this sense, Edwards's soteriology is internally consistent, despite its meager

---

100. Article 24, "Of Man's Sanctification and Good Works," in *Creeds of Christendom*, 3:411; see also French Confession, Article 22, in *Creeds*, 3:372.
101. Following in the wake of Haroutunian, Jenson tries to portray Edwards as a Karl Barth of the eighteenth century for whom "revival" was "not a means to promote religion" but "the surprising result of a *critique* of religion" (*America's Theologian*, 63). Such a sharp contrast of religion and gospel, however, is alien to Edwards's language and conceptualization.

references to the relations between the phases of redemption. In conversion, the indwelling Holy Spirit establishes in human nature a new creation. In justification, this regenerate human goodness, though not counted as the qualification for justification, is given due recognition.

In the meantime, God's economy of salvation is advanced to a higher stage. In conversion, the recipients of grace are totally passive; "natural" persons are spiritually dead and immobile, hence their conversion is compared to resurrection. In contrast, sinners in justification are awakened and made to realize their own state as well as of God's antecedent acceptance, so that with the explicit act of faith they conclude the union with Christ, exercising their ability of voluntary choosing. A definite step forward is made toward the ultimate goal of redemption in terms of human participation. In Chapter 6, the step will be further advanced in sanctification and perfected in glorification, where human beings participate in God's self-repetition and self-enlargement by their conscious activities.

Viewed in this totality, Edwards's soteriology appears to be a unique echoing of the old Augustinian dictum, "When God rewards our merits, he crowns his own gifts." Edwards at times describes faith as "one holy act of ours."[102] To those critics whose primary concern is to defend the "Protestant" character of his theology, such a choice of words can only mean an "unfortunate" exception.[103] In fact, it is neither "unfortunate" nor an exception in his soteriology. Edwards does not show any sign of hesitation in calling faith "one holy act of ours," because he knows that this faith is nothing but an antecedent gift of God. It is true that we do have to close with Christ with our own act of faith, but, "it is God that gives us faith whereby we close with Christ."[104] In preaching he exhorts his parishioners to come to faith, but at the same time he does not forget to add that coming to faith is itself Christ's purchase: "We must *believe* in the Lord Jesus Christ, and *accept* of him as offered in the gospel for a Saviour. But, as we cannot do this of ourselves, Christ has purchased this also for all the elect. He has purchased, that they shall have faith given them; whereby they shall be actively united to Christ, and so have a pleadable title to his benefits."[105] For this reason—and only for this reason—he could call faith "holy" and remain completely at ease. It is a

---

102. "Miscellanies," no. 1070, Yale MSS (emphasis mine).
103. Cherry, *Theology of Jonathan Edwards*, 96.
104. "God Glorified in Man's Dependence," 170.
105. "Wisdom of God," 145 (emphasis original).

human endeavor in which the "divine given" operates. In faith God's self-communication flows back to God via humanity. That is to say, human exercise of faith is an integral part of the divine process of emanation and remanation. It is in this sense that Edwards says that "our faith itself is not of ourselves, but is God's gift."[106] God crowns his own gift of faith with the reward of justification.

My task in the remaining part of this chapter is to explain this structure of divine giving and rewarding in Edwards's dispositional view of reality. Consider a very suggestive entry from his "Miscellanies" notes, entitled "Free Grace." At first sight it appears to be an outright denial of the doctrine of justification by faith alone. Since "God does everything beautifully," he starts writing, "it would be a grating, dissonant and deformed thing for a sinful creature to be happy in God's love."[107] Therefore, God first gives them "holiness, which holiness he really delights in . . . and so, when given, induces God in a certain secondary manner to give them happiness." This is tantamount to saying that God must be "induced" to give happiness to creatures! Creatures have to "induce" God with their holiness in order to receive grace!

This could be a very offensive remark to those trying to portray Edwards as a conventional Reformed theologian. The fact that he was more than that is plainly shown in the following:

> [God] wills their happiness antecedently, of himself, and he gives them holiness that he may be induced to confer it; and when it is given by him, then he is induced by another consideration besides his mere propensity to goodness. For there are these two propensities in the divine nature: to communicate goodness absolutely to that which now is nothing, and to communicate goodness to that which is beautiful and holy, and which he has complacence in. He has a propensity to reward holiness, but he gives it on purpose that he may reward it; because he loves the creature, and loves to reward, and therefore gives it something that he may reward.[108]

---

106. "Efficacious Grace," 576.
107. "Miscellanies," no. 314, Yale MSS.
108. Ibid. See also "Miscellanies," no. 589, Yale MSS. Similar arguments can also be found in *Institutes*, 3.17.5; *Summa Theologica*, 1–2.110.1.

Certainly there must be holiness and goodness in the human creature for God to reward, but this holiness and goodness that he rewards is nothing but what he has given before, with the intention of rewarding it afterward. It is a double structure of prior giving and later rewarding. According to Edwards's explanation, this structure is grounded in the twofold propensity, or disposition, within the nature of God.

God has within his nature two dispositions: to communicate goodness to "that which now is nothing," and to communicate goodness to "that which is beautiful and holy." The first disposition is exhibited in his work of creation out of nothing and re-creation of the fallen creature. The entire creation is a product of this divine disposition to communicate his own goodness absolutely *ad extra* (outward). Naturally there was nothing whatsoever to induce God in this first self-communication, as this happens before creation, neither was there anything that could induce God to reward before re-creation. Yet God has this internal disposition to communicate his own goodness ad extra, with no regard whatsoever to the recipient. Or rather, this internal disposition is itself the cause and force of his act of creating and re-creating its recipients, hence creation out of nothing and re-creation of the fallen nature.

Upon the exercise of this first disposition, God's second disposition is exerted. In other words, the second disposition (to reward goodness to that which is beautiful and holy) presupposes the first disposition to communicate goodness to sheer nonentities. The first disposition is exerted "without any consideration of anything that is good of one kind or other to incline him."[109] If one does not take note of this antecedent disposition, it would be very difficult to understand why this fragment is titled "Free Grace." Out of his own propensity to communicate goodness freely and absolutely ad extra, God first causes the recipient to exist out of nothing, and exist in beauty and holiness. Only after this first communication, is the same divine propensity exerted to reward the recipient with happiness. The second time around, God is now induced "in a *secondary* manner to give them happiness." It is called "secondary," because God is induced by what he himself has given first. God's eros for what is holy and amiable is based on God's disinterested agape that is exerted in advance. In agape God elects and creates antecedently the recipients of salvation, and then rewards in eros what he himself has given. This is why Edwards does not vacillate in talking

---

109. Ibid.

about "beauty and holiness" as residing within the creature prior to justification. It is given by God, precisely with the intention to reward it afterward.

This double structure of giving and rewarding is deeply ingrained in Edwards's theology, and is translated into a number of expressions. For one, there is a distinction often used by the moralists of his day, that is, "love of benevolence" and "love of complacence." The "love of benevolence" is a rough equivalent of the first propensity, or agape, that communicates goodness without presupposing beauty in the recipient, and the "love of complacence" is the second propensity, or eros, that takes delight in the goodness that is there in the object.[110] The genius of Edwards is that he applies the distinction not only to human psychology but also primarily to God. God, out of the "love of benevolence," desires first that there should be recipients of his overflowing goodness, and second, out of the "love of complacence," he desires that the goodness thus communicated should be rewarded with happiness. In another context, Edwards also comments that "God's act in rewarding righteousness is grounded on a foregoing act of his in giving righteousness." Justification in Edwards's soteriology means this rewarding of God's prior giving. God "rewards righteousness in such a person, because he hath given righteousness to such a person."[111] With Edwards, therefore, the existence of creaturely goodness and holiness prior to justification need not be denied in favor of the gratuitousness of salvation and the prevenience of God. In justifying, God simply exerts his internal disposition to further communicate his own happiness and reward the goodness "in the secondary manner," that is, based upon the goodness he himself has communicated beforehand.

Edwards's paradigm of justification thus exhibits a remarkable consistency with the rest of his soteriology. In retrospect, it points to the electing love of God that precedes every act he actually executes in time; in prospect, it points to the ultimate end of God in creating the world and intelligent beings in it. Justification occupies the middle step in this economy of salvation. By rewarding faith with justification, what has emanated from God remanates to God. Faith is assigned an indispensable role in this scheme: it is through human faith that God emanates

---

110. *Charity and Its Fruits*, WY, 8:212–13; *Nature of True Virtue*, WY, 8:542–43; *Treatise on Grace*, 49; "Miscellanies," no. 92, Yale MSS.

111. "Concerning the Divine Decrees in General and Election in Particular," WW, 2:544.

and remanates his goodness, fulfilling his ultimate purpose of creation. Though it may be a human act, faith is nothing but a fraction of the continuous and unfrustratable flow of divine goodness. Its foundation is in God's nature, namely, in his intrinsic disposition to communicate himself ad extra.

My concern in this chapter has been to understand Edwards's relatively isolated pronouncements on justification in a way harmonious with the rest of his soteriology. His Justification discourse was first examined in the light of its polemic setting, confirming his conception of "by faith alone" and "forensic imputation" as directed against the Arminian scheme of justification, not against the Roman Catholic soteriology. Some of the distinctive features of Edwards's justification theory were then highlighted. Edwards put strong emphasis on the active role of faith in justification, and he did not deny the existence of goodness and holiness even prior to justification. Ultimately, however, his scheme of justification is a new rendition of the Augustinian concept of God rewarding his own gifts. All the virtuous dispositions, including faith, are nothing but God's antecedent gift given with the intention to reward afterward. Herein lies the secret of Edwards's confidence. Justification occupies a middle step in the economy of salvation, between God's emanation and remanation.

5

Justification
Systemic Comparison

In this chapter I submit the basic structure of Edwards's soteriology to systemic analyses, particularly by comparing it to Roman Catholic soteriology. In Chapter 1 I mentioned some of the questions raised in Edwards scholarship concerning his suspected "deviation" from Protestant doctrines. These questions are obviously diverse and overlap one another, yet for the sake of argument they can be classified into three major categories: (1) those concerning Edwards's strong emphasis on the ontological reality of salvation as such; (2) those concerning the order of justification and sanctification; and (3) those concerning the relation of faith to love, or the Roman concept of "faith formed by love."

Comparing different theological systems, however, requires careful attention to the value-judgment that is involved in the task. One cannot of course interpret a text without having some frame of evaluation. The task is therefore not to wipe out one's own interpretive bias, but to make it explicit. Edwards interpretation has hitherto been under the untold pressure of making his theology *look* "Protestant," with no appreciation of the obvious affinity it has with the Roman Catholic theology. In this chapter I suggest making a paradigm shift from suppression to open recognition of this affinity. This shift is indeed compelled by the radical developments in recent Protestant–Roman Catholic dialogues. The fruits of these dialogues urge Edwards scholarship seriously to reexamine its unquestioned assumption, namely, that between Protestant and Roman Catholic theories of salvation lies an incompatibility that cannot be overcome. The Edwards reader must now come out of a long-entrenched camp of preconceived "Protestantism" and bring the subject out into the open field for mutual appreciation. It is on this redrawn map where a fair reassessment of Edwards's soteriology should be presented.

The recent advancement of ecumenical dialogue is so remarkable that a few decades ago no one could expect to see such a dwindling of the divergence between the two "siblings" of Christianity. The result has been especially encouraging in the field of soteriology since the publication of Hans Küng's epoch-making monograph on justification. Küng's conclusion that there is "fundamental agreement" between Karl Barth and the Roman understanding on the theme is striking.[1] While Küng's study was conducted as a comparison of Barth and the Council of Trent, its undisguised presupposition is that these two represent Protestant and Catholic theories of justification in their own right.[2] Küng has rendered a great service in breaking through the paralyzing insensitivity toward each other that has lasted over four centuries. A number of scholastic reexaminations have been published since then, generally confirming the irreversible trend of mutual understanding and appreciation. As it stands now, curiously enough, what was most divisive at the time of the Reformation—justification—seems to be the point at which ecumenical dialogue looks most auspicious. Our interpretation of Edwards cannot remain uninfluenced by such a new paradigm of theology.

---

1. Hans Küng, *Justification: The Doctrine of Karl Barth and a Catholic Reflection*, trans. Thomas Collins, Edmund E. Tolk, and David Granskou (New York: Thomas Nelson & Son, 1964; reprint, Philadelphia: Westminster Press, 1981), 282.

2. Küng's opinion must be distinguished from the official teaching of the magisterium. See Alister McGrath, "Justification: Barth, Trent, and Küng," *Scottish Journal of Theology* 34 (1981): 517–29. For a favorable review of Küng's monograph, see Karl Rahner, "Questions of Controversial Theology on Justification," in Rahner's *Theological Investigations*, trans. Kevin Smyth (Baltimore: Helicon Press, 1966), 4:189–218.

Realistic Infusion versus Declaratory Imputation

Our first focus here is Edwards's insistence on the ontological transformation that occurs through the infusion of grace. Does his position, by Protestant standards, violate the Reformers' understanding of justification that is declarative and juridical? A classic but rather unsophisticated example of such an apprehension is furnished by Tryon Edwards. Preparing Edwards's manuscript *Charity and Its Fruits* for publication, Tryon Edwards was dismayed at the frequent and emphatic use of the word "infusion," which to him sounded too Roman Catholic. Urged by a noble sense of duty to defend his great forefather's honor and "orthodoxy," he omitted and paraphrased the word quietly with the kind of liberty that no editor of the twentieth century would think to exercise. The alteration is found fourteen times in the published text, testifying to what Paul Ramsey calls "the growing Protestant aversion to what came to be deemed a Roman Catholic error."[3]

It was a preeminent achievement of Ramsey's critical editorial work in the Yale edition to uncover Tryon Edwards's clandestine attempt to defend Edwards's "Protestantism." Ramsey then went on to present, in one of his appendices, his own version of vindication, affirming a "deep family resemblance" between Calvin and Edwards concerning the use of the word "infusion."[4] This vindication is suggestive, but somewhat pointless, since the argument is presented still under the same old presupposition of antithesis. In confronting Tryon Edwards's textual tampering, Ramsey's attention is understandably directed toward the use of the word itself, namely, *whether* Calvin and other Reformed theologians used it or not. More important is to examine *how* and *in what sense* the word is used in given contexts.

Use of the Word "Infusion"

As for the Protestant lineage of the word "infusion," first of all, Ramsey is right in pointing out that it is not the exclusive property of Roman

---

3. See Ramsey's Introduction to *Charity and Its Fruits*, WY, 8:59–60 n. 5. On three minor occasions, Tryon Edwards let the word appear in print. See *Charity and Its Fruits*, WY, 8:132 n. 8.
4. Appendix 4 to WY, 8:750. Ramsey also tried to salvage Edwards's "Protestantism" by making him an occasionalist. See my argument against this reading in Chapter 3.

Catholic theology. Calvin, for one, used it once in his *Institutes*.⁵ Thomas Ridgeley, one of Edwards's theological sources, stated (much like Edwards) that "concerning this principle of grace, let it be observed that it is *infused*, and not acquired."⁶ Neither did the Synod of Dort hesitate a moment to adopt the word "infusion" to denote the supernatural change wrought within human nature.⁷ Turretin, while preferring "physical predetermination" or "supernatural operation," still did not think it imperative to avoid using "infusion."⁸ Similarly, Mastricht said that the mode of the regenerating grace is "a physical act powerfully *infusing* spiritual life into the soul."⁹ These usages should not be surprising, after all, in view of the fact that it is first employed in Scripture: "God's love has been *poured into* our hearts through the Holy Spirit that has been given to us" (Rom. 5:5).

As is evident in these quotations, however, the Protestant use of the word "infusion" is rather strictly limited to the context of conversion and regeneration. Infusion is necessary for one to be converted and have faith, but it is not directly related to the cause of justification as it seems to be in Roman soteriology. Edwards, too, affirmed the necessity of supernatural infusion, since he believed that sinners cannot convert themselves on their own. Nonetheless, he did not think that justification is achieved by this infused grace. Despite his frequent use of the concept of "infusion" elsewhere, it should be noted, Edwards never mentioned it in his treatise on justification. Little can be accomplished, therefore, by merely locating the precedent *use* of the word irrespective of the context. When the word is used in conjunction with conversion or regeneration, perhaps no Protestant would disagree; it is used simply to affirm the necessity of divine grace in order for a person to be converted and have faith.

Presupposed Contrast

Underlying these arguments is a presupposed contrast of Catholic justification by realistic infusion and Protestant justification by forensic

---

5. *Institutes*, 3.6.2. But the Latin word is *perfundo*.
6. Thomas Ridgeley, *A Body of Divinity*, 2:64 (emphasis mine). For Edwards's relation to Ridgeley, see *Original Sin*, 410 n. 9.
7. "The Third and Fourth Heads of Doctrine," Articles 11 and 14, in *Creeds of Christendom*, 3:590, 591 (Latin, *infundo*).
8. Turretin, *Institutio Theologiae Elencticae*, 15.4.13 (Latin, *infundo*).
9. Mastricht, *Theoretico-Practica Theologia*, 4.3.9 (Latin, *introduco*). Also in ibid., 6.8.7 (Latin, *infundo*).

imputation. Though this kind of contrast is common in what Arvin Vos called "the Protestant textbook tradition,"[10] it is rapidly losing force in the recent reconsideration of both Catholic and Protestant traditions. Edwards underscored the reality of salvation brought forth by the infused grace, but such a concern is by no means absent in Protestant tradition.

The misunderstanding is perceptible already in the Council of Trent.[11] Canon 11 issued by the Sixth Session states that "if anyone says that men are justified either by the sole remission of sins, to the exclusion of the grace and the charity which is poured forth in their hearts by the Holy Ghost, and remains in them, or also that the grace by which we are justified is only the good will of God, let him be anathema."[12] The scheme of justification anathematized here allegedly maintains that there is no alteration made in reality, but that only God's good will *(favor Dei)* is granted in justification. Against this scheme of "justification by divine favor," the Tridentine Fathers contrasted their own scheme of justification, in which the infused grace provides the "formal cause" for the remission of sins. This alleged contrast has continued to dominate the minds of modern Catholic theologians down to the twentieth century. According to Ludwig Ott's contemporary compendium of Roman theology, the Reformers' concept of justification is "a juridical act by which God declares the sinner to be justified, although he remains

10. Arvin Vos, *Aquinas, Calvin, and Contemporary Protestant Thought: A Critique of Protestant Views on the Thought of Thomas Aquinas* (Grand Rapids, Mich.: Wm. B. Eerdmans, 1985), 124.

11. Prior to the Council of Trent there was a moment of genuine rapprochement at the Colloquy of Regensburg in 1541. The Colloquy produced the formula of "double justification," which, however, could secure approval neither from Rome nor from Wittenberg. Luther described it tartly as a piecemeal work of *zusammenleimen* (glueing together). Calvin was a little more appreciative of the movement, but remained equally skeptical about its juxtaposing solution. More promising was the draft of the agreement, prepared by Bucer and Gropper and received favorably by Cardinal Contarini at the Colloquy. McGrath sees in it a lost possibility of reconciliation between the Catholic emphasis on interior renewal and the Protestant exclusion of justification *on account of* that interior renewal *(Iustitia Dei,* 2:57-60). See also Hastings Eells, "The Origin of the Regensburg Book," *Princeton Theological Review* 26 (1928): 355-72; Hubert Jedin, *A History of the Council of Trent,* 2 vols., trans. Dom Ernest Graf (London: Thomas Nelson and Sons, 1961), 1:381-91; Peter Matheson, *Cardinal Contarini at Regensburg* (New York: Oxford University Press, 1972), 97-113, 171-81; H. George Anderson, T. Austin Murphy, and Joseph A. Burgess, eds., "Common Statement," *Justification by Faith: Lutherans and Catholics in Dialogue VII* (Minneapolis: Augsburg, 1985), 32-33.

12. *The Canons and Decrees of the Council of Trent,* trans. H. J. Schroeder (Rockford, Ill.: Tan Books, 1978), 43.

intrinsically unjust and sinful . . . not a real eradication of sin, not an inner renewal and sanctification, but merely an external imputation of Christ's justice."[13] In fact, the same antithetical thinking is implicit in Küng's groundbreaking work as well. By praising Barth for giving up "the purely extrinsic declaration of justice" in favor of "the *interior justifying* of man," Küng repeated the assumption that the Protestant justification is a purely extrinsic declaration of justice.[14]

However, a number of scholars have recently pointed out that the delegates at the Council, in drafting these anathemas in confrontation with the Reformers, either were not fully acquainted with, or did not fully understand, the exact teaching of the Reformers.[15] Had they really had access to the Reformers' actual teachings firsthand, they would have understood Luther's conviction of the unmerited character of God's forgiving grace that is also creative and effective in humanity, as well as Calvin's insistence on the twofold grace of justification and sanctification.[16] Furthermore, recent scholarship on such Reformers as Bullinger and Bucer has revealed a considerable diversity within Reformation theology. The supposition that all the Reformers were homogeneously concerned with the forensic and declaratory aspects of justification, McGrath says, "cannot be sustained on the basis of the evidence available."[17] Bullinger, for example, insisted that "justification did not mean the imputation of righteousness, but the actualization of righteousness." Bucer, much like the Tridentine Fathers, included sanctification in justification.[18]

Protestant Orthodoxy also helped to spread and perpetuate this ill-defined contrast. In their effort to meet the challenges from Rome as

---

13. Ludwig Ott, *Fundamentals of Catholic Dogma*, ed. James Canon Bastible, trans. Patrick Lynch (St. Louis: B. Herder, 1954), 248. The Calvinist understanding of justification was officially condemned in 1713 with the papal constitution *Unigenitus* (DS 2400–2502). See McGrath, "Justification: Barth, Trent, and Küng," 527–29.

14. Küng, *Justification*, 69, 282 (emphasis original).

15. Tavard, *Justification*, 71–72, 128 n. 14; McGrath, *Iustitia Dei*, 2:85; Peter Toon, *Justification and Sanctification* (Westchester, Ill.: Crossway, 1983), 72–73; Theodore W. Casteel, "Calvin and Trent: Calvin's Reaction to the Council of Trent in the Context of his Conciliar Thought," *Harvard Theological Review* 63 (1970): 110.

16. See Calvin's reply to Cardinal Sadoleto: "You very maliciously stir up prejudice against us, alleging that by attributing everything to faith, we leave no room for works." John C. Olin, ed., *A Reformation Debate: John Calvin and Jacopo Sadoleto* (New York: Harper & Row, 1966; reprint, Grand Rapids, Mich.: Baker Book House, 1976), 66.

17. McGrath, *Iustitia Dei*, 2:39.

18. Ibid., 34, 35.

well as from internal heterodoxy, Protestant theologians were gradually inclined to describe justification as an external and forensic transaction, perhaps with a sense of self-assurance that they were merely deepening what the original Reformers had said.[19] Reinhold Seeberg found Melanchthon to be the progenitor of justification as understood "strictly as a forensic act, and hence clearly discriminated from renewal," thus breaking "the inseparable connection, which is in Luther always maintained between regeneration, justification, and sanctification."[20] David Hollaz, one of the most influential theologians of the late seventeenth-century Lutheran Orthodoxy, delineated justification as "not taken in a physical sense, so as to signify to insert, to implant, but in a moral, judicial, and declarative sense, so as to signify to adjudicate, to attribute, to ascribe, to transfer, confer, devolve upon another the effect of a voluntary act by one's own estimate and decision."[21] Similar distortion has been detected in Reformed theology after Calvin, largely within the legal framework of federal theology. As a result of confessional systematization, a wedge was driven "between justification and sanctification in order to clearly distinguish imputed from inherent righteousness."[22] Mastricht, perhaps the most articulate on this matter, declares: "Protestants *never* think that justification denotes an inward change in man, but always an outward one procured by declaration."[23] The Reformed doctrine is criticized sometimes, not without reason, as a "legal fiction."[24]

Yet the fact remains that neither Luther nor Calvin drew such a radical conclusion in their own teachings. For Luther, justification is not just

19. See Wilhelm Niesel, "Calvin wider Osianders Rechtfertigungslehre," *Zeitschrift für Kirchengeschichte* 46 (1928): 410–30.
20. Reinhold Seeberg, *Text-Book of the History of Doctrines*, trans. Charles E. Hay (reprint, Grand Rapids, Mich.: Baker Book House, 1977), 2:360. See also Toon, *Justification and Sanctification*, 62–66.
21. Heinrich Schmid, *The Doctrinal Theology of the Evangelical Lutheran Church*, 3d ed., trans. Charles A. Hay and Henry E. Jacobs (Minneapolis: Augsburg, 1961), 433. See also Tillich, *Systematic Theology*, 3:115–16, for Protestant suspicion against the concept of infusion.
22. Toon, *Justification and Sanctification*, 87. See also Holmes Rolston, *John Calvin Versus the Westminster Confession* (Atlanta: John Knox Press, 1977), 80–85.
23. Mastricht, *Theoretico-Practica Theologia*, 6.6.19. English translation from *Reformed Dogmatics*, 544 (emphasis mine).
24. Stephen Strehle, *Calvinism, Federalism, and Scholasticism: A Study of the Reformed Doctrine of Covenant*, Basler und Berner Studien zur historischen und systematischen Theologie, Band 68 (Bern: Peter Lang, 1988), 314–22, 386–92.

an act of God but also its effect in humanity, not a declaration that has no corresponding reality but itself God's creating Word. "Justification is in reality a kind of rebirth in newness," he wrote in 1535.[25] Terms such as *gratiae infusio* (infusion of grace) or *infusio amoris* (infusion of love) belong to young Luther's frequent vocabulary.[26] Justification is for him at once *Gerechtsprechung* (declaring righteous) and *Gerechtmachung* (making righteous).[27] Calvin is no less expressive in this aspect.[28] As is well known, his *Institutes* postpones the discussion of justification until after that of regeneration. His weightiest concern is, in fact, neither justification nor sanctification; it is the *unio cum Christo* (union with Christ) or *insitio in Christum* (implantation in Christ) that forms the basis for the double grace *(duplex gratia)* of justification and sanctification.[29] "Actual holiness of life, so to speak, is not separated from free imputation of righteousness."[30] Justification for Calvin was neither the only nor the most important aspect that should be discussed in the greater question of human salvation. Calvin did not even think it necessary, in the 1536 edition of his *Institutes*, to give an independent section to the discussion of justification.[31]

Particularly interesting from our perspective is Calvin's quiet affirmation of the Thomist view of justification that includes regeneration in it. Presumably with Thomas and later Thomists in mind, Calvin calls those with whom he has "no quarrel," "the sounder Schoolmen."

---

25. "Theses Concerning Faith and Law," in *Luther's Works*, ed. Jaroslav Pelikan, Helmut T. Lehmann, and Lewis W. Spitz (Philadelphia: Concordia Publishing House and Muhlenberg Press, 1960), 34:113.
26. Horst Georg Pöhlmann, *Rechtfertigung: Die genenwärtige kontroverstheologische Problematik der Rechtfertigungslehre zwischen der evangelish-lutherischen und der römisch-katholischen Kirche* (Gerd Mohn: Gütersloher Verlagshaus, 1971), 316.
27. Walter Kreck, "Zum römisch-katholischen Verständnis der Rechtfertigung," in his *Grundfragen der Dogmatik* (Munich: Chr. Kaiser Verlag, 1970), 292.
28. Calvin and Calvinism are often maligned on this point. Thomas Coates, "Calvin's Doctrine of Justification," *Concordia Theological Monthly* 34 (1963): 325–34, characterizes Calvin's doctrine of justification as "cold, abstract, systematic and legal," in contrast to Luther's realist concern for *Christus in nobis*. Strehle, *Calvinism, Federalism, and Scholasticism*, 318, 392, finds the same fault with Calvinism.
29. *Institutes*, 3.11.1.
30. Ibid., 3.3.1. See also his reply to Cardinal Sadoleto: "We deny that good works have any share in justification, but we claim full authority for them in the lives of the righteous. . . . It is obvious that gratuitous righteousness is necessarily connected with regeneration." Olin, *A Reformation Debate*, 68.
31. See François Wendel, *Calvin: The Origins and Development of His Religious Thought*, trans. Philip Mairet (New York: Harper & Row, 1963), 257.

That a sinner freely liberated from condemnation may obtain righteousness, and that through the forgiveness of sins; *except* that they include under the term "justification" a renewal, by which through the Spirit of God we are remade to obedience to the law. Indeed, they so describe the righteousness of the regenerated man that a man once for all reconciled to God through faith in Christ may be reckoned righteous before God by good works and be accepted by the merit of them.[32]

From the word "except," Calvin seems to have only one point to argue with "the sounder Schoolmen." Actually, the French edition counts two points: "C'est que *premièrement* sous le mot de justification ils comprennent le renouvellement de vie, ou la régénération . . . *Secondement*, que quand l'homme est une fois régénéré, ils pensent qu'il soit agréable à Dieu, et tenu pour juste par le moyen de ses bonnes oeuvres."[33] The first point concerns the term "justification," and the second concerns meriting God's acceptance by good works. Although Calvin continues on to refute the second point, he does not register any complaint against the first point. His only dissatisfaction is about the choice of the word—he would rather distinguish justification from regeneration, though of course without separating them in reality.[34] But then again he does not insist on this issue of terminology, since he knows that there is no substantial difference between him and his opponents. Indeed, for Calvin as well, "Christ justifies no one whom he does not at the same time sanctify."[35] Calvin, and Edwards after him, rejects any possibility of earning salvation by human meritorious works, but the existence of the reality of regeneration is not thereby denied.

After all, the good we have is nothing but the gift of God. Though Calvin did not make any concession to the idea of meritorious works performed by the justified, a question still lingers as to whether he did in fact affirm something equivalent to it with his concept of "double

32. *Institutes*, 3.14.11 (emphasis mine). Careful scholars have noted that Thomas may not be the theologian Calvin is in dialogue with here: E. David Willis, "Notes on A. Ganoczy's *Calvin, Théologien de l'Église et du Ministère*," *Bibliothèque d'Humanisme et Renaissance* 30 (1968): 197; Vos, *Aquinas, Calvin, and Contemporary Protestant Thought*, 38–40.
33. John Calvin, *Institution de la Religion Chrétienne*, ed. Société Calviniste de France (Geneva: Labor et Fides, 1956), 3:243.
34. *Institutes*, 3.9.6: "Scripture, even though it joins them, still lists them separately."
35. Ibid., 3.16.1.

justification" or "justification of works." "Believers are, after their call, approved of God *also in respect of works*. For the Lord cannot fail to love and embrace *the good things that he works in them* through his Spirit. But we must always remember that God 'accepts' believers by reason of works only because he is their source and graciously, by way of adding to his liberality, deigns also to show 'acceptance' toward *the good works he has himself bestowed*."[36] Believers are first justified by faith alone, but, after this justification, their works, though still tainted with sin and imperfection, are now accepted as righteous, because "God deigns to show acceptance toward the good works he has himself bestowed." Works do not earn justification, but they are now rendered good and righteous. According to John Hesselink, the Reformed doctrine that human beings are "worthless and capable of no good" is one of the persistent misunderstandings about the Reformed faith.[37] A true Augustinian-Calvinist view holds to the transformative concept of regeneration: a regenerate person, though still sharing the depravity of nature, is transformed by the power of the indwelling Spirit. "Something new" is brought forth in the person.[38]

On the other hand, the Protestant textbook tradition is often too quick to attack the Roman concept of merit as Pelagian, as if Roman theology was teaching that unaided human free will can merit grace. As far as the Council of Trent or Thomas is concerned, this is not the case. The Tridentine phrase, "they convert themselves by freely assenting to and cooperating with that grace," should not be separated from the preceding passage, "through His quickening and helping grace."[39] Likewise, Thomas never imagines that one can earn merit on his or her own. Justification in Thomas's theory is one of the two "effects" that grace brings forth. A person is first justified by "operating grace," and then this justified person is enabled to perform meritorious works to earn eternal life with the help of "co-operating grace." This first grace, he clearly states, cannot be merited.[40] Human works are meritorious only

---

36. Ibid., 3.17.5 (emphasis mine). See Wendel, *Calvin*, 260–62, for the concept of "double justification" or "justification of works."
37. John Hesselink, *On Being Reformed: Distinctive Characteristics and Common Misunderstandings* (Ann Arbor, Mich.: Servant Books, 1983), 45–50.
38. Ibid. See Chapter 7 for a contemporary Catholic reflection on the issue.
39. *Canons and Decrees*, 6th sess., chap. 5.
40. *Summa Theologica*, 1–2.113–14; especially 114, 5. See also idem, *Summa Contra Gentiles*, 4 vols., trans. Anton C. Pegis et al. (Garden City, N.Y.: Hanover House, 1956; reprint, Notre Dame: University of Notre Dame, 1975), 3.149.

in cooperation with grace, as the works of one who has already been accepted by God and reconciled with God, which is what Calvin taught under the rubric of "justification of works." Thomas does say that one earns merit by the exercise of his or her free will; yet, as I argued in Chapter 3, it is precisely in this human free will that grace becomes operative. Thomas's remark that follows should promptly relieve Protestants of their suspicion about the Roman Pelagianism: "God does not justify us without ourselves, because whilst we are being justified we consent to God's justification by a movement of our free-will. Nevertheless this movement is not the cause of grace, but the effect; hence the whole operation pertains to grace."[41]

Edwards, too, affirmed the existence of goodness that God is inclined to reward. But, as with Calvin, this goodness is rewardable only because God is "the source" from whom all good things flow forth. In a "Miscellanies" entry, Edwards presents an argument for "the justification of works" in a manner not unlike that of Calvin.[42] Despite his avowed opposition to the idea of merit, Edwards's zeal for giving recognition to the concept of "reward" is well beyond doubt.[43] There is no inconsistency, he maintains, to say that believers are made heirs of eternal life "by Xs [Christ's] righteousness recieved [sic] by faith," and to say that it is "in reward for their good works as lovely to God in X."[44] Thomas stands on Edwards's side on this topic as well. His often-neglected assertion is that because of the greatest inequality between God and human beings, human works are meritorious only "on the presupposition of the Divine ordination, so that man obtains from God, as a reward of his operation," for which God also has given humanity the power of acting.[45]

These comparisons amount to show that Edwards, in emphasizing the existence of goodness in human nature that becomes rewardable in

---

41. *Summa Theologica*, 1–2.111.2, ad 2.
42. "Miscellanies," no. 671, Yale MSS: "That the holiness & good works of the saints are rewardable is what is merited and purchased by the righteousness of X. His righteousness not only purchased the holiness it self but also purchased that it should be rewardable. Tis from X righteousness that their holiness derives the value that it has in the eyes of God."
43. See, for example, "Justification by Faith alone," 423–24; "Miscellanies," nos. 403, 627, 671, 672, 780, Yale MSS.
44. "Miscellanies," no. 793, Yale MSS.
45. *Summa Theologica*, 1–2.114.1. Based on this passage, Willis hints at the possibility of further reconciliation between Calvin and Thomas. See his "Notes on A. Ganoczy's *Calvin*," 197.

God's sight, actually coincided with Calvin and even with Thomas. The idea of "reward," if taken out of context, can be fatally Pelagian, whether Roman Catholic or Protestant. But neither Thomas nor Edwards is Pelagian. Their common rule of understanding is the Augustinian dictum: when God rewards, he crowns his own gift. Edwards did not negate the existence of goodness in humanity that is brought forth by God's regenerating grace, yet he did reject the scheme of justification by meritorious works, as did Thomas and Calvin. His insistence on the human reality of salvation, therefore, does not pose a threat to his evangelical faith. Such a concern should not be denigrated within the Protestant perspective, especially in view of the recent findings that the original Reformers were of the same mind.

The Order of Justification and Sanctification

The second category of criticism concerns the order of justification and sanctification in Edwards's soteriology. The first inquiry showed that justification and sanctification are *inseparable* in both Protestant and Roman Catholic traditions; the second inquires into whether there is any temporal or logical order between the two.

The criticism that Edwards is reversing the Protestant order to a Roman Catholic understanding was first voiced by George Boardman, who suspected that in Edwards "faith as a personal act precedes justification," and that "only those first regenerate are justified."[46] Perry Miller and Thomas Schafer share this suspicion, both referring to Edwards's much misunderstood phrase, "what is real" as the foundation of "what is legal." Miller detected in this sentence a suggestion that Edwards felt an urge of "saying something more," namely, something more than legal and forensic justification, to go with the age's increasing demand for a touch of empiricism in theology as well.[47] Schafer wrote, based on the same phrase, that Edwards "went beyond the doctrine of justification, which had agitated the reformers, to the 'real' acts and relations which underlie it."[48] I have critically reviewed these interpretations with regard to the actual context of the words, but the direction in

46. Boardman, *A History of New England Theology*, 155, 156.
47. Miller, *Jonathan Edwards*, 76.
48. Schafer, "Jonathan Edwards and Justification by Faith," 64.

which their argument leads deserves attention. Schafer also pointed out that, from the dispositional understanding of the nature of faith, the reality of sanctification must necessarily exist in the soul prior to faith and justification, since faith as a virtue is defined as "flowing from antecedent inclination."[49]

To these critics, Conrad Cherry proposed a way to circumvent the aporia: whenever the word "sanctification" occurs in Edwards's text, Cherry suggests reading "regeneration" for it.[50] As the standard Reformed theology teaches that regeneration comes before justification, his emphasis on sanctification can thus be conformed to the Protestant pattern. However, this proposal does not address the question straight on, let alone solve it. The fact remains that, in Edwards, the reality of regeneration must be present prior to the declaration of pardon, thus endangering the Protestant tenet of "justification of *the ungodly*." It is important to reexamine the presupposition of these arguments.

Protestant Perspective

The belief that in Protestantism sanctification follows justification both temporally and logically and in Catholicism it is the other way around belongs to the heart of the Protestant textbook tradition. This assumption is worth reconsidering in both the Roman Catholic and Protestant perspectives.

I have already mentioned that, for Calvin, justification and sanctification are two aspects of one and the same grace *(duplex gratia)*. Actually, they are not only one and the same in substance, but take place simultaneously as well.

> The whole of the gospel is contained under these two headings, repentance and forgiveness of sins . . . the Lord freely justifies his own in order that he may *at the same time* restore them to true righteousness by sanctification of his Spirit.[51]

> We confess that while . . . God by free remission of sins accounts us righteous, his beneficence is *at the same time* joined with such a mercy that through his Holy Spirit he dwells in us and by his

---

49. Ibid., 59, 60, 63.
50. Cherry, *Theology of Jonathan Edwards*, 42–43.
51. *Institutes*, 3.3.19 (emphasis mine).

power the lusts of our flesh are each day more and more mortified; we are indeed sanctified.[52]

There is no priority or means-end relationship between the two: neither is justification a preparatory stage for sanctification, nor is the latter for the former. If, as the Protestant textbook tradition teaches, sanctification is to be preceded by justification, it is so only because "sanctification begins with justification but extends beyond it as a continuing process never completed in this life."[53]

This last point is indicative of an important systemic difference. In Calvin, and in Protestant theology in general, justification is conceived of as an instantaneous and once-and-for-all event of declaration, which is necessarily *accompanied* by sanctification. In Catholic soteriology justification is a long and gradual process of transformation that *includes* sanctification in it.[54] Justification in Catholic theology is to be completed only by means of good works that flow from faith, just as in Protestant theology justification entails and concurs with the work of sanctification. It was within the context of this gradual justification that the Tridentine decrees spoke of the "second justification" that "increases" the received justification, of the "forfeit" of justification through sin, and of its "restoration" by the sacrament of penance.[55] The whole event is described by the Council of Trent as a gradual process of ontological transition.

Edwards and other Protestants insist that justification begins and ends at once, but they also insist that this instantaneous justification is always accompanied by sanctification. And they unanimously teach that if faith is genuine good works necessarily follow.[56] If so, one wonders after all

---

52. Ibid., 3.14.9 (emphasis mine).
53. Willis, "Notes on A. Ganoczy's *Calvin*," 196.
54. Cf. *Reformed Dogmatics*, 565, for Riisen and Wolleb on justification as a once-and-for-all act of God and sanctification as a gradual process; *Summa Theologica*, 1–2.113.9, for a notable inclusion of "sanctification" in "justification."
55. *Canons and Decrees*, chaps. 10 and 14. For "second justification," see Jedin, *History of the Council of Trent*, 2:308.
56. "We, indeed, willingly acknowledge, that believers ought to make daily increase in good works." John Calvin, "Acts of the Council of Trent, With the Antidote," in *Tracts and Treatises in Defence of the Reformed Faith*, ed. Thomas F. Torrance, trans. Henry Beveridge (Edinburgh: Calvin Translation Society, 1851; reprint, Grand Rapids, Mich.: Wm. B. Eerdmans, 1958), 3:128. Mastricht, *Theoretico-Practica Theologia*, 6.8.27: "The Reformed deny the necessity of good works for obtaining the right to eternal life. . . . But they declare that they are necessary by divine prescript for receiving possession of

these comparisons, is there any difference other than of terminology? Catholics speak of justification in a broader sense that includes sanctification within, while Protestants speak of justification that is distinguishable but inseparable from sanctification. George Tavard's comment on the difference between Trent and Luther applies here with regard to Trent and all Reformed theologians including Edwards: "It differs somewhat in words, but not truly in substance."[57] Calvin's reaction against the Tridentine proceedings reveals more about their latent compatibility than his apparent rejection.

> The whole dispute is as to the Cause of Justification. The Fathers of Trent pretend that it is twofold, as if we were justified partly by forgiveness of sins and partly by spiritual regeneration; or, to express their view in other words, as if our righteousness were composed partly of imputation, partly of quality. I maintain that it is one, and simple, and is wholly included in the gratuitous acceptance of God.[58]

The difference between the two boils down to this: while the Tridentine Fathers include in "justification" both "forgiveness" and "regeneration," or "imputation" and "quality," Calvin wants to separate them and reserve the term "justification" for "forgiveness" and "imputation," although "regeneration" and "quality" is an absolute accompaniment of justification in this narrower sense. The Council of Trent uses the word "justification" in a broader and gradual sense, including what Calvin would call "sanctification"; Calvin uses the word in a narrower sense, referring to the judicial declaration of forgiveness that takes place instantaneously but is necessarily accompanied by good works of the justified.

It is true that in the ontological perspective of Catholic theology the judicial aspect of justification recedes to the background; together with sanctification, justification forms an integral stage in the unique process of liberation. According to the Catholic definition, justification is "a translation from that state in which man is born a child of the first Adam, to the state of grace and of the adoption of the sons of God

---

life, as conditions without which God refuses to bestow salvation upon us." For similar arguments by Heidegger and Riisen, see *Reformed Dogmatics*, 580.

57. Tavard, *Justification*, 76.
58. Calvin, "Acts of the Council," 116.

through the second Adam, Jesus Christ, our Saviour."[59] But this systemic difference can be reduced in great part to a semantic difference. The long and gradual process of justification in Roman Catholic soteriology is virtually affirmed in Protestant soteriology under the name of sanctification, which indeed continues throughout life. Edwards also affirms this long and gradual process of sanctification, as I will argue in Chapter 6.

In accordance with this semantic difference, there is in Catholic soteriology a notable absence of the locus for sanctification as such. Sanctification has no specific place—neither in Thomas nor in Trent—because it is not a single subject but rather the whole of the process of salvation in Catholic soteriology.[60] In the Tridentine definition, sanctification is subsumed in the proceedings on justification. Thomas does often speak of "sanctifying grace," but this grace is primarily a supernatural help that enables men and women to attain "eternal happiness" beyond their natural endowments.[61] "Justification" in Thomist metaphysics is another name for this incessant procession of the earthly *viator* toward the eternal goal, for which the sanctifying grace is needed as complement to human nature. The sanctifying grace is necessary, not to serve as the basis for any specific phase of this pilgrimage, but as a help to attain the ultimate goal for which human beings are originally ordained to strive. Justification in the narrower sense, or remission of sins, occupies only a small part of this pursuit of transcendental happiness.

It was Protestant Scholasticism that elevated and absolutized justification to the state of "the chief article of faith" with which the church stands and falls, at the expense of other important soteriological phases.[62] "Justification" became the practical equivalent of "salvation" in the full sense, relegating "sanctification" to a subdivision and making

---

59. *Canons and Decrees*, chap. 4. Cf. Thomas's definition in *Summa Theologica*, 1.113.1; Ott, *Fundamentals of Catholic Dogma*, 248.

60. For Ott, "The Doctrine of God the Sanctifier" is the section in which justification (in its broader sense) is to be discussed. See Ott, *Fundamentals of Catholic Dogma*, 217–67.

61. *Summa Contra Gentiles*, 3.147–53.

62. *Die Bekenntnisschriften der evangelisch-lutherischen Kirche: Herausgegeben im Gedenkjahr der Augsburgischen Konfession 1930*, 5 Aufl. (Göttingen: Vandenhoeck & Ruprecht, 1963), 415, 416; Martin Chemnitz, *Justification: The Chief Article of Christian Doctrine as Expounded in Loci theologici*, ed. Delpha Holleque Preus, trans. J. A. O. Preus (St. Louis: Concordia, 1985), 18. See also *Reformed Dogmatics*, 543, for Leiden Synopsis and Walaeus.

it something that attains its meaning only in reference to justification. Despite his intensive learning from the masters of Protestant Orthodoxy, Edwards is not susceptible to this error. Justification for him is not an article that defines the whole system; it does not command methodological domination. It is rather a part that is integral to the gradual and ontological transition of the soul from the state of sin to the state of grace.

Catholic Perspective

A further reconsideration is called for from the Catholic perspective. The Protestant textbook tradition interprets Catholic soteriology as claiming that the infusion of righteousness is the basis of justification, or that God's *making* the sinners just is the cause of God's *declaring* them just. Such an allegation is by no means warranted by reference to the Tridentine decree or to Thomas's theology. Thomas conceives of justification as a movement of the soul toward the remission of sin through the exercise of free will.[63] The infusion of grace is required in this process in order for the free will to move from sin (repentance) toward God (faith), thus fulfilling the end (the remission of sin).

What should be noted here is that the infused grace is not directly accounted for as the basis on which justification is to be achieved. The infusion of grace is necessary, not because God justifies only those who are already just, but because God is the ultimate mover of human free will, whose exercise is indispensable for human beings to attain the remission of sin. It is not "righteousness" per se that is infused; rather, the operating and cooperating grace is infused in order to enable the free will to move toward justification.

As for the temporal sequence, the infusion of grace comes before the remission of sin "in the order of nature," says Thomas, but "in the order of time," justification (in the narrower sense of the word) and the infusion of grace "are simultaneous"; there is no before or after, since "by the same act God bestows grace and remits sin."[64] Or better yet, they are but two ways of expressing one and the same alteration: "Sin is forgiven because grace is infused, and grace is infused because sin is forgiven."[65] It is the expulsion of one state by the installation of another.

63. *Summa Theologica*, 1–2.113.1.
64. Ibid., 1–2.113.8, esp. ad 1; 113.6, ad 2.
65. Article, "Justification," by P. De Letter, *New Catholic Encyclopedia*.

Thomas even states explicitly that, from the viewpoint of the justified, justification comes *prior to* the infusion of grace, since "the being freed from sin is prior to the obtaining of justifying grace."[66]

This Thomistic scheme is restated in the Tridentine decree on justification. It was quite unfortunate that the formulations by the Council of Trent gave the impression that the infusion of grace would itself constitute the cause of the remission of sin (justification). Particularly difficult for Protestants to agree with was its teaching on the formal cause of justification. The Council defined it as "the justice of God, not that by which He Himself is just, but that by which He makes us just, namely, with which we . . . are renewed in the spirit of our mind, and not only are we reputed but we are truly called and are just."[67] One must remember, however, that a pronouncement in the same chapter declares that the infusion of grace, the remission of sin, and sanctification, are all simultaneous.[68] The Council did not resolve this incongruity concerning the temporal order: faith is defined in chapter 6 as the initial stage of "preparation" for justification, whereas chapter 7 states that faith is infused at the same time as justification. It might be said that the Council deliberately left a degree of latitude for the sake of maintaining harmony among delegations representing various schools at the Council.[69] More likely, however, is the interpretation that the Council did not deem it advisable to itemize each phase of salvation in a successive order.[70]

It also has to be remembered that in Aristotelian causation theory, which characterizes the language of the Council, "causes" do not necessarily precede "effects" in time.[71] An oak tree is the "final cause" of an acorn: this final cause is at work throughout the growing process of the acorn, but is realized only after the acorn has fully grown to a tree. So is the "formal cause" in the Tridentine definition of justification. It is defined as "the glory of God and of Christ and life everlasting," but this formal cause takes its form only as the actual event of justifica-

---

66. *Summa Theologica*, 1–2.113.8, ad 1. See also Anderson et al., *Justification by Faith*, 51, 332 n. 181.

67. *Canons and Decrees*, sixth sess., chap. 7, 33.

68. It must be remembered that Thomas did not consider the process to take place successively. *Summa Theologica*, 1–2.113.7.

69. See Jedin, *History of the Council of Trent*, 2:179–80; and McGrath, *Iustitia Dei*, 3:63–68, for the composition of the Council. Among the fifty-five delegates at the sixth session, there were only seven Dominicans.

70. See Tavard, *Justification*, 75–79.

71. See article "Causation," by Richard Taylor, *Encyclopedia of Philosophy*.

tion proceeds. All the Tridentine definition teaches is that the transforming justice of God is the distinctive property of the justified. It is that by which the justified are what they are. Specifying the temporal order is outside the purpose of the article. By denoting the essential character or property without which the justified lose their quality of being just, the article teaches that there is an organic and necessary connection between the infusion of grace and the remission of sin. The article does not presuppose the infusion of righteousness per se as the basis of justification, neither temporally nor logically, and, in that sense, it is in accordance with Thomas's teaching.

Upon these considerations, I think it pertinent to conclude the second inquiry with Georges Bavaud's remark concerning Calvin and the Council of Trent: "Au moment où la divergence sur la nature de la sanctification est résolue, il ne faut pas inviter les chrétiens à *choisir* entre l'interprétation calviniste de la justification et celle du Concile de Trente."[72] As it is not necessary to choose between Calvin and Trent, so neither is it necessary to choose between Edwards and Trent. The second inquiry into the order of justification and sanctification thus comes to a conclusion similar to the one reached at the end of the first, namely, a mutual attestation of authenticity. Those days are over when Edwards's soteriology was viewed as disturbing or in need of apology because of its affinity to Roman Catholic soteriology. It makes a rather good illustration of the fact that one does not have to surrender or compromise his or her theological tradition in order to promote ecumenical harmony.

Faith Informed by Love?

The third category of criticism directed to Edwards's soteriology has to do with the nature of faith. In Schafer's reading, Edwards's concept of faith does not sufficiently exclude the possibility of dissolving itself into love; it is to repeat the Catholic delusion of *fides caritate formata* (faith informed by love), which the Reformers strongly rejected with the axiom of *sola fide* (by faith alone). Schafer concluded that in Edwards "the conception of 'faith alone' has been considerably enlarged—and

72. Georges Bavaud, "La doctrine de la justification d'après Calvin et le Concile de Trente: Une conciliation est-elle possible?" *Verbum Caro* 22 (1968): 91 (emphasis original).

hence practically eliminated."[73] Another critic, Arthur Crabtree, suspects that Edwards deliberately circumvented the problem. With regard to the meaning of "by faith alone, apart from the works of love," Crabtree says, "Edwards never makes his meaning clear, and his whole doctrine remains shrouded in obscurity."[74]

The question overlaps partly with the preceding ones. The Catholic concept of *fides caritate formata* becomes a problem for Protestants, after all, because it implies that justification is based on something that is within the possession of the believer. It also shares some aspects with the second question of order, since it means that faith must first be formed by love in order to be justifying.

Here a quick review of Edwards's treatment of the relation of faith and love is in order. The crucial passage Schafer quotes in his argument is from a "Miscellanies" entry:

> 'Tis the same agreeing or consenting disposition that according to the divers objects, different state or manner of exerting, is called by different names. When 'tis exerted towards a Saviour, faith or trust; . . . when towards unseen good, . . . hope; when towards persons excellent, love; when towards commands, obedience; when towards God with respect to changes . . . resignation, when with respect to calamities, submission.[75]

The entry unmistakably states that faith, trust, hope, and love are all "the same agreeing or consenting disposition." They are distinguished only by the objects to which this disposition is directed. In another context, *Charity and Its Fruits*, Edwards places love at the center of the hub and explains in similar fashion that all other virtues derive from it: love will dispose a person "to give honor to God," "to worship and adore him," "to all acts of obedience to God," and "to all duties towards their neighbors."[76] Edwards also writes in a number of places that "love is the essence of faith."[77] Since "the graces of Christianity" are all "concatenated," faith and love cannot be separated, either in

---

73. Schafer, "Jonathan Edwards and Justification by Faith," 60.
74. Arthur B. Crabtree, *The Restored Relationship: A Study in Justification and Reconciliation* (London: Carey Kingsgate Press, 1963), 151–52.
75. "Miscellanies," no. 218, Yale MSS.
76. *Charity and Its Fruits*, WY, 8:134–35.
77. Ibid., 139, 330; *Treatise on Grace*, 40; "Concerning Faith," 617, 619, 623; "Notes on the Bible," WD, 9:511; "Miscellanies," no. 820, Yale MSS.

concept or in reality.⁷⁸ Faith will not be complete if it does not arise from love or if it is not united with love.

Particularly noticeable in these utterances is that Edwards shows no sign of apprehension about the direction in which his teaching is leading. As I hinted in Chapter 1, it is not unlikely that he did not realize the vulnerability of his teaching—even with his thorough reading of the polemical writings of the preceding generation.⁷⁹ At one point while reading Thomas Goodwin's well-circulated book, Edwards encounters a standard Protestant criticism of the concept of "faith informed by love," and wonders in an innocent and unsuspecting tone why it is called "wicked" and "wretched."⁸⁰

One cannot say, however, that the issue completely escaped Edwards's attention. Evidence shows that some efforts were made on his own to differentiate faith from love. In a "Miscellanies" entry entitled "Justification by Faith Only," he poses a critical question to himself: "It may be objected that if it be allowed that God promises mercy of the mercifull & forgiveness to the forgiving & love to the loving . . . this will be to make love, & mercy, & meekness & all graces the condition of justification & salvation in the same manner as faith."⁸¹ But, according to his conclusion, this cannot be the case, and for three reasons: (1) faith is "a *direct* according, suiting or closing of the soul with the Saviour"; (2) faith is the soul's according to "the *whole* of salvation," while other graces are "more partial" and suitable only to "particular part of salvation"; and (3) faith not only has "an harmony of similitude, but that of *actual* unition." These characterizations of faith—direct, whole, and actual—appear in other contexts as well to serve as distinguishing marks of genuine faith.⁸² The major difference in his view, therefore, lies in that faith is a more comprehensive term than love when describing the condition of justification. The act that constitutes an organic union with Christ is "something else besides mere love," which can only be termed as faith.⁸³ This is as far as Edwards goes in differentiating faith from love, and

---

78. *Charity and Its Fruits*, WY, 8:327. See also "Miscellanies," no. 393, Yale MSS.

79. Turretin has a section devoted to the subject. See 15.13, Title Question: "Whether the Form of justifying Faith is love. . . . We deny against the Romanists and Socinians."

80. "Concerning Faith," 625.

81. "Miscellanies," no. 714, Yale MSS.

82. "Concerning Faith," 606, 607, 611; "Justification by Faith alone," 370, 430; *Qualifications*, 179; "Miscellanies," nos. 315, 329, 412, Yale MSS.

83. "Concerning Faith," 617.

evidently it was not far enough for those who were disconcerted by his undetermined attitude toward the Roman Catholic concept.

To the relief of these anxious readers, Conrad Cherry affirmed that Edwards was not quite so un-Protestant, if only a distinction is made between love as the indwelling holiness of God himself (uncreated grace) and love as a human act. The love that Edwards underscored, according to Cherry, is not "a human faculty nor a human work but is the Holy Spirit himself."[84] This argument was reviewed in some detail in Chapter 3. By making such a distinction, Edwards might *look* Protestant, but then his concern for the reality of new creation in the regenerate will have to remain unaccounted in the background. While not abandoning the Lombardian concern of "uncreated graced" given anew each moment, Edwards underscores the enduring reality of "created grace," the transformation that is brought forth by this uncreated grace. Affirming the presence of created grace does not always mean denying the presence of uncreated grace. Regenerate human reality is affirmed in Edwards *in addition to* the presence of the Holy Spirit who works through it. The love "as human holy act" and the love "as the Holy Spirit himself," therefore, are not in disjunction, as Cherry describes them to be. There must be another path to address the question.

Different Terms

My suggestion here is to reexamine the concept of *fides caritate formata* and find out why it constitutes a problem in the Protestant perspective. For Calvin, the concept is questionable because it means that faith is attained first through purely intellectual assent, to which love is later superadded as its "form." No, says Calvin, faith is from its very beginning not merely intellectual. Parker points out that "to allow that *fides informis* is a real faith, though needing to be 'formed by love,' is to separate arbitrarily the intellect from the soul."[85] Faith for Calvin, as I reviewed in Chapter 2, is always "more of the heart than of the brain, and more of the disposition than of the understanding,"[86] not something to which love is superadded later. There cannot be such a thing as "unformed" faith, "for even assent rests upon such pious inclination."

---

84. Cherry, *Theology of Jonathan Edwards*, 40–41.
85. Parker, *Doctrine of the Knowledge of God*, 107.
86. *Institutes*, 3.2.8. Passages of similar import can be found in 1.5.9; 3.2.33; 3.2.36.

"Christ cannot be known apart from the sanctification of his Spirit," and hence "faith can in no wise be separated from a devout disposition."[87]

But one might ask if this is a fair denunciation of the concept. The case is presented by Thomas Aquinas in a somewhat different way. His definition of the concept runs as follows: "Charity [love] is called the form of faith in so far as the act of faith is perfected and formed by charity."[88] It may sound as if there are two kinds of faith, one formed and the other unformed. Yet the reader must be reminded that faith in Thomas's conception, too, is a joint act of the intellect and will. Faith is "an act of the intellect assenting to the Divine truth," but unlike other acts of the intellect, it assents to the truth "at the command of the will."[89] Moreover, it is charity, as a preeminent act of the will, that commands, determines, and disposes the intellect to the particular object proper to faith.[90] When Thomas says that charity "perfects" and "forms" faith in the above definition, therefore, he means that the act of the assenting intellect is now "directed" and "guided" by charity to its proper object.[91] There are neither two kinds of faith nor is the nature of faith altered by charity. Faith, whether formed or unformed, is of one kind; the change is rather "in the soul."[92] That is to say, a person who has formed faith has faith together with love, thus involving not only his or her intellect, but the whole soul with the movement of the will. It is essential for Thomas to have the will involved in this way, for that is what makes an act "virtuous" and hence "meritorious." Faith must be "formed" because it must be of saving nature.

Now Calvin has little patience with this kind of scholastic argument; he quickly rejects it as "worthless . . . childish babble."[93] But the deeper one looks into the matter, the more difficult one finds it to substantiate Calvin's rejection. Comparing these two representative theologians, Arvin Vos comments that "Aquinas is in fact not far from Calvin in

---

87. Ibid.
88. *Summa Theologica*, 2–2.4.3. See also Thomas Aquinas, *Commentary on Saint Paul's Epistle to the Galatians*, trans. F. R. Larcher (Albany, N.Y.: Magi Books, 1966), 156: "Faith is a knowledge of the word of God—which word is not perfectly possessed or perfectly known unless the love which it hopes for is possessed."
89. *Summa Theologica*, 2–2.2.9.
90. Ibid., 2–2.2.1, ad 3.
91. Charity "directs" other virtues to its proper end (ibid., 2–2.23.8, ad 3).
92. Ibid., 2–2.4.4, ad 4.
93. *Institutes*, 3.2.8.

essential matters."⁹⁴ While Calvin disapproves of Thomas's distinction of the formed and unformed faith, he, too, admits that there are "divers forms of faith." There is what he calls "historical faith," that is, faith that believes only that "there is a God," or that "the gospel history is true." Such a faith is but a "shadow" and "image" of faith, says Calvin, and "does not deserve to be called faith."⁹⁵ To this Thomas would give full endorsement. Had he heard Calvin say that those who boast of the unformed faith "are no better than the devils," Thomas would have chimed a snappy "Amen," since he also argues that demons do have faith, but that their faith is not virtuous.⁹⁶ The difference between Calvin and Thomas, therefore, converges into a taxonomic one: while Calvin thinks that "unformed faith" does not deserve the name "faith," Thomas, while allowing the name "faith," thinks that it does not deserve the name "virtue." Both concur in content: the genuine, virtuous, and saving faith must involve the whole human personality, both the intellect and will.

Another critic, Robert Scharlemann, compares Thomas with Johann Gerhard on the issue and concludes that there is no substantial difference between them—besides terminology.⁹⁷ A Lutheran Orthodox theologian, Gerhard shows certain variance from Calvin's argument, yet the comparison hits the same note. Gerhard's main concern is to emphasize the element of *fiducia* (trust) in faith as essential over *notitia* (knowledge) and *assensus* (assent).⁹⁸ The "form" of justifying faith, if the word is to be employed, is for Gerhard not *caritas* but *fiducia*. He does concede, however, like Calvin, that there are incomplete faith and complete faith—or "historical" and "saving" faith—a familiar distinction for Edwards and other Puritan divines. The difference between Thomas and Gerhard, according to Scharlemann, converges again upon the difference in terminology: Gerhard calls the faith that does not save *fides historica*,

---

94. Vos, *Aquinas, Calvin, and Contemporary Protestant Thought*, 35. Vos suggests that Calvin "had no more than a passing familiarity with the writings of Aquinas." This might explain why Calvin did not realize the obvious similarity between him and Thomas.

95. *Institutes*, 3.2.9, 10. Later Reformed theologians largely followed in Calvin's wake. Turretin (15.13.3) says that the concept of "faith formed by love" rests upon an incorrect foundation that "there is any true unformed faith." See also *Reformed Dogmatics*, 535, for Ursinus and Burmann.

96. *Summa Theologica*, 2-2.5.2, esp. ad 1.

97. Scharlemann, *Thomas Aquinas and John Gerhard*, 183–99.

98. Ibid., 191. See Anderson et al., *Justification by Faith*, 30, for Melanchthon's argument against *fides caritate formata* in the Apology of the Augsburg Confession.

while Thomas calls it *fides informis,* by which both theologians mean the faith that does not involve the movement of the will. Gerhard calls saving faith *fiducialis apprehensio,* or faith with a cordial assent, and Thomas calls it *fides caritate formata.* Both agree that "the bare knowledge . . . is not sufficient to be a principle of actions which attain the ultimate end."[99] The difference that has been looming hitherto now dwindles to nominal.

Edwards's position on this issue cannot be clearer. His repeated and ubiquitous contention is that "saving faith" is more than "a mere assent to the doctrines."[100] It is "a sense of glory and excellency" or "a spiritual taste and relish of what is excellent and divine," and it is only natural for him to describe it as arising "from a charitable disposition of heart, or from a principle of divine love."[101] All in all, it boils down to the affirmation of what both Thomas and the Reformers, under different terminology, tried to affirm—namely, faith, if it is genuine, is an act that involves the whole human personality, not just the intellect or will. Whether this is tantamount to the elimination of "by faith alone," as some suspect, is a question to be discussed within the context in which the statement occurs. I now come to the last phase of my comparative analysis.

Different Contexts

Once again recent reconstruction of the Reformers' teaching must be taken into account. George Tavard, in anticipation of the kind of conclusion I draw, lamented Luther's attack on the concept of informed faith as "particularly disastrous," because "this concept had originally no other purpose than to embody the concern that faith must be a living faith—Luther's very concern."[102] How could such a gross misunderstanding happen? The most likely guess, from what has been established so far, is that the parties involved were not quite cognizant of the systemic difference that was at issue. In his second lecture on Galatians in 1531, Luther was particularly at pains to demonstrate that the

---

99. Ibid.
100. "Concerning Faith," 602, 632.
101. Ibid., 601, 604.
102. Tavard, *Justification,* 103. Tavard is summarizing here Louis Bouyer's effort to rehabilitate Luther's theology in Catholic thought.

passage "faith working through love" does not occur in the context of justification:

> They read this passage through a colored glass, and they distort the text to suit their own dreams. For Paul does not speak of "faith, which justifies through love," or of "faith, which makes acceptable through love." . . . He says that works are done on the basis of faith through love, not that a man is justified through love. . . . Being justified is one thing and working is another. . . . It is an obvious trick when they suppress the true and genuine meaning of Paul and interpret "working" to mean "justifying" and "works" to mean "righteousness."[103]

There is for Luther no question about faith working only through love. But he believes that this is no place for Paul to speak of justification; Paul simply describes here how faith works through love as instrument. As is obvious from his distinction, however, Luther's criticism is pertinent only insofar as he lines up conversion, justification, and sanctification in his own context.

Calvin is of the same mind when he points out in his commentary on Galatians that Paul is not treating justification here. He underscores the importance of "by faith alone," while not forgetting to enunciate the inseparable connection of faith and love. "It is not our doctrine that the faith which justifies is alone," he says. Faith is always joined with good works. His only contention is that "faith avails by itself for justification."[104] It also frames a point of disagreement in his otherwise mild comments on the acts of the Council of Trent: "When they quote the passage of Paul, 'faith which worketh by love,' they do not see that they are cutting their own throats. . . . I must remind my readers that that passage is irrelevantly introduced into a question about Justification, since Paul is not there considering in what respect faith or charity avails to justify a man, but what is Christian perfection."[105] Both Luther and Calvin raise objections about citing that particular passage of Paul in the

---

103. *Luther's Works*, 27:28. Luther's first lecture on Galatians in 1519 has no reference to the question (333–36).
104. John Calvin, *The Epistles of Paul the Apostle to the Galatians, Ephesians, Philippians and Colossians*, eds. David W. Torrance and Thomas F. Torrance, trans. T.H.L. Parker (Edinburgh: Oliver and Boyd, 1965), 96.
105. Calvin, "Acts of the Council of Trent," 119.

context of justification, while they both agree that faith does work with love. Working faith is not without love, yet love does not "avail" in justification.

Evidently presupposed in their objection is their own framework of justification, in which justification is considered to be an instantaneous declaration of righteousness. Transferred to the Roman Catholic framework, however, the concept of "faith that works through love" by no means sounds out of context. Since justification in the Roman framework is a comprehensive term that subsumes the whole process of sanctification, making reference to the concept of informed faith is quite logical in that framework. It is part of the continuing process of transformation, which Protestant theology also affirms as "sanctification" that flows forth from justification. Once this contextual difference is taken into consideration, one cannot fail to notice their substantive agreement.

Edwards, too, affirmed that there is an inseparable connection between faith and love, and in that sense agreed not only with Luther and Calvin but also with Thomas. But notably he did not touch on this connection in his Justification discourse. He never asserted that without love faith does not justify; as far as I know, not once does he allude to the importance of love in his treatise on justification. In this sense, his frame of reference remained that of the standard Protestant doctrine. One may safely conclude now that the third category of criticism also fails in the face of these observations. Edwards may have had little knowledge of the Reformation controversy over the concept of "informed faith," yet his theological instinct commanded different emphases in different contexts.

Thus I have shown in all three cases that, once misunderstandings are resolved and semantic or systemic differences decoded, the issues that have been considered as threatening Edwards's "Protestantness" can no longer be so viewed. Recent Catholic-Protestant dialogues on justification are especially helpful in reshaping some of the longstanding patterns of Edwards's interpretation. Indeed, as Horst Pöhlmann says, "The doctrine of justification is today not a problem of theological controversy any more, but is a hermeneutical problem."[106] If Schafer feels that

---

106. Horst Georg Pöhlmann, *Abriss der Dogmatik*, 3 Aufl. (Gütersloh: Gütersloher Verlagshaus Gerd Mohn, 1980), 257.

there is nothing that keeps Edwards from becoming a Roman Catholic except for his rejection of the concept of merit, he is quite right in his interpretation.[107] This perception may once have been disconcerting to some, but it is no longer the case. My conclusion proposes to appreciate Edwards's theology precisely for that reason. It signals for Protestant soteriology a much-needed reappraisal of the biblical understanding of the power of God's transformative grace. What is reclaimed in every phase of Edwards's soteriology, as strongly as in Scripture, is that grace means at once God's gratuitous favor and a gift that effectuates itself in the person to whom it is given. "Righteousness" is at the same time imputatory and effective. Edwards's soteriology is thus a new envisioning of Paul's insight that "God is the source of . . . our righteousness and sanctification and redemption" (1 Cor. 1:30). God's word is God's deed.[108]

---

107. Schafer, "Jonathan Edwards and Justification by Faith," 61.
108. I have found, besides those cited, the following book especially helpful on the theme of Protestant and Catholic justification: Hanfried Müller, *Evangelische Dogmatik im Überblick* (Berlin: Evangelische Verlagsanstalt, 1978), 189–99.

6
Sanctification and Glorification

Having outlined the basic configuration of Edwards's soteriology in relation to conversion and justification, I will now examine how the reality of new creation is given preeminent emphasis in sanctification and glorification. In this emphasis Edwards's soteriology shows a remarkable consistency throughout the four stages of the application of redemption.

Sanctification

Sanctification in Relation to Regeneration

Sanctification in early Reformed theology was not always given an unquestioned place in soteriology. Some theologians took it as synonymous with regeneration, others included it under justification, and still others called the whole process of human salvation by this name.¹ Edwards, too, confuses sanctification with conversion or regeneration at times, giving the impression that he undervalued or bypassed justification.² This was unavoidable, given that he curtly summed up the entire work of grace as the infusion of a divine principle. Yet when he takes up sanctification as a theme in relation to other loci of soteriology, he is basically in agreement with the standard understanding of the Reformed *ordo salutis:* While recognizing the essential continuity, Edwards distinguishes sanctification from regeneration and places it after justification.³ Regeneration and sanctification are, in essence, one and the same operation of the Holy Spirit that renews a person from within by means of infused and internalized grace, yet are named differently depending on the way they are viewed. In a long "Miscellanies" entry titled "Regeneration," Edwards explains the difference: The work of the Holy Spirit is "sometimes spoken of as done when men are *first* savingly called as soon as they become believers or faithfull in X Jesus or *begin* to be saints" (regeneration), but the same work is named "sanctification" when it is "spoken of as yet remaining to be sought & prayed for by the saints after they are become saints."⁴ In this latter sense, it is "done gradually through the whole work of the sanctification of the Spirit" and lasts "as long as the Xtian lives," because "there is as it were an unregenerate part still in man after the first regeneration that still needs to be regenerated." It is this continuing phase of regeneration that deserves careful analysis in this chapter.

Fundamental to Edwards's concept of sanctification, then, is that it is a continuation of the work that has already begun in the regenerate persons. It is "to carry on the work of his grace which [God] has begun in them."⁵ The Holy Spirit continues to dwell in the regenerate as the "internal vital principle," communicating his divine nature and regenerating the "unregenerate part" that still remains in them.⁶ Hence

---

1. See Witsius, *Oeconomy of the Covenants*, 2:635. According to Witsius, the first opinion is that of Leyden Synopsis, the second, of Gomarus, and the third, of Polanus.
2. See, for example, "Efficacious Grace," 570; *Religious Affections*, 391, 398; "Miscellanies," nos. 77, 78, 847, Yale MSS.
3. See *Reformed Dogmatics*, 565–80. Cf. Shepard, *Sound Believer*, 123.
4. "Miscellanies," no. 847, Yale MSS (emphasis mine).
5. *History of the Work of Redemption*, 121.
6. *Religious Affections*, 392.

the psalmist's prayer: "Do not take your holy Spirit from me" (Psalms 51:11).

However, sanctification is not merely a touch-up job added onto regeneration. In Edwards's soteriology, the two are coordinated purposefully in the paradigm of antecedent qualification and anticipated reward. Sanctification is an integral part of God's purposive progression toward his ultimate goal of redemption, "for 'tis the very end of it, with a view to which the whole work is wrought."[7] The infusion that takes place in regeneration is "calculated and framed" in such a way that it provides the ontological ground for sanctification. In his "Wisdom of God" sermon, Edwards describes this relation with the following words: "Christ has purchased all, both objective and inherent good: not only a portion to be enjoyed by us; but all those inherent qualifications necessary to our enjoyment of it. He has purchased not only justification, but sanctification and glorification; both holiness and happiness."[8] This passage is so dense and arcane that it opens itself to deciphering only when one remembers the structure of his justification paradigm: Edwards is saying here that "holiness" is the qualification necessary to enjoy "happiness," and that "inherent good" is the qualification necessary to enjoy "objective good."[9] And yet, both the qualification and the enjoyment are the purchase made by Christ and given to the regenerate, not something that one must build up in one's own capacity. In other words, God rewards his own gift of holiness with the enjoyment of happiness. God crowns his own gift of regeneration and justification with sanctification and glorification. Sanctification is thus considered an elevated stage of regeneration. In a purposive progression God brings to completion the work he began in the regenerate.

Christian Practice

What is operative in the work of sanctification, then, is the goodness that resides within the regenerate as the new internal principle of action.

---

7. Ibid., 398.
8. "Wisdom of God," 145.
9. The same structure appears in "Miscellanies," no. 671, Yale MSS: "the whole of mans salvation it self so far as consequent on the saints' holiness is *given as a reward of their holiness & good works. Mens happiness is in great measure the natural consequent of mens holiness.* . . . The sum of salvation includes the saints conversion & justification & holiness & good works & also their consequent happiness. X has purchased holiness & happiness both, *but only he has purchased one as consequent on the other*" (emphasis mine).

This principle naturally exerts itself in holy actions. Since being "a principle of holy action" is "the definition of grace," Edwards maintains, "it is absurd to talk of a principle that does not tend to practice."[10] It may sound strange to hear a theologian, who is so preoccupied with the celestial mystery of grace, preach on the utmost importance of practice in this world, but that is exactly the case with Edwards. His notion of "practice" may not encompass all the concerns of today's praxis-oriented theologians; one cannot expect him to answer questions that were not on the agenda of his time. Yet Edwards's theology, like all other great theologies of history, provides an important basis for the kind of practice that is needed today.

His insistence on practice culminates in his widely-known argument concerning the twelfth sign of genuine religious affections: "gracious and holy affections have their exercise and fruit in Christian practice."[11] Of all twelve signs of gracious affections, this sign is the "greatest," "highest," "principal," "best," and "chief" sign, and is "the most proper evidence" by which one can judge the sincerity of godliness.[12] As a matter of fact, these emphatic characterizations he gave to the twelfth sign indicate that more than a "sign" is at stake. Christian practice, in Edwards's conception, is not just an outward symptom by which one can diagnose inward godliness. It has an ontological dimension: it brings grace to perfection. "Grace is said to be perfected or finished in holy practice," in the sense that it is brought to "its proper effect."[13] The new principle of grace infused at conversion is brought to its proper effect in Christian practice, just as the production of fruit, being the "end" of the tree, brings the life of the tree to perfection. As it is the "design" of the tree to bear fruit, so grace perfects the end for which human beings were originally ordained. Edwards is thoroughly convinced of the existence of such a purposeful design. Not only is conversion brought to its proper end in practice, but practice is even "the aim of that eternal election." The whole scheme of redemption provides the basis. God "elects them that they may live holy," and

---

10. *Charity and Its Fruits*, WY, 8:298.
11. *Religious Affections*, 383.
12. Ibid., 406–7, 411, 434, 443.
13. Ibid., 435, 434. Conrad Cherry, again in an attempt to portray Edwards as orthodox as possible, elaborates here that "works perfect faith not in the sense of making perfect something that was imperfect, but perfect it by demonstrating its true character" (see his *Theology of Jonathan Edwards*, 137). However, practice for Edwards means more than a "demonstration." It brings grace to ontological perfection.

Christ "redeemed the elect and purchased grace for them to that end, that they might walk in holy practice."[14] Edwards deftly cites a scriptural passage, "I have chosen you, and ordained you, that ye should go and bring forth fruit" (John 15:16, KJV), to show the teleological relationship between election and practice.[15] Obviously, more than a cognitive sign or external demonstration is involved here. The entire scheme of redemption, the "wonderful contrivance of redemption" as he used to say,[16] is made to serve as the ground for Christian practice, without which neither election nor redemption can achieve its ordained *telos*.

With regard to the enhanced status of practice in Edwards's soteriology, a pair of contrasting interpretations have been proposed. On the one hand, there is a forthright reading of "Edwards the moralist." John Smith found in Edwards's argument the inception of American pragmatism, which refuses to admit any existence beyond perceptible manifestation and outward expression. "[It] pushes Edwards's empiricism in the direction of a pragmatism in the sense that the religious virtues are now seen as tendencies that can be known only in and through their active expression. Whether a man truly has love, for example, is not to be determined merely by direct inspection, for love is not a static quality to be apprehended in an instant, but an affection that . . . manifests itself in some overt and living way."[17] An unavoidable deduction from this pragmatism, in Smith's view, is that practice "came to be regarded not primarily as the sign of the sincere heart but rather as a virtue in its own right." Edwards—or at least his distorted image—expedited religion to dissolve into morality, or piety into practice, and in so doing gave rise to the "American character."[18]

On the other hand, Norman Fiering objects to such a reading of Edwards as a "do-gooder" of the conventional Puritan mold.[19] According to Fiering, Edwards "cared primarily about internal states and exercises, not results or consequences in the world in and for themselves." In Fiering's reading, the causal connection that "a good tree

---

14. *Charity and Its Fruits*, WY, 8:294–95.
15. *Religious Affections*, 398–99.
16. "Wisdom in the Contrivance of the World," WY, 6:307–10; "Wisdom of God," 133–68; "Miscellanies," nos. 554, 571, Yale MSS.
17. John E. Smith, "Jonathan Edwards: Piety and Practice in the American Character," *Journal of Religion* 54 (1974): 172.
18. Ibid., 177. The development was clearly contrary to Edwards's intention. "He opened the door," writes Smith, "for precisely what he sought to exclude."
19. Fiering, *Jonathan Edwards's Moral Thought*, 346.

will yield good fruit" is "incidental to his reasoning," for "purity of soul was ontologically of supreme importance for him and preceded any strictly ethical considerations."[20]

My proposal is to reconcile these two views by reinterpreting Edwards's text in light of the concept of disposition, which has its own ontological dimension. According to Edwards, a disposition has a mode of reality apart from its actual exercise, and it necessarily and purposively exercises itself on specified occasions. What really counts here is the presence of the saving disposition. "The disposition is all that can be said to be absolutely necessary," and the holy act that arises out of this disposition, as Edwards plainly put, "cannot be proved to be absolutely necessary" in order for one to be counted in the state of salvation.[21] This is because the infused habit as an active tendency has its own mode of reality, apart from and even prior to its actual exercise. It is not that the disposition achieves its reality only when or only after it is triggered into actual exercise. Edwards's concept of "habit," unlike the conventional understanding of the word, is given a status of ontological reality that exceeds mere recognition of the lingering residual of habitual actions and events. In this sense, Fiering's objection to seeing Edwards as a pragmatic moralist is legitimate. Edwards is concerned more with the "internal states and exercises," rather than with the "results or consequences in the world in and for themselves."

But if the sum and substance of such "internal states" and the "purity of soul" consists in the reality of the new principle, it must necessarily come to be exercised as a conditional and prescriptive law when the specified occasion does arise. The causal connection that "a good tree will yield good fruit," far from being *"incidental"* as Fiering supposes,[22] belongs to the very nucleus of Edwards's theological conviction. It is indeed inconceivable for an internal disposition not to be exercised outwardly at the time and circumstances it is preordained to do so. "Godliness in the heart," says Edwards, "has as *direct* a relation to practice, as a fountain has to a stream, or as the luminous nature of the sun has to beams sent forth . . . or as a habit or principle of action has to action."[23] Christian practice is nothing but the saints' new disposition being exercised spontaneously and outwardly, thus bringing religion out

---

20. Ibid., 348.
21. "Miscellanies," no. 27b, Yale MSS. See Chapter 3 for detail.
22. Fiering, *Jonathan Edwards's Moral Thought*, 348.
23. *Religious Affections*, 398 (emphasis mine).

into a public arena. In this sense, John Smith is right in pointing out the indispensable importance of practice in Edwards.

As I argued in Chapter 4, Edwards confidently affirms the reality of inherent goodness that resides in the regenerate, not only publicly but also and primarily before God. Clearly, this inherent goodness owes its existence and operation to God. God has antecedently determined that, by the infusion and indwelling of the Holy Spirit, the regenerate should have this inherent goodness as the source of their good works. God directly and unceasingly exercises his power of causation in and through this human goodness. The work of sanctification, therefore, is not just a human affair.[24] At the same time, sanctification is not an operation totally alien to the human subject, for it is only by human participation that this work is carried out. Again, it may be likened to a tree yielding fruit.[25] The fruit is, in one sense, totally the product of the tree; it is brought forth by the exercise of the tree's disposition to yield it, thus fulfilling the tree's ordained *telos*. And yet what becomes manifest in the fruit is not from the tree itself but from the soil, the air, and the sunlight, without which it cannot exercise its disposition to bear fruit. Likewise, the fruition of the regenerate disposition in holy practice is at once the result of the autonomous human exertion *and* God's direct and immediate causation. In Christian practice, the saints are united closer and closer with God, and in this union they become ontologically more and more conformed to the image of God. They participate in God's own holiness.

As I will discuss below, glorification is also the result of the increasing communication of the fullness of God. At work in and through the human disposition is God's own disposition to glorify and enlarge himself in time. Sanctification and glorification, accordingly, is a continuous process of this self-enlargement of God in time, in which human beings participate by increasing degrees.

Perseverance

If "Christian practice" is characterized as the continuing work of *conversion,* "perseverance" can be called the continuing work of *justifi-*

---

24. See, for example, "Miscellanies," no. 739 (*Philosophy of Jonathan Edwards*, 207). Other Reformed theologians place similar emphasis on God's initiative in perseverance, but, unlike Edwards, they are not prepared to affirm its crystallization in human reality. See Berkhof, *Systematic Theology*, 546; *Reformed Dogmatics*, 584.

25. Edwards often likens the exercise of dispositions to the growing of a tree. See, for example, *End of Creation, WY*, 8:435, 439.

cation.²⁶ Christian practice and perseverance are close correlatives under the common rubric of sanctification, yet in Edwards's terminology perseverance is linked more often with justification than with conversion. Christian practice publicly manifests one's saving disposition *before human eyes*, whereas perseverance manifests one's justifying faith *in foro Dei*.²⁷ Naturally, justification as it is taught in Reformed dogmatics is an instantaneous act of declaration and cannot be a "continuing" event. But the faith on which justification depends has to be of a persevering kind, not a temporary or short-lived one. Here justification meets the aspect of duration, and "perseverance" is the term Edwards prefers to denote this enduring aspect.

The problem of temporary versus persevering faith troubled many Puritan minds, and Edwards was no exception.²⁸ "Perseverance" is a subject-heading frequently appearing in his private notes. According to the basic tenet of Protestant justification, a sinner is justified on the very spot when he or she begins to have genuine faith. But what will happen if this person later loses faith? Yes, the faith that justifies must be persevering faith, but the problem is that it takes the whole lifetime to find out if one's faith is truly persevering or not. If justification is dependent upon perseverance, then, no living person on earth can have the assurance of salvation. Edwards's answer to this aporia is strikingly blunt and even provocative: "The condition of justification in a sense remains still to be performed even after the first conversion and the sentence of justification in a sense remains still to be passed, & the man remains still in a state of probation for heaven which could not be if his justification did not still depend on what remain'd to be done."²⁹ Here Edwards seems to be advancing a daring thesis of "pending justification." Luther would be thrown back into terror—terror of losing his hard-earned *certitudo salutis*—if he were told that justification is still conditional upon future works. Certainly this was not Edwards's

---

26. Edwards himself speaks of "continuance in justification." "Miscellanies," no. 1188, Yale MSS. (See "Concerning the Perseverance of Saints," *WW*, 3:514–15, for text.) The relationship is especially visible in the fact that it is his Justification discourse that contains his most extensive argument on perseverance. See "Justification by Faith alone," 410–15.

27. For Christian practice, see *Religious Affections*, 432, 441; "Miscellanies," no. 467, Yale MSS; for perseverance, see "Miscellanies," nos. 695, 711, 729, 755, Yale MSS.

28. For Calvin, Beza, Perkins, Sibbes, Ames, Cotton, Hooker, and others on the subject, see Kendal, *Calvin and English Calvinists*.

29. "Miscellanies," no. 847, Yale MSS.

intention. Again, I propose that the passage be understood in light of Edwards's concept of disposition. A clue to better understanding of this daring remark lies in the reality of the transformed disposition that would necessarily issue into good works.

Edwards's way of handling the subject is not uniform. A chronological survey of the "Miscellanies" numbers reveals that there were two preliminary stages of understanding before Edwards reached the third and definitive answer to it. His earlier remarks on the theme indicate that he was not acutely aware of the complexity involved. His remarks in this first stage amount to no more than assuring that perseverance is the "condition of justification" and that the gift of justification is granted only to the persevering kind of faith.[30] A practical syllogism, about which he later comes to harbor some doubts, carries no hint of suspicion at this stage: Since "true grace shall persevere" (major premise), if a person finds his or her faith persevering (minor premise), the person can be certain about his or her salvation (conclusion). Perseverance is therefore "a certain evidence of their election."[31] Obviously Edwards is more concerned here with upholding the post-justification obligation to "earnest endeavors" and "steadfastness" than with theoretical consistency. Perseverance has a value and a place in soteriology, primarily because it serves as the "evidence" and "sign" whereby a person knows his or her saving status.[32]

However, Edwards gradually leaves this naive view behind and works out a theory that is more consonant with his own paradigm of justification. Perseverance is no longer designated as the "condition" of justification, for he now realizes that it would cause a number of complications. First, calling perseverance the "condition" of justification makes it difficult to understand why God had to install a new covenant, the covenant of grace, in which the reward of life is not dependent on "the strength & steadfastness of his [the believer's] own will." Second, an overemphasis on human strength and steadfastness encourages self-dependence, "which would be very dissonant from the gospel scheme." Third, this would "deprive the believer of the comfort, hope & joy of salvation"—young Luther's most anxious concern. It would imply that "there are none on this side the grave, that are admitted as his children

---

30. "Miscellanies," no. 428, Yale MSS. (See *WW*, 3:510, for text.)
31. "Miscellanies," no. 415, Yale MSS. (See *WW*, 3:509, for text.) See Chapter 2 for "practical syllogism."
32. "Miscellanies," nos. 84, 467, Yale MSS. (See *WW*, 3:509, 510, for text.)

or people, because they hant [*sic*] yet actually persevered to the end of life."³³ He instead proposes to see perseverance in a Christological perspective. It is the scheme of federal imputation extended to the continuing phase of justification. The saints shall surely persevere, Edwards now asserts, because Christ has already earned perfect perseverance, which is now imputed to the saints "as if they had performed it." God knows that the saints would all fall away if left to themselves. Christ's work of redemption must come with perseverance in the same package, so that it may not be rendered void in the future. Christ is "our second surety" in perseverance as he was in justification—this was his solution in the second stage.³⁴

Edwards's treatment reaches its third and final stage when this federal scheme is given an ontological ground in his dispositional view of reality. He again calls perseverance the "condition" of justification, but this time he does so with deliberation. It is at this stage that he advances the daring theory of "pending justification." The condition of justification remains to be performed, and the sentence of justification is still pending the result of probation. This does not pose any threat to the evangelical doctrine of justification, however, for the initial faith as the saving disposition necessarily and without fail comes to be exercised in perseverance. It is not because of the forensic imputation of Christ's perseverance: justifying faith is in and of itself a persevering faith because it is a disposition that comes into exercise when so specified. God knows, even before a person does actually persevere, that "by divine establishment" perseverance will necessarily flow out of the initial faith. "The first act of faith . . . *virtually* contains perseverance," says Edwards.³⁵ The word "virtually" here is of special importance. It means that although the saints' perseverance is not fully actualized yet, it nonetheless possesses a mode of reality called "virtuality." Justification is dependent on this virtual perseverance. He repeats the word in another

---

33. "Miscellanies," no. 695, Yale MSS. (See *WW*, 3:510–14, for text.) The argument reappears in *Charity and Its Fruits*, *WY*, 8:346.

34. *Charity and Its Fruits*, *WY*, 8:347. This is still the standard teaching of conservative Reformed theology today. See Berkhof, *Systematic Theology*, 547.

35. "Miscellanies," no. 729, Yale MSS. (See *WW*, 3:516, for text.) For the meaning of the word "virtual," see my review of Edwards's dispositional ontology in Chapter 3. The dispositional understanding of perseverance is not limited to what I call here the third stage of his theoretical development. The transition is gradual with overlaps in between—just as in justification the federal imputation theory does not vanish all at once with the beginning of the ontological understanding.

context: "Future faith and repentance are beheld, in that justification, as *virtually* contained in that first faith and repentance; because . . . the continuance of that habit and principle in the heart that has such an actual repentance and faith in its nature and tendency, is now made sure by God's promise."[36] With Edwards, a habit or disposition is not just a description of the likelihood that faith *usually* perseveres. By divine establishment, the disposition of the regenerate is programmed to exert itself, and do so unfailingly. It is God's prescriptive law that assures "the continuance of that habit and principle" in "after acts of faith."[37] This law is ontologically present, whether in full manifestation or not, in the objective reality of the regenerate. As I argued in Chapter 3, Edwards is not an occasionalist. The existence of a chair when unperceived, for instance, is secured by a nexus of established laws of nature according to which the chair must be supposed to exist precisely in the same manner as it does when perceived. Likewise, perseverance is already ontologically real in the initial faith as an active and purposive disposition. Edwards can therefore remain completely at ease in advancing what seems to be "pending justification." It is another expression of his conviction that faith as a saving disposition, once infused, has its own mode of reality, and that it is actualized at the preordained time and circumstances, which is the definition of disposition.

Furthermore, according to a related "Miscellanies" entry, in order to give the saving disposition time and occasion to actualize itself, believers are given earthly life as a time of probation. God could have created all the saints in heaven from the beginning of their regenerate life, dispensing altogether with the trouble of sustaining them on earth in perseverance. However, that would be contrary to God's design, says Edwards, for then "this disposition could not be exercised & manifested under its proper trials."[38] In other words, there must be a time for sanctification through probation because it provides faith with the occasion to exercise itself and become fully actual, thus manifesting and magnifying God's glory in time. Creation and its temporality are necessary, not because God is powerless to accomplish his purposes in an instant, but because

---

36. "Justification by Faith alone," 412 (emphasis mine).
37. "Miscellanies," no. 729, Yale MSS. The 1843 Reprint Edition alters Edwards's often-repeated but awkward phrase "*after* acts of faith" to "*subsequent* acts of faith" (*WW*, 3:516). See also *Original Sin*, 390–91, for a comparable concept of "after operations" resulting from an evil disposition.
38. "Miscellanies," no. 1129, Yale MSS.

in and through the temporary exercise of their disposition God further glorifies himself.[39] This leads me to the last subject of this study.

Glorification

Glorification in soteriology means what traditional Reformed dogmatics has called—somewhat awkwardly—"individual eschatology," and as such it is contrasted with "general eschatology," which includes such topics as the second coming of Christ, the millennium, and the consummation and renewal of the world.[40] Edwards also makes this distinction at the outset of his Redemption discourse. Glorification is carried on in two respects, he says: first, "with respect to particular persons," and second, "with respect to the grand design in general as it relates to the universal subject and end of it."[41] In this study of Edwards's theories of salvation, attention is focused as much as possible on the first sense, the glorification of individual believers.

Individual Eschatology

In the previous subsection I pointed out the overwhelming significance of sanctification among Edwards's soteriological concerns. Sanctification, however, is not the ultimate *finis* of the work of God that has begun in the regenerate. The work of sanctification cannot terminate

---

39. For James Martin, this is not a satisfactory answer to the question as to why the Kingdom of God should take so much time to establish itself. In Martin's view, Edwards's answer does not do justice to the concept of *Deus absconditus* (see Martin, *The Last Judgment in Protestant Theology from Orthodoxy to Ritschl* [Grand Rapids, Mich.: Wm. B. Eerdmans, 1963], 85). However, the concept of *Deus absconditus*, though not entirely absent, sounds very remote to Edwards's scheme of theology in which God unceasingly manifests and communicates his own glory to his creatures.

40. Ames discusses individual "glorification" separately from "the End of the World" (*Marrow of Theology*, 1.30, 1. xli). Similarly, Mastricht concludes his chapter "de redemptio applicatione" with glorification, and treats "de dispensatione foederis gratiae sub aeternitate" separately (*Theoretico-Practica Theologia*, 6.9; 8.4). Turretin discusses "de consummatione seculi," along with individual aspects of glorification, in an all-inclusive chapter "de novissimis" (*Institutio Theologiae Elencticae* 20.1–13). Heppe treats both individual and general eschatology under one heading, "glorification" (*Reformed Dogmatics*, 695–712).

41. *History of the Work of Redemption*, 120–21.

there but must be carried on further into glorification, for it is never complete in this life. Even with the continuing work of the indwelling Spirit that keeps working on "the unregenerate part" of the regenerate, the stain of corruption persists. Edwards has no illusion of the earthly *viator* attaining perfect holiness in his or her life.[42] The work of restoring the ruined image of God in humanity must continue beyond death. Glorification in the individual sense, therefore, means "to bestow upon them when their bodies die that eternal glory which is the fruit of the purchase of Christ."[43] It is the time when the work of conversion and sanctification is brought to completion. With its sting removed, death is made into an occasion for glorification. Edwards is convinced that God's design is "to restore the soul of man in conversion . . . and to carry on the restoration in sanctification, and to perfect it in glory."[44]

Yet even death as the termination of one's bodily life is not quite the *terminus ad quem* of the work of restoration. Underneath the idea of individual glorification lurks the problem of soul and body. In the words of William Ames, perfect glorification is granted to the soul "immediately after the separation from the body," but the body has to wait for glorification "until that last day when all the faithful shall in one moment be perfected in Christ."[45] This duality of soul and body should not be quickly pushed aside as unscriptural Hellenistic thinking, since in Scripture the redemption of the body is closely associated with the redemption of the whole creation. Only when the body is glorified together with the soul, is redemption fully actualized. It is the time when "the creation itself will be set free from its bondage to decay and will obtain the freedom of the glory of the children of God," for which "the whole creation has been groaning in labor pains until now" (Rom. 8:21–22). The ultimate redemption, then, cannot be realized until our bodies are redeemed.

Edwards counts the transposition of Enoch into heaven (Gen. 5:24) as the first instance of restoring the body, which was followed by another instance of Elijah (2 Kings 2:11) and a number of the bodies raised and glorified at Christ's resurrection. These instances are the

---

42. See "Hope and Comfort," 87; *Religious Affections*, 390.
43. *History of the Work of Redemption*, 121.
44. Ibid., 124. Here Edwards follows the Reformed tradition, in which glorification is viewed as the "achievement of complete sanctification." See Ames, *Marrow of Theology*, 1.41.1; *Reformed Dogmatics*, 696.
45. Ames, *Marrow of Theology*, 1.30.34.

"pledge or earnest" of future glorification, indicating that it is God's design that the body of all the elect be glorified at the end of the world. Thus individual death gives us a glimpse of what the general eschaton will be like. The church has thereby "a clearer manifestation of a future estate and of the future glorious reward of the saints in heaven."[46] The work of redemption is finished only when "all the bodies of the saints shall be saved and glorified together . . . in the whole man, and the soul and body in union one with another." Until then, redemption is "but incomplete and imperfect."[47] Glorification in the individual sense means for Edwards the time of completion and fruition of the work of sanctification, both in the soul and body.[48]

Furthermore, glorification is the time when not only sanctification but also justification is brought to completion. The two graces of justification and sanctification are consummated in the grace of glorification. This is particularly noticeable in Edwards's treatment of the Last Judgment. As Protestant Orthodoxy placed increasing emphasis on justification, the doctrine of the Last Judgment lost its edge of imminence it possessed in the Reformers' teaching. The doctrine came to be viewed in theoretical conflict with justification: If justification becomes central and controlling, the Last Judgment is inevitably rendered superfluous and peripheral; but if the Last Judgment is thrust to the forefront in its own right, it tends to obscure the finality of the grace of justification in this life.[49] By viewing the Last Judgment as the completion of justification and sanctification, Edwards could see both doctrines as not mutually detrimental. On the one hand, he does not disregard the biblical account according to which the ultimate verdict will be based on *works*: "The Scripture so fully teaches us that we are to be judged by our works."[50] But the works according to which this last verdict is sentenced are foreseen, promised, preordained, and therefore *virtually* contained in the initial disposition of faith. In other words, the works

---

46. *History of the Work of Redemption*, 145, 146.
47. Ibid., 498, 497.
48. Ibid., 507–8; "Miscellanies," no. 571 ("Heaven" in *WD*, 8:546).
49. For the place of the Last Judgment in Protestant Orthodoxy, see Martin, *Last Judgment*, 1–86. See also *Reformed Dogmatics*, 704–5, for Wendelinus, Bucanus, Wollebius, Ames, and Turretin on the subject.
50. "Miscellanies," no. 289, Yale MSS. Also in nos. 671, 856, 859, 861, 996, Yale MSS. Most of these are entitled "how works justify." See also "Excellency of Christ," 186; *Charity and Its Fruits*, *WY*, 8:309. For scriptural references on the importance of works, see Matthew 25:31–46, Romans 2:6, and Revelation 20:12.

are already an ontological reality in the act of faith upon which the first justification is sentenced. The Last Judgment is therefore characterized as "a declarative judgment . . . not God's forming a judgment within himself, but the manifestation of his judgment."[51] And yet it does not lose significance in face of justification, since this virtual reality is still expected to actualize what it is ordained to actualize. If perseverance is called "*continuing* justification," the Last Judgment should be called "*completed* justification."

To speak of justification and sanctification in the context of glorification is to speak of them in the eschatological perspective that characterizes the New Testament vision of justice and holiness. Thus far, I have been speaking of the "stages" of the application of redemption: conversion, justification, and sanctification. With Edwards, however, these are not self-contained stages of pilgrimage through which one journeys step by step; rather, they are one seamless and unceasing flow that achieves its ultimate meaning only in reference to glorification. Any potential rift between the two graces of justification and sanctification in Edwards's thought is given a definitive solution: he sees the dialectic of justification and sanctification *sub specie aeternitatis*. In his Redemption discourse, he divides the entire history after Christ into two phases: "in grace" and "in glory."[52] The economy "of grace" represents the age of the church in which the outward means of grace are adopted, in order to make the saints ready for the economy "of glory," that is, the economy administered on the last day. In other words, the entire history from Christ's resurrection to the end of the world is but preliminary for this last day of glory. "All that is before this, while the church is under means of grace, is only to make way for that, to prepare that success that is to be accomplished in the bestowment of glory. The means of grace are to fit for glory, and God's grace itself is bestowed on the elect to make them meet for glory."[53] In the economy of grace, both justification and sanctification are significant as such, yet when they are taken in the broader economy of glory, the two graces are but a necessary preparation for the last day of glorification. In this, Edwards's soteriology is distinctively eschatological.

In view of this eschatological character of Edwards's soteriology,

---

51. *Religious Affections*, 441.
52. *History of the Work of Redemption*, 362.
53. Ibid., 493, 509.

there is one commanding question: Does the work of glorification ever come to its *terminus ad quem*? It does not come to fruition in this life, or at death. As a matter of fact, Edwards thinks that it will not come to an end in heaven, or even at the eschaton. If glorification is yet another operation of the saving disposition, this disposition cannot cease to be a disposition there: it continues to seek further occasions for exercise. For this reason, Edwards speaks of the "eternal fruits" of the work of redemption. The work of redemption itself is not eternal. It has "an issue," and once the issue is achieved, it comes to an end. But the "fruits" of this work will have no end and continue even "after the end of the world . . . to all eternity."[54] The saving disposition, which God has implanted in the saints at conversion and has continued to tend in justification and sanctification, is not something that achieves its reality once and for all and finishes its exercise. It continues to achieve its own ordained *telos* again and again in a never-ending process of fuller actualization, each time with increased actuality than before.

Edwards's marked interest in "heaven" is probably a result of this understanding. In a Thanksgiving day sermon, he takes up the intriguing subject of "heavenly employment." We are not to suppose, he says, that the saints will have nothing to do in heaven. Heaven is of course a place for rest, but that is not inconsistent with the saints "being continually employed" and in "exceedingly full of action."[55] The saints in glory are as active as the saints on earth, or even more active than the saints here, for "they shall serve God day and night, continually or without ceasing," being freed from all other cares and labors that would interfere on earth. Their principle of holiness is the same principle that is at work in the saints on earth, and it is "a most active principle" that shall not cease working. Edwards elaborates on the "increase" of happiness in a "Miscellanies" entry on "heaven": "It seems to be quite a wrong notion of the happiness of heaven that it is in that manner unchangeable, that it admits not of new joys upon new occasions . . . their joy is continually increased as they see the purposes of God's grace unfolded in his wondrous providences towards his church. Their happiness is increased as they see their number increases."[56] Throughout the duration of the world, and even "beyond" the eschaton, Edwards believes, the saints

---

54. Ibid., 119. See Lee, *Philosophical Theology*, 237.
55. Sermon, "Praise, one of the chief employments of heaven," WD, 8:307.
56. "Miscellanies," no. 372 ("Heaven," WD 8:536). Edwards also speaks of "degrees of glory" in heaven. See "Miscellanies," no. 431, Yale MSS.

will increase their happiness and glory, for the disposition in them is "a most active principle" that continues to operate ever and ever for greater communication with God. "The degree and manner of the creature's glory" increases, by "greater and greater communion and participation with him [God] in his own glory and happiness," and this process of increase continues indefinitely "in constant progression, throughout all eternity."[57] This is Edwards's concept of glorification. Like two converging lines that come ever closer and closer but never meet, the saints will be in ever-increasing union and communion with God. They become more and more conformed to God and one with God, and yet, "the time will never come when it can be said it has already arrived at this infinite height."[58]

The End of Creation

As I mentioned earlier, glorification in Reformed dogmatics is described in two ways: individual and general. The distinction, however, ultimately proves to be no more than an expedient for systematic description. In reality, the glorification of individual believers cannot be separated from the glorification of God, for, in Edwards's words, "one necessarily supposes the other."[59] His Redemption discourse, for example, forthrightly aims to describe "the grand design" of the general course of history, yet in order to describe it Edwards had to give an account of how God perfected the glory of individual human beings. God's design "to complete and perfect the glory of all the elect" is integral to his design "to accomplish the glory of the blessed Trinity."[60] Or better yet, God is glorified precisely through the glorification of human beings. What is achieved in their glorification is nothing short of the glorification of God. God is glorified in the attainment of all the objectives he had as the end of creation. The glorification of the elect is not a Christian glorification, unless it issues into the glorification of God: "When all things are subjected to him . . . God may be all in all"

57. *End of Creation*, 459.
58. Ibid., 534, 536. See Ramsey's footnote for another example of editorial constraint to make Edwards "look" Protestant. Ramsey indicts the image of asymptotic lines as "a gross one" for suggesting "merger with the divine." His effort to recast Edwards in the Protestant mold of the dialectic of union and distance, however, is consonant neither with the text on which he comments nor with the text that he quotes for warrant.
59. *History of the Work of Redemption*, 122.
60. Ibid., 125. See also ibid., 345, for another expression of this duality.

(1 Cor. 15:28). What is distinctive about Edwards's treatise on the history of redemption, as John Wilson notes, is that the "objective or divine side" of redemption is not neglected at the expense of the "subjective or human side."[61] How these two sides are related to each other in Edwards's theology can itself be the subject of another book. Only a glimpse at the problem is provided here in order to conclude my analysis of his soteriology.

That the glorification of himself was God's ultimate end constitutes the pivotal thesis of Edwards's theology. God has this design of glorifying himself from all eternity, and God accomplishes it by communicating his own goodness to his creatures. God has designed and decreed everything in order that all the divine attributes should be exercised and that none should remain dormant.[62] The exercise of his attributes was the ultimate purpose of all the decrees concerning the economy of salvation. Even sin is given a place within this scenario of God's self-glorification, because "the display of the glory of God could not but be imperfect and incomplete without it."[63]

In fact, God's self-glorification is already in exercise even before the foundation of the world, for, according to Edwards, it belongs to the very nature of God to glorify himself. Edwards applies here the category of disposition to God's being: "It is God's essence to incline to communicate Himself."[64] God's disposition to communicate or diffuse his own infinite fullness is part of the "perfection of his nature."[65] In the dispositional category, God's being is translated into God's action. It is not that God first exists in a perfectly still vacuum and then begins to exercise his power; God *is* as God *acts*. God does not exist without exercising his divine power. For God to exist is to act as God, that is, to exercise his power and perfection. This exercise of divine power results

---

61. Wilson's Introduction to *History of the Work of Redemption*, 56. Also in 30–32, 100.

62. *End of Creation*, 428–35; "Miscellanies," nos. 553 (*Philosophy of Jonathan Edwards*, 136–37), 1218 (ibid., 149–52); "Concerning the Divine Decrees," 541–42.

63. "Concerning the Divine Decrees," 517. See also "Efficacious Grace," 586–87; "Miscellanies," nos. 581 (*Philosophy of Jonathan Edwards*, 137), 586.

64. "Miscellanies," no. 107, Yale MSS. See Lee, *Philosophical Theology*, 175–77.

65. *End of Creation*, 434. The word "fullness," in most cases, is used interchangeably with such other words as "perfection," "beauty," "joy," "glory," "happiness," and "goodness." See, for example, "Notes on the Bible," 527. For further philological information, see Delattre, *Beauty and Sensibility*, 137–39. In my reading, "holiness" and "happiness" seem to have more distinct shades of nuances against each other.

in the manifestation of his own glory. "God *is*" means, therefore, "God *glorifies himself.*"

Edwards explains this in two senses, not without complaining about the shortcomings of language: God is glorified, first, in "God's infinite perfection being exerted" *(in se)*, and second, in "His infinite happiness being communicated" *(ad extra)*.[66] In the first sense, God's self-glorification is the exercise of his infinite perfection within the eternal Trinity. In the second sense, the same exercise of his perfection results in the outward work of creation. "God is glorified within Himself these two ways: 1. By appearing or being manifested to Himself in His own perfect idea, or in His Son who is the brightness of His glory. 2. By enjoying and delighting in Himself, by flowing forth in infinite love and delight towards Himself, or in his Holy Spirit."[67] By the internal glorification, God the Father has "His own perfect idea" (the begotten Son) and the "infinite love and delight towards Himself" (the Holy Spirit). Within this immanent Trinity, God's glory is already infinitely being exercised and manifested, since it is his own nature to exercise his perfection. God's self-glorification is already fully actual in se, without any outward movement. This is the first phase of God's self-glorification.

However, the same inclination must be further exercised ad extra in creating the world, because "to incline to communicate Himself" belongs to his very "essence," and hence must continue to operate.[68] His infinite perfection, in other words, consists not in self-contentment but precisely in communication. God is not circumscribed in his eternal bliss. God enjoys "infinite happiness and perfect bliss," and yet, "he is not inactive, but is himself in his own nature a perfect act, and is continually at work in bringing to pass his own purposes and ends."[69] By the very nature of his being, God continues to manifest and communicate his perfection outwardly, which is the second phase of his self-glorification. The link between "God *an sich* [in himself]" and "God *für*

66. "Miscellanies," no. 1066 *(Philosophy of Jonathan Edwards,* 139). For Edwards's theological reflections on the Trinity, see *Observations Concerning the Scripture Oeconomy of the Trinity, and Covenant of Redemption* and *An Essay on the Trinity,* in *Treatise on Grace,* 77–98, 99–131; Herbert W. Richardson, "The Glory of God in the Theology of Jonathan Edwards: A Study in the Doctrine of the Trinity" (Ph.D. diss., Harvard University, 1962), 220–90; Lee, *Philosophical Theology,* 185–96.
67. "Miscellanies," no. 448 *(Philosophy of Jonathan Edwards,* 133).
68. "Miscellanies," no. 107, Yale MSS.
69. "Praise," 307.

sich [for himself]," as George Hendry perceptively states, is in the original disposition of God to emanate his own infinite fullness. It is "inherent in the nature of God, not only to be God, but to reveal himself as God."[70] By the exercise of the same disposition that was "from eternity, within Himself and toward Himself," God repeats himself outwardly, and thus creates the world.[71] In this work of creation, God "delights in seeing those exercises of His perfection." God's glory is thereby "repeated," "increased," and "multiplied," because now it is "known and seen by other beings besides himself."[72] God's communication of his infinite fullness *ad extra*, therefore, is essential to God's further self-glorification. Just as his self-glorification within the immanent Trinity resides in the manifestation and communication of his perfection, so does his self-glorification in time reside in the communication and emanation of the perfection he has in *se*.[73]

What, then, is the role of human beings in the self-glorification of God? The distinctive character of Edwards's soteriology of participation reappears in his answer to this question. Human beings are not passive receptacles of the grace of glorification; here again, they are given an active role to play. They participate in the process of God's self-glorification through their knowledge, love, and faith. God glorifies himself by increasing human holiness. The glorification of elect human beings is so thoroughly assimilated into God's self-glorification that without the former the latter would be rendered "imperfect." To put it another way, God achieves his purpose of glorifying creatures by communicating his internal glory and perfection to them, thereby increasing and multiplying his own glory *ad extra*. The overflowing

70. George Hendry, "The Glory of God and the Future of Man," *Reformed World* 34 (1976): 150.
71. Here again, Edwards concurs with Thomas, who says that "to create belongs to God according to His being, that is, His essence." *Summa Theologica*, 1.45.6. In the Protestant circle, Paul Tillich is another who understands the work of creation as belonging to the very nature of divinity. *Systematic Theology*, 1:252.
72. "Miscellanies," no. 553 (*Philosophy of Jonathan Edwards*, 136–37); *End of Creation*, 411–33.
73. In an effort to synchronize Edwards's terms with his own interpretation scheme, Richardson seems to confine the word "communication" to God's emanation *ad extra* (see his eclectic quotations from "Miscellanies," no. 1066, in Richardson, "Glory of God," 1,316–21). However, Edwards does apply the word to the inner-trinitarian relationships as well. God's primordial disposition to communicate is operative both in *se* and *ad extra*. See Lee, *Philosophical Theology*, 170–210.

communication of his internal glory ad extra is at once the glorification of the creature and of himself, because the creature's glorification consists entirely in the communication of God's fullness to them and their participation in it. This process takes place as the emanation of the divine fullness to them and the remanation of it back to God in their knowledge, love, and faith.[74] Here I shall explain the soteriological significance of these three in Edwards's paradigm.

Intelligent beings are created to glorify God and further increase his glory, first, through their knowledge of God, which is their taxonomic difference from "senseless matter" or "beasts."[75] Their end is "to behold and admire the doings of God and magnify Him for them, and to contemplate His glories in them"; and so without them the world would be "altogether useless."[76] They are created to be "the consciousness of the universe," or "the eye of the creation to behold the glory of God" and "the mouth of the creation to praise him and ascribe him the glory that is displayed in them."[77] For this purpose, they are endowed with the faculty of understanding—to know God in his being and acting. Here "knowing" comprises more than a cognitive activity: it ontologically increases their conformity to God, for their knowledge of God is nothing but "a communication of God's infinite knowledge which primarily consists in the knowledge of himself."[78] In order to know God properly—to know God in admiration and exaltation—they have to be conformed to the image of God. The more they know God in adoration, the more they are transformed and drawn closer to the Son who is the perfect Image of God. They are ontologically transformed, because to know God is to receive more communication of God's own knowledge of himself.[79] They are glorified by having God's own knowledge communicated to them, and precisely in their glorification, God's glory increases through time.

74. *End of Creation*, 531.
75. "Miscellanies," no. gg (*Philosophy of Jonathan Edwards*, 237); *End of Creation*, 472; "The Mind," no. 59 (*WY*, 6:374). By "intelligent beings," Edwards primarily means human beings, but also in the category are angels, who are created to perform the same function with elevated capacity. See "Miscellanies," no. 555 ("Heaven," *WD*, 8:545).
76. "Miscellanies," no. gg (*Philosophy of Jonathan Edwards*, 237).
77. "Miscellanies," no. 87 (*Philosophy of Jonathan Edwards*, 128); no. 104, Yale MSS; Sermons, "Watchman's Duty and Account," *WD*, 7:182; "Natural men in a dreadful condition," 7.
78. *End of Creation*, 441. Lee remarks that God's self-communication is "ontologically productive." *Philosophical Theology*, 174, 180, 191.
79. "Miscellanies," no. 1225 (*Philosophy of Jonathan Edwards*, 152–53).

In the same manner, second, human beings participate in the ever-increasing process of God's self-glorification ad extra by reflecting and reiterating God's immanent love of the Trinity in their love of God.[80] Their knowledge of God is not a real knowledge of God unless it is accompanied by love, admiration, and exaltation. But the love that accompanies their knowledge is originally "the mutual love of the Father and the Son" within the Trinity.[81] This immanent love of God is communicated to human beings, thus increasing their holiness. For this reason, one can say that human beings are ontologically more real than senseless matter. They become what they are, or what they are intended to be, by having this immanent love of God communicated to them. Again, God's glorification advances through this communication of divine love and the remanation of it back to God, thus achieving at once both the glorification of human beings and of God himself.[82]

This pattern of primordial fullness in se and its communication ad extra also explains the origin of the holiness in sanctification: the holiness with which the saints are transformed is the divine holiness that is fully actual in God and is diffused from God. This holiness emanates immediately from God to the creature, "so that hereby the creature partakes of God's own moral excellency."[83] Creaturely holiness is "a conformity to, and participation of it [divine holiness]"; when the creatures exercise their holiness, it returns to God, and God takes delight in it. Sanctification, therefore, is this process of "increasing communication of [God] himself."[84] In reflecting and remanating the increasing holiness and excellency of God, the elect creatures repeat and magnify the glory of God. God is all the more glorified now in the emanation and remanation of his own knowledge, love and holiness, because these are all "the excellent brightness and fullness of the divinity

---

80. Edwards is delighted to find a similar thought in "Ramsays Principles," vol. 1, 309–15. The excerpt reads: "the supernatural love by which we can love God is an emanation of the holy Ghost and a participation of that love by which he loves himself." See "Miscellanies," no. 1254, Yale MSS.

81. "The Mind," 45 (WY, 6:364).

82. God's self-love merges here with God's love for creatures. See *End of Creation*, 457. Likewise, human love "of benevolence" coalesces with that "of complacence." *Charity and Its Fruits*, WY, 8:258.

83. *End of Creation*, 442. See also "Miscellanies," no. 187, Yale MSS: "virtue and holiness are given by way of immediate emanation from God."

84. *End of Creation*, 443.

diffused, overflowing, and as it were enlarged; or in one word, *existing ad extra*."[85]

The communication or emanation of these divine virtues and excellencies, third, can be summed up as faith (knowledge and love joined) and its exercise in practice. For Edwards, faith is a kind of ontological transformation through which human beings are more and more conformed to the image of God. It is to become "partakers of the divine nature" (2 Pet. 1:4, KJV). Herein lies the marrow of Edwards's soteriology. He sees in faith an unceasing and ever-increasing flow of divine fullness return to where it came from. God's "infinite fullness," or his internal knowledge and love and holiness in se, emanates ad extra to the elect creatures, resides within them in a relatively independent form, glorifying them as they exercise it, and finally remanates back to God himself, all the while repeating and increasing God's glory in time. This communicated fullness in exercise is the human reality of salvation. Precisely in order to repeat and further increase, the glory of God has to be exercised in time, *outside* the trinitarian Godhead. It has to take place *outwardly*, apart from God's being, in a relatively independent and spontaneous activity of "intelligent creatures" who stand as the real *Gegenstand* of God's communication over against him. Edwards's concern for the creaturely reality of salvation is thus embedded in the grand scheme of the theology of divinization *(theosis)*.

This dynamic flow of divine emanation and remanation also explains in what sense human participation is "necessary" or even "indispensable" for God to glorify himself. The word "necessary" here must be qualified in two senses. First, human participation is necessary only in the *second* phase of God's self-glorification. God's self-glorification is already fully and eternally actual in the *first* phase, that is, in the communication and manifestation of perfection within the immanent Trinity: "Being already infinitely happy, He does not need any manifestation of His glory to make Him more happy."[86] Second, human participation is necessary—to use Edwards's term—only "consequentially."[87] This communication and manifestation of the internal glory ad extra is a spontaneous overflow of the same primordial disposition of

---

85. Ibid., 527 (emphasis original).
86. "Miscellanies," no. 1182 (*Philosophy of Jonathan Edwards*, 140).
87. See *Freedom of the Will*, 152–53. I owe this explanation of "consequential necessity" to Richardson, "Glory of God," 322.

God in se, and as such it is not dependent on its being received by others. A fountain overflowing, in Edwards's superb metaphor, is no sign of the deficiency of the fountain.[88] In fact, as Lee argues, it is peculiar to God's disposition that it creates even the occasion for itself to exercise, thus creating the world as the receiver of his communication.[89] In this sense, God is "ab-solute" and stands in no need of human participation.

Yet, having thus qualified, one must say that human participation is indeed "necessary" for God to glorify himself. When human beings receive the emanation of divine fullness and remanate it back to God in faith, God's glory becomes *more perfect*, if there can be such an expression. Since creaturely holiness is nothing but what has emanated from himself, God's joy in receiving the remanation is "rather a rejoicing in his own acts," and therefore "dependent on nothing besides his own act." Nevertheless, "God has *the more delight and pleasure* for the holiness and happiness of his creatures," for now his glory is repeated in time.[90] By converting, justifying, and sanctifying, God glorifies his creatures, taking delight in their holiness; and this glorification of his creatures is integral to further glorification of God himself. It is in this sense, Edwards believes, that the church is called in Scripture "the fullness of Christ" (Eph. 1:23). The church adds "fullness" to Christ's glory, "as though he were not in his most complete and glorious state without it."[91] Christ's glory is already perfect within the immanent Trinity from all eternity, hence Edwards's remark "as though" in the quotation. But in the second phase of God's self-glorification, that is, in the economy of salvation in time, the church *does* contribute to the fullness of Christ's glory. Human participation is necessary in this sense.

Finally, this dynamic flow of emanation and remanation corroborates the Augustinian scheme I employed to interpret the fundamental structure of Edwards's soteriology: God crowns his own gift. Edwards was

---

88. *End of Creation*, 448.

89. Lee, *Philosophical Theology*, 182–83, 197. See Lossky, *Mystical Theology*, chap. 4, for a comparable thought in Eastern theology.

90. *End of Creation*, 447.

91. Ibid., 439. See also "Miscellanies," no. 104, Yale MSS: "The church is said to be the completeness of Christ, as if Christ were not complete without the church." "Notes on the Bible," 528: "Until he had attained this [church], he was pleased not to look on himself as complete, but as wanting something." An interesting parallel is found in modern Roman Catholic understanding of the church as expressed in Pius XII's 1943 encyclical, *Mystici corporis* (DS 3805).

certainly aware of it when he made the following remark: "The refulgence shines upon and into the creature, and is reflected back to the luminary. The beams of glory come from God, and are something of God, and are refunded back again to their original. So that the whole is *of* God, and *in* God, and *to* God; and God is the beginning, middle and end in this affair."[92] This trinitarian formula is one of his long-cherished expressions, as it appears from the very early stage of his theological writings. Yes, God is everything: he is the beginning, middle, and end. But it does not mean that there is no human participation. The argument can be restated in the following way. On the one hand, God is in need of human participation in order to repeat and increase his glory. It all has to go through human knowing and loving, in their faith and practice. It has to take place *outside* the trinitarian Godhead, through intelligent creatures' active participation. This means that there has to be a reality of salvation in human nature that stands in relative independence. On the other hand, this creaturely reality of salvation does not endanger the prevenience and sovereignty of God, because it is nothing but God's antecedent gift being in exercise. God sees and takes delight in human holiness and goodness, but that does not make an argument for God's dependence on his creation. Edwards is very articulate on this point:

> Though he has real pleasure in the creature's holiness and happiness; yet this is not properly any pleasure which he receives from the creature. For these things are what he gives the creature. They are wholly and entirely from him. Therefore they are [sic] nothing that they give to God by which they add to him. His rejoicing therein is rather a rejoicing in his own acts, and his own glory expressed in those acts, than a joy derived from the creature.[93]

The passage affirms the existence of "the creature's holiness and happiness." God takes delight in seeing his creatures exercise their holiness and happiness, outside and apart from himself, because God's glory is indeed repeated and enlarged thereby. In that sense, God's self-glorification is dependent upon them. Yet it is no more than God "rejoicing in his own acts," since it is "what he gives the creature." God simply

---

92. *End of Creation*, 531 (emphasis original).
93. Ibid., 447.

enjoys the remanation of what has emanated from himself. God is eternally holy and happy already in himself, but nonetheless God invites human beings to be a part of this blissful circle. They are made genuine subjects who contribute to a further increase of God's glory in time. This is what it means to be "partakers of divine nature."

Our journey through Edwards's soteriology has thus come to culmination. Under the rubric of sanctification, "Christian practice" is characterized as the continuation of conversion, and "perseverance" as the continuation of justification, both of which coalesce in the grace of glorification. Through these "stages," the operation of grace makes a purposive progression, bringing to completion what is begun in regenerate humanity. The grand design of Edwards's soteriology, however, manifests itself not in the glorification of individual believers but in the ever-advancing and ever-increasing process of God's self-glorification, which is God's ultimate end in creation. Here, this study touches on a much larger theme of Edwards's theology. Based on the inner-trinitarian disposition to communicate his own fullness in se, God further communicates it ad extra, creating the universe as the occasion to exercise his own dispositions, and exercising them through the reality of regenerate humanity. Human exercise of holy disposition, therefore, ultimately proves to be part of the divine exercise of emanation and remanation. Within this paradigm of circular movement, human beings are given an indispensable role to further increase the glory of God in time and to make even more perfect what is already perfect within God. One might say that, with Edwards, human salvation is integral to God's glory. God's glory is greater than human salvation. In this emphasis, Edwards is distinctively Reformed.

7

Conclusion

I have examined Edwards's soteriology in four "stages" of the application of redemption. His soteriology has now emerged as an integrated whole that is internally consistent and rich in implication.

Edwards's soteriology is first of all consistent internally as a system that envisages the whole economy of salvation under a unified perspective. Throughout the four stages, the abiding ontological reality of the new creation is consistently maintained in the form of a new disposition. In particular, his pronouncements on justification have hitherto been either quietly neglected or regarded as anomalous in his theology, but they can now be viewed as constituting an integral part of his soteriology. Justification in Edwards's theology, far from "occupying a precarious place," is an indispensable phase of the process of salvation in which God crowns his own gift. God rewards his antecedent giving of faith with a further communication of his own goodness. With Edwards, not only justification but all the phases of individual salvation are conceived of organically as an unceasing and ever-increasing process of God's self-communication and human participation in it. They are not merely stacked one on top of another without an overall scheme. Conversion provides the fundamental infrastructure of the renewal in the form of a new disposition. This new disposition functions in justification as the ontological ground of the forensic imputation. The same disposition continues to operate in sanctification, resulting in Christian practice and perseverance. Finally, in glorification, these phases will be brought to completion in God's self-glorification, fulfilling his ultimate end in creation. It is a purposive progression from one degree of divine communication to another, each time with more participation in God's own nature. Salvation for Edwards means becoming "partakers of the divine nature" in increasing degrees.

Edwards's soteriology also shows a remarkable conformity with his general ontology. There is a structural correspondence between the order of nature and the order of grace in his thought. My contention is that the fundamental axiom linking these two realms is the dispositional view of reality. It is the key to understanding not only the being of corporeal entities but also of spiritual reality. The axiom by which he affirmed the relative permanence of the material world in ontology is also applicable to his soteriology, giving relative permanence to the reality of salvation in human nature. From the early stage of his theological development, Edwards was convinced that it is "laws that constitute all permanent being in created things, *both corporeal and spiritual.*"[1] The ultimate objective of his theology, he once wrote, is "to shew how all arts and sciences, the more they are perfected, the more they issue in divinity, and coincide with it, and appear to be as parts of it."[2] It was this conviction that also sustained his youthful interest in the new sciences of Locke and Newton. In view of these remarks, it is hardly surprising to see such a consistency in his overall paradigm of ontology and soteriology.

In neither realm, however, did Edwards compromise God's sovereign prevenience in favor of the reality of creation and re-creation. God is sovereign in establishing, upholding, and exerting the laws, and the reality of creation and new creation is totally dependent on God's activity. Yet this does not demolish the relative independence and

---

1. "The Mind," no. 36 (*WY*, 6:391).
2. "Outline of 'A Rational Account,' " *WY*, 6:397. See also Anderson's Introduction, 27, 50.

integrity of creaturely reality. It can even be argued, as I did in Chapter 6, that such independence and integrity of creation and new creation is integral to God's design, and in a sense "necessary" for God to fulfill his ultimate purpose.

Also highlighted in the course of my analysis was the wide relevance of his theology. Edwards's soteriology is not only "Puritan" or "Reformed," but profoundly ecumenical as well by implication. This study moves beyond Edwards scholarship per se to a broader context of the Protestant reformulation of soteriology. There still may be points of greater divergence—such as Mariology and Papal authority—between Protestant and Roman Catholic theologies today, yet as far as soteriology is concerned, our age is now witnessing a greater potential for mutual understanding and appreciation. Our interpretation of Edwards cannot remain uninfluenced by this auspicious climate. To be sure, Edwards himself may not have anticipated such a burgeoning of ecumenical dialogues. But his theology makes it acutely evident that being Protestant does not prevent one from being "catholic" in the Apostolic sense of the word. The suspicions hitherto voiced concerning Edwards's affinity with Roman Catholic soteriology serve only to illuminate a possible convergence that both traditions can appreciate. Edwards's theology, one might say, helps Protestants rediscover and reclaim the original ecumenicity that Reformation theology possessed, but which remained unavailing up until recently. The theology of Northampton in reality is just as ecumenical as that of Wittenberg or Geneva was in intention. The ontological transformation effected by infused grace, in particular, is no longer to be viewed as an exclusive *proprium* of Roman Catholic soteriology.

In support of such a reformulation of Protestant soteriology, I quote from two representative Roman Catholic theologians who seem to corroborate the direction in which Edwards urges us to move. The first is Hans Küng, whose comparative study on justification I referred to in Chapter 5. His question throughout the study was: What does the "bestowal of grace upon man" mean? And his answer is: "It means that God opens Himself and imparts Himself, and that He thereby allows man to have a share in His divine life. . . . God does this through His own indwelling, but in such a way that in the sphere of created being something actually happens and becomes reality."[3] God dwells in

3. Küng, *Justification*, 201.

humanity in such a way that "something actually happens and becomes reality," which is called in Catholic tradition "created grace." Küng does not stop there, however. He further states that this created grace should not take the "principal position," which is due only to uncreated grace, the Holy Spirit. The affirmation of created grace does not deny the presence of uncreated grace. Rather, he argues, created grace can be operative only by the power of uncreated grace.

Based on this understanding of the relationship of created and uncreated grace, Küng dismisses as "unfounded" Barth's fear that "God's grace might become, perniciously, *my* grace" in Catholic theology. Grace, in Roman understanding as well, must be given "each day as something completely new."[4] But, turning to the Protestant side, Küng also points out that Protestant theology (including Barth himself) has also known and affirmed the reality of created grace under different names. Küng's suggestion is therefore twofold. First, Protestant theology should be more open to recognizing the reality of created grace as it is expressed in the New Testament with such words as *charisma*, *doron*, and *dorema* (gifts).[5] Second, however, this does not mean that it should violate or sacrifice the vital doctrine of Protestant faith: from the very beginning of its history, Protestant theology has also known and implicitly affirmed the gift of created grace. It simply means to retrieve and deepen what Reformation theology originally had.

Karl Rahner is another contemporary theologian who seeks to restore a balanced relationship between created and uncreated grace. In reviewing the Reformation formula of justification, *simul iustus et peccator* (justified and sinner at the same time), Rahner finds the Catholic rejection of the formula partly legitimate and partly unadvisable. It is legitimate and necessary to reject it in the Catholic perspective, because "salvation-history is a really genuine history," not only in "the order of objective salvation" but also as "the individual history of salvation."[6] To affirm the reality of the individual history of salvation, in Rahner's view, means to affirm the fact that "something happens and takes place here which is now but was not before." There is in this affirmation a decisive

---

4. Ibid., 205.
5. Ibid., 204.
6. Karl Rahner, "Justified and Sinner at the Same Time," *Theological Investigations*, trans. Karl-H. and Boniface Kruger (Baltimore: Helicon Press, 1969), 6:222–23. By "the individual history of salvation," Rahner implies what I have called by the Reformed-Puritan term, "the application of redemption."

moment of transition from the old to new creation. The Reformation formula *simul iustus et peccator* does not do full justice to this transition to the new creation. The justified are not suspended in the dialectic of sinfulness and holiness, for salvation is "not merely an ideological fiction" described with "as if." God's act of justification "transfigures and divinises" the justified to the deepest roots of their being; they have "really crossed the boundary."[7]

At the same time, however, Rahner thinks that Catholic theology can and must say "yes" to the same Reformation formula, insofar as it teaches that this justice is not "a purely static possession or static quality in man."[8] Such a static understanding of created grace, in Rahner's judgment, is an unfortunate result of the Tridentine reaction against what seemed to them Protestant "extrinsicism," and therefore must be corrected today by "a greater and profounder idea of 'uncreated grace.'"[9] The Reformation formula of *simul* is a proper expression of the importance of this uncreated grace. "The grace of justification must always be accepted and exercised anew again, since basically it is always given anew again by God."[10] In that sense, the Reformation formula can be taken as decisively important in the Catholic perspective as well. Rahner's effort to restore the integral relationship of uncreated and created grace is fundamentally consonant with the biblical testimony of God's transforming presence in humanity.[11]

The import of these arguments should be clear to the reader. In Edwards's soteriology there are elements that say both "yes" and "no"

---

7. Ibid., 221, 222, 223. Strehle's criticism of the point has been mentioned. For him, the Reformed doctrine of justification means "an external and fictious predication," "a divine fantasy" and "a divine fabrication," with no ontological reality (*Calvinism, Federalism, and Scholasticism*, 316, 317). See Chapter 5 for my argument.

8. Rahner, "Justified and Sinner," 228.

9. Karl Rahner, "Nature and Grace," *Theological Investigations*, trans., Kevin Smyth (Baltimore: Helicon Press, 1966), 4:168, 172–73.

10. Rahner, "Justified and Sinner," 228. See also Scharlemann, *Thomas Aquinas and John Gerhard*, 214; Yarnold, *Second Grace*, 53, for Thomas Aquinas on the same issue. In this respect, there is some room to reconsider Lee's contrasting remark in *Philosophical Theology*, 143 n. 61. Thomas did not deny the presence of uncreated grace, just as Edwards did not deny the presence of created grace.

11. See also Avery Dulles, "Justification in Contemporary Catholic Theology," in *Justification by Faith: Lutherans and Catholics in Dialogue*, 7:259, who finds in the category of uncreated grace "a path toward rapprochement not only with Orthodox but also with Protestant Christians." George Lindbeck is of the same opinion in "A Question of Compatibility: A Lutheran Reflects on Trent," in *Justification by Faith*, 240.

to the Reformation formula of *simul iustus et peccator*. When grace is infused, something new happens in the person; it transforms the person in a decisive way. Grace does not stay merely extrinsic to the human subject. The redeemed person has, as Edwards maintained, not only the "objective good" but also the "inherent good." Salvation is not just a status into which they are promised entry, but is already a tangible and objective reality *hic et nunc*—a reality of "being made excellent by a communication of God's excellency," and "being made holy by participating in God's own holiness."[12] And yet, this does not mean that divine sovereignty and prevenience is compromised, since, precisely as the result of God's constant communication, this reality of new creation is not a creaturely property independent of divine communication. It must always be given anew immediately from above, and in that sense never becomes encapsulated in human static possession. The gift of new life never ceases to be the giver of the gift.

I have explained these dynamics in terms of Edwards's concept of disposition. Infused grace brings forth a new disposition. As a law established and upheld by God, this new disposition certainly comes into exercise on specified occasions, and this certainty gives it a measure of abiding and enduring character. At the same time, however, this new disposition requires God's constant and direct power of causation, for it is the prime and indispensable condition for actualizing itself. *Gratia creata*, in other words, cannot operate without *gratia increata*, the Holy Spirit, who works in and through it. Edwards's concept of the new disposition thus preserves the truth of both Protestant and Catholic concerns in one form.

Furthermore, salvation as understood in this dispositional view can be extended even beyond the boundary of Judeo-Christian tradition. There is no hard division between Christians and non-Christians in terms of the grounds on which they are saved. Those who do possess the disposition are all saved on account of that disposition, regardless of their explicit or conscious religious affiliation, or lack thereof. This is a paradigm of soteriology that is radically inclusive and yet theologically responsible. The Christian message will bear the task of offering an occasion for their God-given disposition to bloom in full faith. It is an invitation for self-realization.

---

12. "God Glorified in Man's Dependence," 174.

Grace is really *in-fused;* it comes *into* the innermost of our being, in such a way that it is internally *fused* with human nature, transforming it from within and providing a renewed power to live and act in Christian freedom. At the same time, this internal renewal is not something that can be maintained by human endeavor. It is entirely dependent, moment by moment, on the power of God that works through it. Indeed, as Bonaventure once aptly put, *"habere est haberi":* we do not "possess" grace without being "possessed" by it.

Bibliography

Primary Sources

Jonathan Edwards

Collected Works

WD: *The Works of President Edwards in Ten Volumes.* Dwight Edition. New York: S. Converse, 1829–30.
  1. *Life of President Edwards* (by Sereno E. Dwight)
  5. "Justification by Faith alone"
  7. Sermons
  8. Sermons; "Heaven" in "Miscellaneous Observations"
  9. "Notes on the Bible"

WW: *The Works of President Edwards in Four Volumes.* Reprint of the Worcester Edition (1808–1809). New York: Jonathan Levitt and John F. Trow, 1843.
  1. *An Humble Inquiry into the Rules of the Word of God; Concerning the Qualifications Requisite to a Complete Standing and Full Communion in the Visible Christian Church;* "Concerning the Necessity and Reasonableness of the Christian Doctrine of Satisfaction for sin"
  2. "Concerning the Divine Decrees in General and Election in Particular"; "Concerning Efficacious Grace"; "Observations Concerning Faith"
  3. "Concerning the Perseverance of Saints"
  4. Sermons

WY: *The Works of Jonathan Edwards.* 12 vols. New Haven: Yale University Press, 1957– .
  1. *Freedom of the Will,* ed. Paul Ramsey, 1957.
  2. *Religious Affections,* ed. John E. Smith, 1959.
  3. *Original Sin,* ed. Clyde A. Holbrook, 1970.
  4. *The Great Awakening,* ed. C. C. Goen, 1972.
  5. *Apocalyptic Writings,* ed. Stephen J. Stein, 1977.
  6. *Scientific and Philosophical Writings,* ed. Wallace E. Anderson, 1980.

8. *Ethical Writings*, ed. Paul Ramsey, 1989.
9. *A History of the Work of Redemption*, ed. John F. Wilson, 1989.

Individually Published Writings

The Philosophy of Jonathan Edwards from his Private Notebooks, ed. Harvey G. Townsend. Westport, Conn.: Greenwood Press, 1955.
"Six Letters of Jonathan Edwards to Joseph Bellamy," ed. Stanley T. Williams. *New England Quarterly* 1 (1928): 226–42.
Treatise on Grace and Other Posthumously Published Writings, ed. Paul Helm. Greenwood, S.C.: The Attic Press, 1971.

Unpublished Manuscripts

"Miscellanies." Beinecke Library, Yale University.

Others

Ames, William. *Conscience with the Power and Cases Thereof*. N.p., 1639; reprint, in "The English Experience: Its Record in Early Printed Books Published in Facsimile," no. 708. Amsterdam: Theatrum Orbis Terrarum, 1975.
———. *The Marrow of Theology*, ed. and trans. John Dykstra Eusden. Boston: Pilgrim Press, 1968; reprint, Durham, N.C.: Labyrinth Press, 1983.
Aquinas, Thomas. *Commentary on Saint Paul's Epistle to the Galatians*, trans. F. R. Larcher. Albany, N.Y.: Magi Books, 1966.
———. *Summa Contra Gentiles*, trans. Anton C. Pegis et al. Garden City, N.Y.: Hanover House, 1955–1956; reprint, Notre Dame: University of Notre Dame Press, 1975.
———. *Summa Theologica*, trans. Fathers of the English Dominican Province. New York: Benzinger Brothers, 1911; reprint, Westminster, Md.: Christian Classics, 1981.
Aristotle. *Nicomachean Ethics*. In *The Basic Works of Aristotle*, ed. Richard McKeon. New York: Random House, 1941.
Bellarmine, Robert. *Opera Omnia*, vol. 4. Neapolis, 1856.
Berkeley, George. *A Treatise Concerning Principles of Human Knowledge*. Vol. 2 of *The Works of George Berkeley*. Ed. T. E. Jessop. Dublin, 1710; reprint, London: Thomas Nelson and Sons, 1949.
Breck, Robert, Joseph Ashley, Timothy Woodbridge, and Chester Williams. *A Letter to the Reverend Mr. Hobby in Answer to his Vindication of the Protest, against the Result of an Ecclesiastical Council met at Northampton, &c.* Boston, 1751.
Calvin, John. "Acts of the Council of Trent, with the Antidote." In *Tracts and Treatises in Defense of the Reformed Faith*, vol. 3, ed. Thomas F.

Torrance, trans. Henry Beveridge. Edinburgh: Calvin Translation Society, 1851; reprint, Grand Rapids, Mich.: Wm. B. Eerdmans, 1958.

———. *The Epistle of Paul the Apostle to the Galatians, Ephesians, Philippians and Colossians*, ed. David W. Torrance and Thomas F. Torrance. Edinburgh: Oliver and Boyd, 1965.

———. *The Epistles of Paul The Apostle to the Romans and to the Thessalonians*, ed. David W. Torrance and Thomas F. Torrance, trans. Ross Mackenzie. Edinburgh: Oliver and Boyd, 1960; reprint, Grand Rapids, Mich.: Wm. B. Eerdmans, 1990.

———. *Institutes of the Christian Religion*, ed. John T. McNeill, trans. Ford Lewis Battles. Library of Christian Classics, vols. 20–21. Philadelphia: Westminster Press, 1960.

———. *Institution de la Religion Chrétienne*, vol. 3, ed. Société Calviniste de France. Geneva: Labor et Fides, 1956.

———. *Iohannis Calvini Commentarius in Epistolam Pauli ad Romanos*, ed. T. H. L. Parker. Studies in the History of Christian Thought, vol. 22, ed. Heiko A. Oberman et al. Leiden: E. J. Brill, 1981.

———. *A Reformation Debate: John Calvin and Jacopo Sadoleto*, ed. John C. Olin. New York: Harper & Row, 1966; reprint, Grand Rapids, Mich.: Baker Book House, 1976.

Flavel, John. *The Method of Grace in the Holy Spirits Applying to the Souls of Men, the Eternal Redemption Contrived by the Father and Accomplished by the Son*. London, 1699; reprint, London, 1820.

Hooker, Thomas. *The Application of Redemption By the Effectual Work of the Word, and Spirit of Christ, for the bringing home of lost Sinners to God: The Ninth and Tenth Books*. London, 1657.

Hume, David. *A Treatise of Human Nature*. London, 1739–40; reprint, London: Scientia Verlag Aalen, 1964.

Kant, Immanuel. *Religion Within the Limits of Reason Alone*, trans. Theodore M. Greene and Hoyt H. Hudson. New York: Harper & Row, 1960.

Lombard, Peter. *Sententiae, IV Libris Distinctae*. Collegii S. Bonaventurae ad Clarus Aquas, ed. Rome: Grottaferrata, 1971.

Luther, Martin. "Lectures on Galatians, Chapters Five and Six." In *Luther's Works: American Edition*, vol. 27, ed. Jaroslav Pelikan and Walter A. Hansen. St. Louis, Mo.: Concordia Publishing House, 1964.

———. "Theses Concerning Faith and Law." In *Luther's Works: American Edition*, vol. 34, ed. Jaroslav Pelikan, Helmut T. Lehmann, and Lewis W. Spitz. Philadelphia: Concordia Publishing House and Muhlenberg Press, 1960.

Mastricht, Peter van. *Theoretico-Practica Theologia*. Reprint. Amsterdam, 1715.

———. *A Treatise on Regeneration: extracted from his system of divinity called theologia theoretico-practica and faithfully translated into English*. New Haven, n.d. [1769].

Ridgeley, Thomas. *A Body of Divinity: Wherein the Doctrines of the Christian Religion are Explained and Defended*. London, 1731; reprint, New York, 1855.

Shepard, Thomas. *The Parable of the Ten Virgins Opened & Applied; Being the Substances of divers Sermons on Matth. 25:1–13.* Reprint edition, Jonathan Mitchell and Thomas Shepard [Thomas's son], n.p., 1695.

———. *The Sound Believer: or a Treatise on Evangelical Conversion, Discovering the Work of God's Spirit, in Reconciling a Sinner to God.* London, 1670; reprint, Aberdeen, 1849.

Skelton, Philip. *Deism Revealed; or The Attack on Christianity Candidly Reviewed in its Real Merits, as They Stand in the Celebrated Writings of Lord Herbert, Lord Shaftesbury, Hobbes, Toland, Tindal, Collins, Mandeville, Dodwell, Woolston, Morgan, Chubb, and Others,* 2 vols., 2d ed. London, 1751.

Taylor, John. *The Scripture-Doctrine of Original Sin, Proposed to Free and Candid Examination.* London, 1738 or 1740.

Turretin, Francis. *Institutio Theologiae Elencticae.* Reprint. New York, 1847.

———. *Institutio Theologiae Elencticae,* trans. George Musgrave Giger. Unpublished manuscript. Speer Library, Princeton Theological Seminary.

Wigglesworth, Samuel, and Joseph Chipman. *Remarks on Some Points of Doctrine, Apprehended by many as Unsound, Propogated In Preaching and Conversation, and since Published, by the Reverend Mr. William Balch, pastor of the Second church in Bradford, Humbly Offered to the Consideration of the Ministers and Churches of New-England.* Boston, 1746.

Willard, Samuel. *The Compleat Body of Divinity in Two Hundred and Fifty Expository Lectures on the Assembly's Shorter Catechism.* Boston, 1726.

Williams, William, Isaac Chauncey, Jonathan Edwards, Stephen Williams, Samuel Hopkins, and Peter Reynolds. *A Narrative of the Proceedings of those Ministers of the County of Hampshire &c. That have disapproved of the late Measures taken in order to the Settlement of Mr. Robert Breck, in the Pastoral Office in the first Church in Springfield. With a Defence of their Conduct in that Affair.* Boston, 1736.

Witsius, Herman. *The Oeconomy of the Covenants Between God and Man: Comprehending a Complete Body of Divinity.* London, 1772.

Secondary Sources

Aldridge, Alfred Owen. *Jonathan Edwards.* New York: Washington Square Press, 1964.

Allen, Diogenes. *Christian Belief in a Postmodern World: The Full Wealth of Conviction.* Louisville, Ky.: Westminster/John Knox Press, 1989.

Anderson, H. George, T. Austin Murphy, and Joseph A. Burgess, eds. "Common Statement." In idem, *Justification by Faith: Lutherans and Catholics in Dialogue VII.* Minneapolis: Augsburg, 1985.

Barth, Karl. *Church Dogmatics,* 4.1, trans. G. W. Bromiley and T. F. Torrance. Edinburgh: T. & T. Clark, 1956.

Bavaud, Georges. "La doctrine de la justification d'après Calvin et le Concile de Trente: Une conciliation est-elle possible?" *Verbum Caro* 22 (1968): 83–92.
Berkhof, Louis. *The History of Christian Doctrines*. Grand Rapids, Mich.: Baker Book House, 1937.
———. *Systematic Theology*, 4th ed. Grand Rapids, Mich.: Wm. B. Eerdmans, 1949.
Boardman, George Nye. *A History of New England Theology*. New York: A. D. F. Randolph, 1899; reprint, New York: Garland, 1987.
Boler, John F. *Charles Peirce and Scholastic Realism: A Study of Peirce's Relation to John Duns Scotus*. Seattle: University of Washington Press, 1963.
Bourke, Vernon J. "The Role of Habitus in the Thomist Metaphysics of Potency and Act." In *Essays in Thomism*, ed. Robert E. Brennan. New York: Sheed & Ward, 1942.
———. *Will in Western Thought: An Historico-Critical Survey*. New York: Sheed & Ward, 1964.
Brodrick, James, S.J. *The Life and Work of Blessed Robert Francis Cardinal Bellarmine*. 2 vols. London: Burns Oates and Washbourne, 1928.
———. *Robert Bellarmine: Saint and Scholar*. Westminster, Md.: Newman Press, 1961.
Casteel, Theodore W. "Calvin and Trent: Calvin's Reaction to the Council of Trent in the Context of his Conciliar Thought." *Harvard Theological Review* 63 (1970): 91–117.
Chemnitz, Martin. *Justification: The Chief Article of Christian Doctrine as Expounded in Loci theologici*, ed. Delpha Holleque Preus, trans. J. A. O. Preus. St. Louis: Concordia, 1985.
Cherry, Conrad. *Nature and Religious Imagination: From Edwards to Bushnell*. Philadelphia: Fortress Press, 1980.
———. *The Theology of Jonathan Edwards: A Reappraisal*. Gloucester, Mass.: Peter Smith, 1974.
Coates, Thomas. "Calvin's Doctrine of Justification." *Concordia Theological Monthly* 34 (1963): 325–34.
Crabtree, Arthur B. *The Restored Relationship: A Study in Justification and Reconciliation*. London: Carey Kingsgate Press, 1963.
Delattre, Roland Andre. *Beauty and Sensibility in the Thought of Jonathan Edwards: An Essay in Aesthetics and Theological Ethics*. New Haven: Yale University Press, 1968.
Dowey, Edward A., Jr. *The Knowledge of God in Calvin's Theology*. New York: Columbia University Press, 1952.
Dulles, Avery. "Justification in Contemporary Catholic Theology." In *Justification by Faith: Lutherans and Catholics in Dialogue VII*, ed. H. George Anderson, T. Austin Murphy, and Joseph A. Burgess. Minneapolis: Augsburg, 1985.
Eells, Hastings. "The Origin of the Regensburg Book." *Princeton Theological Review* 26 (1928): 355–72.
Elwood, Douglas J. *The Philosophical Theology of Jonathan Edwards*. New York: Columbia University Press, 1960.

Erdt, Terrence. *Jonathan Edwards: Art and the Sense of the Heart*. Amherst: University of Massachusetts Press, 1980.
Fiering, Norman. *Jonathan Edwards's Moral Thought and Its British Context*. Chapel Hill: University of North Carolina Press, 1981.
———. "Solomon Stoddard's Library at Harvard," *Harvard Library Bulletin* 20 (1972): 262–69.
———. "Will and Intellect in the New England Mind." *William and Mary Quarterly*, 3d ser., 29 (1972): 515–58.
Foster, Frank Hugh. *A Genetic History of the New England Theology*. Chicago: University of Chicago Press, 1907; reprint, New York: Garland Publishing, 1987.
Hardie, W. F. R. *Aristotle's Ethical Theory*. London: Clarendon Press, 1968.
Hendry, George S. "The Glory of God and the Future of Men." *Reformed World* 34 (1976): 147–57.
Hesselink, John. *On Being Reformed: Distinctive Characteristics and Common Misunderstandings*. Ann Arbor, Mich.: Servant Books, 1983.
Hodge, Charles. *Systematic Theology*, 3 vols. Reprint edition. Grand Rapids, Mich.: Wm. B. Eerdmans, 1989.
Hoopes, James. "Calvinism and Consciousness from Edwards to Beecher." In *Jonathan Edwards and the American Experience*, 205–25, ed. Nathan O. Hatch and Harry S. Stout. New York: Oxford University Press, 1988.
———. Review of *The Philosophical Theology of Jonathan Edwards* by Sang Hyun Lee. *Journal of Religion* 70 (1990): 258.
Jamieson, John F. "Jonathan Edwards's Change of Position on Stoddardeanism." *Harvard Theological Review* 74 (1981): 79–99.
Jedin, Hubert. *A History of the Council of Trent*, 2 vols., trans. Dom Ernest Graf. London: Thomas Nelson and Sons, 1961.
Jensen, Robert. *America's Theologian: A Recommendation of Jonathan Edwards*. New York: Oxford University Press, 1988.
Kendall, R. T. *Calvin and English Calvinism to 1649*. New York: Oxford University Press, 1979.
Kolfhaus, W. *Christusgemeinschaft bei Johannes Calvin*. Beiträge zur Geschichte und Lehre der Reformierten Kirche, Dritter Band. Ansbach: Buchhandlungs des Erziehungsvereins Neukirchen Kr. Moers, 1939.
Kreck, Walter. "Zum römisch-katholischen Verständnis der Rechtfertigung." In *Grundfragen der Dogmatik*. Munich: Chr. Kaiser Verlag, 1970.
Küng, Hans. *Justification: The Doctrine of Karl Barth and a Catholic Reflection*, trans. Thomas Collins, Edmund E. Tolk, and David Granskou. New York: Thomas Nelson & Son, 1964; reprint, Philadelphia: Westminster Press, 1981.
———. *On Being a Christian*, trans. Edward Quinn. London: Collins, 1977.
———. *Theology for the Third Millennium: An Ecumenical View*, trans. Peter Heinegg. New York: Doubleday, 1988.
Lee, Sang Hyun. "Mental Activity and the Perception of Beauty in Jonathan Edwards." *Harvard Theological Review* 69 (1976): 369–96.
———. *The Philosophical Theology of Jonathan Edwards*. Princeton: Princeton University Press, 1988.

Lindbeck, George. "A Question of Compatibility: A Lutheran Reflection on Trent." In *Justification by Faith: Lutherans and Catholics in Dialogue VII*, 230–40, ed. H. George Anderson, T. Austin Murphy, and Joseph A. Burgess. Minneapolis: Augsburg, 1985.
Lossky, Vladimir. *The Mystical Theology of the Eastern Church*, trans. The Fellowship of St. Alban and St. Sergius. Cambridge: James Clarke & Co., 1957; reprint, Crestwood, N.Y.: St. Vladimir's Seminary Press, 1976.
MacKintosh, Robert. *Historic Theories of Atonement*. London: Hoder and Stoughton, 1920.
Maloney, George. *A Theology of "Uncreated Energies."* Milwaukee: Marquette University Press, 1978.
Martin, James P. *The Last Judgment in Protestant Theology from Orthodoxy to Ritschl.* Grand Rapids, Mich.: Wm. B. Eerdmans, 1963.
Matheson, Peter. *Cardinal Contarini at Regensburg*. New York: Oxford University Press, 1972.
McDonald, H. D. *The Atonement of the Death of Christ: In Faith, Revelation, and History.* Grand Rapids, Mich.: Baker Book House, 1985.
McGrath, Alister E. *Iustitia Dei: A History of the Christian Doctrine of Justification*, vol. 2: *From 1500 to the Present Day.* Cambridge: Cambridge University Press, 1986.
———. "Justification: Barth, Trent, and Küng." *Scottish Journal of Theology* 34 (1981): 517–29.
Migliore, Daniel L. *Faith Seeking Understanding: An Introduction to Christian Theology.* Grand Rapids, Mich.: Wm. B. Eerdmans, 1991.
Miller, Perry. *Jonathan Edwards.* New York: W. Sloane Associates, 1949; reprint, Amherst: University of Massachusetts Press, 1981.
———. *The New England Mind: The Seventeenth Century.* Cambridge: Belknap Press of Harvard University Press, 1939.
———. "'Preparation for Salvation' in Seventeenth-century New England." *Journal of the History of Ideas* 4 (1943): 253–86.
Morgan, Edmund S. *Visible Saints: The History of a Puritan Idea.* New York: New York University Press, 1963.
Müller, Hanfried. *Evangelische Dogmatik im Überblick.* Berlin: Evangelische Verlagsanstalt, 1978.
Murray, John. "The Imputation of Adam's Sin." *Westminster Theological Journal* 19 (1956): 141–69.
Newbigin, Leslie. *The Gospel in a Pluralist Society.* Geneva: World Council of Churches; Grand Rapids, Mich.: Wm. B. Eerdmans, 1989.
Niesel, Wilhelm. "Calvin wider Osianders Rechtfertigungslehre." *Zeitschrift für Kirchengeschichte* 46 (1928): 410–30.
Oberman, Heiko A. *The Harvest of Medieval Theology: Gabriel Biel and Late Medieval Nominalism.* Cambridge: Harvard University Press, 1963; reprint, Durham, N.C.: Labyrinth Press, 1983.
Olin, John C., ed. *A Reformation Debate: John Calvin and Jacopo Sadoleto.* New York: Harper & Row, 1966; reprint, Grand Rapids, Mich.: Baker Book House, 1976.

Ott, Ludwig. *Fundamentals of Catholic Dogma*, ed. James Canon Bastible, trans. Patrick Lynch. St. Louis, Mo.: B. Herder, 1954.
Parker, T. H. L. *The Doctrine of the Knowledge of God: A Study in the Theology of John Calvin.* Edinburgh: Oliver and Boyd, 1952.
Pelikan, Jaroslav. *Christian Doctrine and Modern Culture (since 1700)*, vol. 5 of *The Christian Tradition: A History of the Development of Doctrine.* Chicago: University of Chicago Press, 1989.
Pettit, Norman. *The Heart Prepared: Grace and Conversion in Puritan Spiritual Life.* New Haven: Yale University Press, 1966.
Pinnock, Clark H. *A Wideness in God's Mercy: The Finality of Jesus Christ in a World of Religions.* Grand Rapids, Mich.: Zondervan, 1992.
Pöhlmann, Horst Georg. *Abriss der Dogmatik*, 3 Aufl. Gütersloh: Gütersloher Verlagshaus Gerd Mohn, 1980.
―――. *Rechtfertigung: Die genenwärtige kontroverstheologische Problematik der Rechtfertigungslehre zwischen der evangelish-lutherischen und der römisch-katholischen Kirche.* Gütersloh: Gütersloher Verlagshaus Gerd Mohn, 1971.
Rahner, Karl. "Justified and Sinner at the Same Time." In idem, *Theological Investigations*, vol. 6, trans. Karl-H. and Boniface Kruger. Baltimore: Helicon Press, 1969.
―――. "Nature and Grace." In idem, *Theological Investigations*, vol. 4, trans. Kevin Smyth. Baltimore: Helicon Press, 1966.
―――. "Questions of Controversial Theology on Justification." In idem, *Theological Investigations*, vol. 4, trans. Kevin Smyth, Baltimore: Helicon Press, 1966.
Reuter, Karl. *William Ames*, trans. Douglas Horton. Cambridge: Harvard Divinity School Library, 1965.
Richardson, Herbert W. "The Glory of God in the Theology of Jonathan Edwards: A Study in the Doctrine of the Trinity." Ph.D. diss., Harvard University, 1962.
Rolston, Holmes. *John Calvin Versus the Westminster Confession.* Atlanta: John Knox Press, 1977.
Rudisill, Dorus Paul. *The Doctrine of the Atonement in Jonathan Edwards and His Successors.* New York: Poseidon Books, 1971.
Sanders, John. *No Other Name: An Investigation into the Destiny of the Unevangelized.* Grand Rapids, Mich.: Wm. B. Eerdmans, 1992.
Schafer, Thomas A. "Jonathan Edwards and Justification by Faith." *Church History* 20 (1951): 55–67.
―――. "Jonathan Edwards' Conception of the Church." *Church History* 24 (1955): 51–66.
―――. "The Role of Jonathan Edwards in American Religious History." *Encounter* 30 (1969): 212–22.
Scharlemann, Robert P. *Thomas Aquinas and John Gerhard.* New Haven: Yale University Press, 1964.

Scheick, William, ed. *Critical Essays on Jonathan Edwards*. Boston: G. K. Hall, 1980.
Seeberg, Reinhold. *Text-Book of the History of Doctrines*, trans. Charles E. Hay. Vol. 2: *History of Doctrines in the Ancient Church*. Reprint, Grand Rapids, Mich.: Baker Book House, 1977.
Shedd, William G. T. *Dogmatic Theology*, 2 vols. New York: Charles Scribner's Sons, 1888.
Simonson, Harold P. *Jonathan Edwards: Theologian of the Heart*. Grand Rapids, Mich.: Wm. B. Eerdmans, 1974.
Smith, John E. "Jonathan Edwards: Piety and Practice in the American Character." *Journal of Religion* 54 (1974): 166–80.
Smith, Shelton. *Changing Conceptions of Original Sin: A Study in American Theology Since 1750*. New York: Charles Scribner's Sons, 1955.
Sprunger, Keith L. *The Learned Doctor William Ames: Dutch Background of English and American Puritanism*. Chicago: University of Illinois Press, 1972.
Strehle, Stephen. *Calvinism, Federalism, and Scholasticism: A Study of the Reformed Doctrine of Covenant*. Basler und Berner Studien zur historischen und systematischen Theologie, Band 58. Bern: Peter Lang, 1988.
Tavard, George H. *Justification: An Ecumenical Study*. New York: Paulist Press, 1983.
Tillich, Paul. *Systematic Theology*, vols. 1 and 3. Chicago: University of Chicago Press, 1951, 1963.
Tomas, Vincent. "The Modernity of Jonathan Edwards." *New England Quarterly* 25 (1952): 60–84.
Toon, Peter. *Justification and Sanctification*. Westchester, Ill.: Crossway, 1983.
Vos, Arvin. *Aquinas, Calvin, and Contemporary Protestant Thought: A Critique of Protestant Views on the Thought of Thomas Aquinas*. Grand Rapids, Mich.: Wm. B. Eerdmans, 1985.
Wendel, François. *Calvin: The Origins and Development of His Religious Thought*, trans. Philip Mairet. New York: Harper & Row, 1963.
Whittemore, Robert C. *The Transformation of the New England Theology*. American University Studies, vol. 23, series 7: Theology and Religion. New York: Peter Lang, 1987.
Willis, E. David. *Calvin's Catholic Christology: The Function of the So-called Extra Calvinisticum in Calvin's Theology*, Studies in Medieval and Reformation Thought, vol. 2, ed. Heiko A. Oberman et al. Leiden: E. J. Brill, 1966.
———. "Notes on A. Ganoczy's *Calvin, Théologien de l'Église et du Ministère*." *Bibliothèque d'Humanisme et Renaissance* 30 (1968): 185–98.
Winslow, Ola Elizabeth. *Jonathan Edwards, 1703–1758: A Bibliography*. New York: Macmillan, 1940.
Yarnold, Edward. *The Second Gift: A Study of Grace*. Slough, Engl.: St. Paul Publications, 1974.

Reference Sources

Die Bekenntnisschriften der evangelisch-lutherischen Kirche: Herausgegeben im Gedenkjahr der Augsburgischen Konfession 1930, 5 Aufl. Göttingen: Vandenhoeck & Ruprecht, 1963.

The Canons and Decrees of the Council of Trent, trans. H. J. Schroeder. Rockford, Ill.: Tan Books, 1978.

The Creeds of Christendom: With a History and Critical Notes, 3 vols., ed. Philip Schaff. New York: Harper & Row, 1931; reprint, Grand Rapids, Mich.: Baker Book House, 1985.

The Doctrinal Theology of the Evangelical Lutheran Church, 3d ed., ed. Heinrich Schmid, trans. Charles A. Hay and Henry E. Jacobs. Minneapolis: Augsburg, 1961.

The Encyclopedia of Philosophy, ed. Paul Edwards. New York: Macmillan, 1967.

New Catholic Encyclopedia, ed. Editorial Staff at the Catholic University of America. New York: McGraw-Hill, 1967.

The Oxford Dictionary of the Christian Church, 2d ed., ed. F. L. Cross and E. A. Livingstone. New York: Oxford University Press, 1974.

The Oxford English Dictionary, 2d ed., ed. J. A. Simpson and E. S. C. Weiner. New York: Oxford University Press, 1989.

Reformed Dogmatics: Set Out and Illustrated from the Sources, ed. Heinrich Heppe and Ernst Bizer, trans. G. T. Thomson. Reprint. Grand Rapids, Mich.: Baker Book House, 1978.

Index

acceptatio or *acceptilatio*, 76
Ames, William, 16–18, 61–62, 87,
    142n.40, 143
Anselm, 15, 16, 63
application of redemption, 10, 72, 131,
    145, 157, 160n.6
Aquinas, Thomas, 5, 26n.60, 42, 43, 51,
    53n.58, 54, 63, 112, 113, 118, 119–20,
    125, 161n.10
  and Edwards, 2, 10, 43, 47, 150n.71
Aristotle, Aristotelian, 16n.16, 40, 120
Arminianism, 9, 19–20, 26, 74–78, 79–81,
    91, 95
Arminius, Jacob, 20
Augustine, Augustinian, 2, 15, 16, 83, 97,
    154

Barth, Karl, 83n.45, 104, 160
Bavaud, Georges, 121
beauty, perception of, 23, 41, 127
Belgic Confession, 96
Bellarmine, Robert, 51
Berkeley, George, 57, 58
Berkhof, Louis, 79n.31, 94n.94
Bernard of Clairvaux, 63
Boardman, George, 8, 114
Boler, John, 56n.73
Bonaventure, 163
Bourke, Vernon, 14n.4, 45
Breck, Robert, 75
Brunner, Emil, vii
Bucer, Martin, 108
Bullinger, Heinrich, 108

calling, 18–19, 31, 52
Calvin, John
  on *duplex gratia*, 108, 110, 115

  and Edwards, 2, 9–10, 13–16, 16n.16,
    21, 25, 41, 105
  on faith, 88, 91, 124–26, 128
  on illumination, 14–16, 16n.16
  on infusion, 14n.3, 42, 106
  on justification, 107n.11, 110–11, 112,
    117
  and Thomas, 110–11, 111n.32, 114,
    124–26
  on *unio cum Christo*, 87, 110
  on works, 112, 116n.56
Catholic concern, 7–8, 61, 162
Chambers, Ephraim, 50n.47
Cherry, Conrad, 8, 46, 49, 54n.62,
    56n.72, 93n.87, 94n.91, 115, 124,
    134n.13
church, adds fullness to Christ, 154
Coates, Thomas, 110n.28
communication, 5, 6, 29–30, 47, 49, 98–
    100, 148, 150–56, 157–58, 162
consent, 82, 90
Contarini, Gasparo, 107n.11
conversion
  as change of disposition, 22–25, 39–40
  effectuated by infusion, 13n.1, 38–39
  habitual and actual, 53
covenant, federal theology, 56, 76, 77–78,
    84, 91, 109, 139
Crabtree, Arthur, 122

De auxiliis controversy, 18–19, 51
deification or divinization (*theosis*), 5,
    153, 161
disposition, habit
  as active tendency, 34–35, 57, 61, 134,
    136, 141, 146–47
  Aristotle's concept of, 40, 61

and faith, 115, 122
in God's nature, 98–101, 137, 148, 149, 154
as inherent quality, 46, 49–50, 52, 94, 137
as laws of being, 6–7, 54–59, 158–59
as principle of perception, 23–24
as virtual reality, 33, 57–59, 61–62, 63, 136–37, 141, 144–45
unexercised, 30–35, 34n.91, 66
Dort, Synod of, 13n.2, 53n.59, 96, 106
Dowey, Edward, 15
Dulles, Avery, 161n.11
Dwight, Sereno (*Life of President Edwards*), 26–27, 79n.31, 82

economy, of grace and of glory, 145
ecumenical dialogue, 2, 10, 104, 121, 129–30, 159
Edwards, Jonathan, Jr., 79n.31, 82n.43
Edwards, Tryon, 8, 105
Elwood, Douglas, 49n.45
emanation and remanation, 98, 100–101, 150, 152–54
enthusiasm, 25, 49
Erdt, Terrence, 14–15
eschatology, individual and general, 142, 147
Eusden, John, 17n.19

faculty psychology, 14, 16–18, 24
faith
  active role, 88–90
  antecedent gift, 97–98
  condition of justification, 73, 91, 123, 128, 138–41
  formed by love, 121–30
  historical and saving, 126–27
  instrumental cause of justification, 88
  as remanation, 153–54
  temporary and persevering, 138
federal theology. *See* covenant
Fiering, Norman, 14n.4, 43n.24, 56n.72, 135–36
fitness, natural and moral, 91, 94–95
Flavel, John, 38n.2, 72n.3
Foster, Frank, 82n.42

Gerhard Johann, 126–27
glorification, 133, 137, 142–56
Goen, C. G., 75

good, objective and inherent, 5, 133, 162
grace
  created and uncreated, 8, 41–47, 61, 124, 160, 161, 162
  intermediary habit, 42, 46
  operating and cooperating, 112, 119
  perfected by practice, 134–35
  as principle of action, 6, 29, 35, 38, 44–47, 48, 52–54, 134
  sanctifying, 118
Grotius, Hugo, 79

habit. *See* disposition
Hampshire Association of Ministers, 75
heaven, 45, 146–47
Heidelberg Catechism, 80n.33
Hendry, George, 149–50
Hesselink, John, 112
Hodge, Charles, 75–76, 94n.94
Holbrook, Clyde, 20n.29
Hollaz, David, 109
Holy Spirit
  assists the unregenerate, 28–30, 41
  indwelling, 6, 28–30, 38, 41–42, 44, 49, 115–16, 124, 132, 159
  as uncreated grace. *See* grace, created and uncreated
  and the Word, 24–25
Hoopes, James, 59n.82
Hume, David, 57

illumination, 13–16, 23–24
imputation
  Adamic, 81–84
  basis of justification, 13n.1, 105–14
  Christological, 76, 77, 84–87, 90
  mediate, 82n.39
  of perseverance, 139–40
inclusivism, 65–68
infusion
  Arminian view, 19–20, 26, 47
  Catholic view, 18–19, 119, 121
  Edwards's concept of, 13–16, 20–22, 24, 28–30
  as indwelling, 28–30, 38
  Luther's concept of, 110
  Mastricht's concept of, 18–19
  and preparation, 26–28
  Protestant view, 8, 19n.27, 105, 106, 109n.21
  Turretin's concept of, 18, 52–54

Index

intellectualism and voluntarism, 14, 16–17n.17
"interest," 37–38, 86

Jenson, Robert, 1, 96n.101
justification
  antecedent acceptance, 91–93
  Arminian, 74–78, 79–80
  as commendation or influence, 86–87
  Edwards's M.A. thesis on, 71n.2
  in Edwards's soteriology, 71–74
  forensic, 74, 78–80
  and human goodness, 93–96
  as pardon, 76, 77
  pending, 138–41
  in Protestant scholasticism, 118
  and sanctification, 4–5, 114–21, 145
  second, 116

Kant, Immanuel, 76n.18
Kendal, R. T., 16–17n.17
knowledge of God, 151
Küng, Hans, 64n.102, 65n.107, 68, 104, 108, 159–60

Last Judgment, 144–45
Lee, Sang, vii, 4, 50n.47, 55, 73n.6, 151n.78, 154, 161n.10
Lindbeck, George, 161n.11
Locke, John, 3, 23, 158
Lombard, Peter, 8, 42, 63
Lossky, Vladimir, 154n.89
love
  of benevolence and complacence, 100, 152n.82
  of God, 152
Luther, Martin, 29, 87, 107n.11, 108, 110, 127–28, 138

MacKintosh, Robert, 76n.16
Martin, James, 142n.39
Mastricht, Peter van, 18–19, 63n.100, 87, 106, 109, 116n.56, 142n.40
  and Edwards, 18, 20, 26, 34n.91, 45, 51n.48
McDonald, H. D., 79n.31
McGrath, Alister, 107n.11
Melanchthon, Philipp, 109, 126n.98
merit, meritorious, 78n.24, 96, 112
Migliore, Daniel, 64n.102, 67n.111
Miller, Perry, 1, 5n.6, 8, 14n.4, 86, 114
Morgan, Edmund, 27

Müller, Hanfried, 130n.108
mysticism, 49–50

Newbigin, Leslie, 65n.107, 67–68
Newton, Isaac, 3, 158

Oberman, Heiko, 76n.16
occasionalism, 56, 58–59, 60n.86, 105n.4, 141
ordo salutis, 10, 132
original sin, 73, 81–84
Ott, Rudwig, 107, 118n.60

Parker, T.H.L., 15
participation, 5–6, 29, 37–38, 46, 53, 83–84, 90, 97, 137, 147, 150–56
Peirce, Charles, 57
Pelikan, Jaroslav, 5n.7
Perkins, William, 17n.19
perseverance, 137–42
Pinnock, Clark, 65, 67n.110
Pöhlmann, Horst, 129
potentia ordinata, 7
practice, Christian, 133–37
pragmatism, American, 135
preparationism, 27, 28, 29, 39
Protestant concern, 7–8, 59–61, 162
Protestant Orthodoxy, 108, 109, 144
Protestantness of Edwards, 8–10, 60, 89, 97, 103–30, 147n.58, 159

qualification controversy, 34–35

Rahner, Karl, 160–61
Ramist logic, 16, 16–17n.17
Ramsey, Paul, 20, 60, 105, 147n.58
Reformation, 13n.1, 87, 104, 160–62
Reformed tradition, 2, 9, 10, 31, 39, 96, 112, 137n.24, 143n.44, 156
regeneration
  and conversion, 31–34
  and sanctification, 31, 115, 117, 131–33
Regensburg, Colloquy of, 107n.11
repentance, evangelical and legal, 29
Reuter, Karl, 16n.17
revival, 74
reward, rewardability, 94, 98–100, 113, 133
Richardson, Herbert, 150n.73, 153n.87
Ridgeley, Thomas, 106
Rudisill, Dorus, 86–87

Sadoleto, Jacopo, 108n.16, 110n.30
salvation
　of adults dying with unexercised disposition, 33
　of ancient Jews, 33, 63–64
　of body and soul, 143–44
　of infants, 30–33, 63
　outside the Christian tradition, 2–3, 64–68, 162
sanctification, 4, 31, 34n.90, 90, 114–21, 128, 131–42, 152
Sanders, John, 33, 64–65, 67n.110
Schafer, Thomas, viii, 8, 20, 86, 114–15, 121–22, 129–30
Scharlemann, Robert, 48, 126
scholasticism, Medieval, 3–4, 14n.5
Seeberg, Reinhold, 109
Shedd, William, 76
Shepard, Thomas, 35, 62, 72n.3
Simonson, Harold, 23
Smith, John, 135–37
Smith, Shelton, 82n.43, 84
Sprunger, Keith, 16–17n.17
Stoddard, Solomon, 32n.86, 43n.24
Strehle, Stephen, 161n.7
syllogism, practical, 28n.67, 139

Tavard, George, 117, 127
Taylor, John, 47–49, 85
Thomas. *See* Aquinas, Thomas
Tillich, Paul, 5, 8, 92, 109n.21, 150n.71
traducianism and creationism, 83n.44
Trent, Council of, 42, 107, 112, 116, 117, 118, 120
Trinity, trinitarian, 41, 43, 147, 149–50, 152, 155
Turretin, Francis, 18, 50–54, 59, 106, 123n.79, 126n.95, 142n.40
　and Edwards, 18, 18n.23, 51

union, 86–87, 89–90, 91–92, 137, 147

Vos, Arvin, 107, 125–26

Westminster Confession, 13n.2, 33, 53–54n.59
Whitby, Daniel, 20
Wigglesworth and Chipman, 80n.33, 95
Willard, Samuel, 80n.33
Willis(-Watkins), David, viii, 25
Wilson, John, viii, 148
Witsius, Herman, 48n.44, 132n.1

Yarnold, Edward, 46n.34, 63

www.ingramcontent.com/pod-product-compliance
Lightning Source LLC
Chambersburg PA
CBHW031552300426
44111CB00006BA/286